Introductory Java for Scientists and Engineers

Introductory Java for Scientists and Engineers

Richard J. Davies

University of Cambridge

▲▼ Addison-Wesley

Harlow, England • Reading, Massachusetts • Menlo Park, California • New York
Don Mills, Ontario • Amsterdam • Bonn • Sydney • Singapore
Tokyo • Madrid • San Juan • Milan • Mexico City • Seoul • Taipei

Pearson Education Limited
Edinburgh Gate
Harlow
Essex CM20 2JE
England

and Associated Companies throughout the world.

Visit us on the web at: http://www.pearsoneduc.com

Cover designed by Designers & Partners, Oxford
Typeset in 10/12 pt Times New Roman by 56
Printed in Great Britain by Henry Ling Ltd., at the Dorset Press, Dorchester, Dorset

First published 1999

ISBN 0-201-39813-3

British Library Cataloguing-in-Publication Data
A catalogue record for this book is available from the British Library

Library of Congress Cataloging-in-Publication Data

Davies, Richard J., 1977-
Introductory Java for scientists and engineers / Richard J. Davies.
        p.   cm.
Includes bibliographical references and index.
ISBN 0-201-39813-3
1. Java. (Computer program language). I. Title.
QA76.73.J38D35   1999
005.13'3–dc21   98-49587
                                                                            CIP

10   9   8   7   6   5   4   3
04   03   02   01   00

To my parents

Contents

Trademark Notice

Preface

What is Java?

Java is an important new programming language, designed by a team at Sun Microsystems. Many of you will have heard of it in the context of the Internet, which is where it made its initial impact. Sun started developing Oak, the forerunner of Java, in 1990. Java was released in 1993 and has grown from nothing to become widely accepted as one of the world's most important programming languages. All major web browsers now support Java and companies such as Microsoft and Apple are already building support into their operating systems. Many of the new **network computers** will run little other than Java programs.

At present, Java is usually thought of as a means of embedding fancy graphics or interaction into web pages. However, it is capable of much more than this. In fact, it is a language comparable to any other: Fortran, C, C++, Pascal or Modula-3. It provides all of the standard language constructs that you would expect and a standard library which goes beyond what any of these provides. It is available on most systems: Windows, Macintosh, Solaris, Linux and many others, including almost all varieties of UNIX.

As you will see later in this book, Java is capable of matrix manipulation, RSA encryption, computing π and all of the other types of computation that a scientific programmer might want to perform.

Why use Java?

If you already know another language or are trying to decide which to learn then you are probably thinking something like 'OK, so Java can do everything that more traditional languages do, but why should I choose it in particular?'

From the point of view of the scientific programmer, Java has several advantages:

- Java is totally platform independent. Your code will compile literally unchanged on any system. In addition the compiled code itself will run on any system. Even languages such as Pascal or C do not provide this degree of portability; in these languages the amount of accuracy that numerical data types store varies and certain pieces of behaviour do not have a defined standard. You will be able to switch systems or share code with colleagues much more easily.

- The Java standard libraries provide support for graphics. This is not true of any other popular language. It means that even graphical code is portable between systems, whereas under other systems it usually needs complete rewriting.

- The Java standard libraries provide arbitrary precision arithmetic in both integers and decimals. This is not true for any of the languages that we have mentioned.

- Java is a modern language. Its many technical virtues range from being object oriented to being multi-threaded, from being dynamic to being architecture neutral, and cover many other buzzwords. This may not mean much to you; in practice it means that Java provides features that are much more powerful than older languages such as Pascal or C, and, since it was designed as a coherent whole, there are fewer strange side-effects than in C++. As a simple example, in any of these three languages, if you allocate memory then you must keep track of it and deallocate it. In Java the memory is automatically tracked and deallocated when you have finished with it. Features like this make it harder to write buggy code.

- Java code run over the Internet is secure. Java is designed so that programs embedded in web pages can have only limited access to your computer. For example, they cannot read or write to the hard disk and cannot access memory allocated to different programs. When running Java code inside a web browser, you are protected from any malicious actions that it may try to perform. The only other technology for embedding programs into web pages, Microsoft's ActiveX, makes no attempt to provide any security at all. This security and its platform independence makes Java the standard for programs on the web. Simultaneously, the need for security does not cripple the Java language: programs that you have explicitly downloaded onto your local system or are writing yourself are as powerful (and potentially as risky) as any other form of program.

- Java is free. This is almost true of C/C++ where any UNIX machine will come with a compiler. However, at present Sun are providing their JDK (Java Development Kit) free of charge for Windows 98/NT and Solaris, and free ports exist to many other platforms. The website accompanying this book, at `http://www.jscieng.co.uk/`, provides pointers to Sun's versions for Windows and Solaris as well as to third-party ports of this software to other platforms. Of course, other companies such as SuperCede, Borland, Metrowerks, Microsoft and Symantec have also written their own competing compilers, some with nicer graphical user interfaces. You can pay and get a fuller service if you want to, but the JDK defines the standard.

- With most of the computer industry backing it, we can expect further exciting developments over the next few years.

In addition, if you are involved in any kind of teaching then Java provides two further benefits:

- Java code can be run in a web browser over the Internet, allowing you to write demonstration programs which your students will be able to run at any connected computer.

- From a student's point of view, knowledge of Java is a very marketable skill. Many courses include computer projects, usually performed in a language such as Pascal. By doing such projects in Java, the student loses nothing, since the basic syntax is as easy to learn, but gains all of the advantages listed above, such as better standard library support. In addition, the student gains experience with a language which is actually used in the computer industry.

Why buy this book?

Java has made such an impact on the programming community that bookshops are currently flooded with books on the subject. The vast majority of these cover exactly the same ground. They are designed for corporate programmers: people who intend to write flashy graphical additions for web pages, standard business applications or networking software. As such, these books discuss the entire standard library, concentrating on issues such as graphics, user interface design and networking. In addition, these books tend to assume quite a high level of expertise and most of the popular titles, such as *Java in a Nutshell* (Flanagan, 1997), assume knowledge of C/C++ and familiarity with object orientation.

This book is different. It is aimed at the scientific programmer and at the increasing number of science students who are being taught Java as their first language. As such, the focus is different and discussion of issues such as user interface components is almost entirely omitted. Indeed, this book makes no attempt to cover the entire standard library. Instead we concentrate on those parts which will be of use to you. For example, the library supports arbitrary precision arithmetic. Most other books would relegate this to an aside. Here, however, this is the second part of the standard library that we discuss (following on from the standard mathematical functions), and we follow our discussion by implementing RSA (large prime number) encryption.

In addition, unlike other Java books, our examples perform the kind of computations that a scientific programmer will be interested in. This book is not intended as a systematic source of good numerical algorithms – the programs are intended to illustrate language features. However, all of the examples perform a scientific computation of some sort and there are brief introductions to more serious numerical algorithms, software engineering and physical modelling in the second part of the book. These introductions are directed towards students who have not encountered these subjects before. We also include a description of Visual Numerics' 'JNL, a numerical library for Java' and a simple library of our own, 'JSGL, a scientific graphics library for Java', to handle graphical output for you so that you do not need to learn the full structure of Java graphics. Both of these libraries are intended for professional numerical work. The JSGL will run on all platforms that support Java, in contrast to most other graphical systems and languages in which you must rewrite your code to switch platforms.

This book has a fast track for those who already know C/C++, which are superficially similar, and also a more elementary introduction for students who have done no previous computing. Whichever category you are in, I have tried to provide an easier introduction to the subject than many other books on Java. No knowledge of any particular programming language is assumed, nor is any familiarity with object orientation.

Acknowledgements

I should like to thank Professor Brian Davies, who acted as my scientific advisor, ensuring that the style did not get too technical and suggesting some of the examples. I should also like to thank Daniel Andor, Alan Bain, Tobias Berger, Sarah Clelland, Andrei Kanaber, Tom Oinn, Andrei Serjantov and Chris Webb, students at Cambridge University who acted as my proofreaders, and Drs Tim Cutts, Andrew Gee and Robert Hunt, members of staff with whom I had useful conversations. I must stress, however, that it is of course the author alone who is responsible for any errors in the final draft.

Richard J. Davies
Cambridge, England
August 1998

PART I

Learning Java

CHAPTER I

Getting started

1.1   Introduction

It is a feature of books on computing that they will be read by people from widely differing backgrounds in the subject. To provide for this, I have tried to write a book with several possible entry points from various levels of previous knowledge. The next section explains these and should help you to choose one that is appropriate to you.

The remainder of the chapter covers the concepts which we will use in our discussion of Java and is recommended to all readers. It ends with the compilation and execution of our first simple program.

1.2   Using this book

The book is structured into two major parts.

- Part I, 'Learning Java', is a language tutorial, covering the Java language itself and its standard libraries. It provides entry points for first-time programmers, programmers experienced in C/C++ and those experienced in other languages. These are explained in Figure 1.1. The book is not all-encompassing, especially in its description of the standard libraries, and concentrates on those features of use to the scientific programmer.

- Part II, 'Scientific applications', moves on to discuss using the Java that you will have learnt. Chapter 7, 'JSGL, a scientific graphics library for Java', and Chapter 8, 'JNL, a numerical library for Java', describe two helpful third-party libraries for this sort of usage. The JSGL was written for this book, and is public domain software. It will run on any platform supporting Java and provides a sophisticated graphical interface to

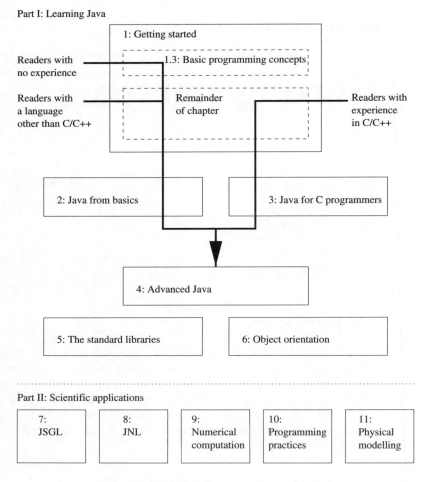

Figure 1.1 Entry points into the book.

your programs without forcing you to learn how to write user interfaces or graphical code in Java. The JNL was produced by Visual Numerics, is also free, and provides support for complex numbers, vectors, matrices and some statistical operations.

Following on from these two libraries, Chapters 9 to 11, 'Numerical computation', 'Programming practices' and 'Physical modelling', introduce specific areas of scientific or engineering use. This book is not intended as a source of good numerical algorithms or as a text on software engineering. However, these chapters do provide an introduction into these and other subjects and discuss the basic ideas involved. The first two of these discussions will probably be at a suitable level only if you have not encountered the subjects before.

Within each chapter we adopt a few conventions. We always start with an introduction, which gives an overview of what the chapter will cover and mentions any prerequisites.

Similarly, we always finish with a section suggesting further reading about a topic or what to move on to next. In addition, we use three typographical conventions:

- Technical terms that we have not previously used appear in bold, **like this**, with a short description.
- Short pieces of program code appear in typewriter font, `like this`, whilst longer pieces of code are displayed in a separate paragraph, also in typewriter font. The longer sections of code use different styles of the font to indicate program syntax: comments are in italics and keywords are in bold to distinguish them from the rest of the program.
- When we need a placeholder to indicate where you should customize some code, it is indicated with angle brackets, like this: `<description of parameter>`. The angle brackets should not appear in your final program. You should remove them and their contents and replace this with the appropriate code of your own. We also use '. . .' to mark large sections of code which have been omitted.

At the time of writing (August 1998) there are three versions of Java: those defined by JDK 1.0.x, JDK 1.1.x and JDK 1.2.x. This book discusses the newest version, JDK 1.2, which will become standard within a few years. This version is also known as the Java 2 Platform. However, many current compilers and web browsers (including Microsoft Internet Explorer 4 and the original release of Netscape Communicator 4) are not fully **JDK 1.0** JDK 1.1 compliant, so we also provide markers in the margin, as shown here, for those **JDK 1.1** using an earlier version of the JDK. The 'JDK 1.0' marker is for features which differ in JDK 1.0, but are the same in JDK 1.1 and 1.2 or later, whilst the 'JDK 1.1' marker is for features which differ in both JDK 1.0 and 1.1 from JDK 1.2 or later. Whilst you can write code that you want to run on your own machine using JDK 1.2 features, any code that you put on the web should probably be restricted to JDK 1.0. The website accompanying this book, at `http://www.jscieng.co.uk/`, contains links to the latest Java compilers for Windows, Solaris and other platforms.

1.3 Basic programming concepts

This section is intended for those new to programming. It aims to describe some of the concepts involved before we start discussion of Java in detail. Those of you with any existing programming experience will probably want to skip straight to the next section. Those with none should read this section, and should concentrate on the concepts involved rather than the technical details of how they are achieved, which will be covered again later.

Programming is the word that we use to describe the process of creating a set of tasks which will be carried out automatically by computer. The set of tasks is called the **program**. At its most simple, a program is simply a list of commands stored in a text file, one per line. The same approach is taken by batch files (ending in `.bat`) under Windows or shell scripts under UNIX which are literally a list of commands that could be typed at the system's command line.

When we have written a program, we **run** (or **execute**) it when we tell the computer to actually step through the tasks that we have written. Our original human-readable program, called the **source code** or **program code**, may need to be **compiled** into a different, more computer-readable form before running it, or it may be **interpreted** directly.

Java programs are more complicated than either batch files or shell scripts. This makes them more powerful, but also means that we must now discuss their structure in greater depth. A Java program consists of a text file, each line of which is called a **line of code**. We refer to lines which perform an action as **statements**. Every statement has a line to itself, which is terminated by a semicolon. An example of a statement is:

```
System.out.println("Hello");
```

which prints the text `Hello` to the command line.

Statements are carried out one after the other, line by line down the file. Thus

```
System.out.println("Message 1");
System.out.println("Message 2");
```

would print first `Message 1` and then `Message 2`.

During execution, the program also has a memory in the form of **variables**. A variable is a name which the programmer has explicitly stated will be used to store a value, rather as in algebra. We must **declare** variables before we can use them – this is a process of formally telling the program that the variable exists and what type of value it stores. For example:

```
int a;
```

is a **declaration** (not a statement – it does not perform an action) saying that we will be using a variable called a which is an integer. Once we have this variable, we can now perform many actions on it, giving a range of new statements. The sequence

```
a = 1;
a = a * 7;
System.out.println(a);
```

would **assign** the value 1 to the variable a, then assign a new value which is the old value multiplied by seven, and then output the final value. Note that in programming, the = sign plays a different role from that in mathematics: it assigns the value on its right to the variable on its left as opposed to testing if their values are equal.

It must be pointed out at this stage that the computer requires an exact specification of what is to be done. A single undeclared variable, a variable that is declared as containing one type of value and then used with another, or misspelling of a command, will cause your program to fail. Missed spaces are also fatal, although extra spaces where one is already present are irrelevant. It is equally likely that you will specify something other than what you intended, and the computer will mindlessly execute your code exactly as written. The process of removing such errors from your code is known as **debugging** after a famous incident in which a dead bug inside an early vacuum-tube computer caused a failure, and the causes of failures are still known as **bugs**.

Programming is not algebra – it's far more wide-ranging in scope. However, mathematical lines like some of those above are designed to look like algebra to help the programmer. You should note some important differences: variables may have names more than one character long (although some words are reserved by the language as commands); only round brackets (and) may be used in maths; and * for multiplication must be used explicitly – variable names placed next to each other will not automatically be multiplied. **Operator precedence** (the order in which operations are carried out in a complicated expression, an **operator** being something like * or +) is the same as in maths.

At this point, our code is still executed from end to end. The true power of programming comes into play when we create code which executes repeatedly or makes decisions about what to do. The key concept to introduce here is that of a **block of code**. This is a group of statements which are grouped together into a unit using curly brackets { and }. Execution of the unit may then be controlled by the commands immediately before and after it. As we have discussed, lines containing statements are terminated by semicolons. However, lines containing curly brackets or execution control commands are not. For example:

```
if (a == 7)
{
   System.out.println("a is 7");
}
else
{
   a = 9;
   System.out.println("a is 9");
}
```

tests the initial value of a, and executes different blocks of code depending on this. Note how we use a different operator == to test for equality from that which we used to assign values earlier. Note also that we use **indentation** to make the code inside the block stand out from the main program. This is not necessary, but is a very good habit to pick up since it makes your code much more comprehensible to others!

Repeated execution is achieved by code such as:

```
while (a < 30)
{
   a = a * 2;
   System.out.println("Multiplying by 2");
}
```

At this point we have introduced statements, variables, blocks of code, and **flow control** commands. There is only one more concept needed before launching into the details later in the book. This is that of a **method, procedure, function** or **subroutine**. When programming, you will often find that you need to perform the same task in more than one place in your program. One option would be to copy out the necessary lines of code twice. This is not desirable! It makes programs large and unwieldy and also puts a burden on the programmer, who will have to try to update both copies of the code every time a bug is found or some improvement or modification to the code is made. The solution is to create a standard piece of code, which is called a method, and then **call** the method when that piece of code is needed. For example,

```
public static void printvalue(int a)
{
   System.out.println("The value of the variable is");
   System.out.println(a);
}
```

creates a method, called `printvalue`, which prints the value of a variable, together with some explanatory text. The words `public static void` will be explained later. We can now call this from anywhere in our code as

```
printvalue(5);
```

The variable a in the declaration of the method is a placeholder representing whatever value is **passed** to the method when it is called. During execution of the method, a will be set to take this value. For example, in the code above, a is set to 5 during execution of `printvalue`.

   You should note that variables declared in a method or as parameters passed to a method are **local** to that method. This means that the association of the variable name with its value is valid only inside the method in which it is declared. Methods are not able to access local variables of another method. We can even use the same name for different local variables in several different methods and these will not affect each other because none of them is valid outside its own method. Thus we can write code such as:

```
int a;
int b;
a = 4;
b = 10;
printvalue(b);
```

and this will output 10, since b's value is passed to the method, and the fact that the name a is also used outside `printvalue` is irrelevant since this is local to a different method.

   It is also possible to have variables that can be accessed inside a method which they are not explicitly passed to. These are called **global** variables, in contrast to local ones. These will be discussed further later.

1.4 How Java works

Java is different from languages such as Pascal or C/C++ in that it is partially **interpreted**. In traditional languages, the programmer writes the program in a textual form, and then runs a tool called a **compiler** to convert this into the native machine code of their system. Java is also in part a compiled language. However, the compiler converts the program into an intermediate language called **byte-code**. This is then run over an **interpreter**, which executes the native machine code instructions corresponding to each instruction in byte-code.

   One of the most important features of Java is that programs are system independent. This is only possible because Java is partially interpreted, as discussed above. Not only is the original program code transferable between systems, but the compiled byte-code is also transferable to any system with a byte-code interpreter. This is one of the major reasons why Java has enjoyed such success as an Internet language, since users of many different types of systems all view web pages and can all run Java programs on the web.

The drawback, of course, is speed. Java is substantially faster than most interpreted languages since the byte-code is rather like a generic machine code, and so can be interpreted very rapidly over any system. However, it is still slower than native machine code. A simple test of repeated floating point operations on my system (JDK 1.1.1 under Linux) showed Java to be about three times slower than C.

This speed difference will decrease. Java compiler and interpreter technology is not yet fully mature, whereas C++ technology is. In addition, there are two developments which are still to appear in a widespread fashion. The first is called **just in time compilation** (JIT). This will enable systems to recompile the byte-code into native machine code before running it. JIT is currently implemented in Microsoft Internet Explorer and Netscape Navigator. The second development is much simpler. The interpretation stage is present only to enable Java to run on many platforms across the Internet. If we are happy to lose this flexibility, then we might as well compile direct to native machine code, as any other language does. SuperCede's Java compiler, SuperCede for Java, currently supports this feature (this compiler used to be produced by Asymetrix). CodeWarrior from Metrowerks also plans to do so.

In short, Java technology is currently fast enough for many applications. Soon, it seems that Java will be almost as fast as any other language.

1.5   Using the JDK

The website accompanying this book, at `http://www.jscieng.co.uk/`, contains links to the latest versions of the JDK from Sun Microsystems. Sun officially supports the versions for Windows 98/NT and Solaris, and third-party ports exist to many other platforms. In addition, other companies, such as SuperCede, Borland, Metrowerks, Microsoft and Symantec, sell their own compilers. This book will assume that you are using the JDK, and will tell you how to use the JDK tools such as `javac`. If you are using a different system, then you should consult your own documentation for instructions on how to compile and run programs. All of the Java code should still work unchanged.

The JDK is a command-line system, providing new commands such as `javac` to compile a file and `java` to run the byte-code interpreter. As such, it does not come with a text editor. You can use any editor of your choosing, but word processors, such as Microsoft Word, are unsuitable since they insert formatting information into their files. Under Windows, Notepad (supplied as standard) or Programmer's File Editor (available free on the Internet) is appropriate. Under UNIX, any editor, such as vi, pico or emacs, will work. You should probably operate in a windowing environment with at least two windows open: one containing the editor and one containing a command prompt to compile programs and run them. Under Windows, you can convert a full-screen command prompt into a window by pressing Alt-Enter. Remember to save all of your files in the editor before trying to compile them at the command line.

At this stage, I suggest that you install Java on your system. You can find the JDK via our website at `http://www.jscieng.co.uk/`. Appendix B contains installation instructions for the JDK under Windows 98/NT and Solaris. If you are on a different platform or are using non-JDK software then consult your own documentation.

1.6 Your first program

At the end of the last section, you should have installed a Java development system. We are now in a position to start writing actual code. We shall start with a very simple example – the traditional 'Hello world' program which outputs a line of text on to the screen.

The code for this program is listed below (lines beginning with `//` are comments):

```java
public class Hello
{
  public static void main(String[] argv)
  {
    // Print out the traditional
    // 'Hello world' message

    System.out.println("Hello world in Java");
  }
}
```

The JDK is not affected by the position of the program files. However, you should probably keep your files together in a directory. If you want to type this example in, then create a directory `Hello` somewhere on your hard disk to store it, type the program into an editor and save it as `Hello.java` in this directory. Alternatively, this code is available on the website at `http://www.jscieng.co.uk/Code/GetStart/Hello/`. If you decide to get it from the website, then you may want to download `http://www.jscieng.co.uk/Code.zip` or `http://www.jscieng.co.uk/Code.tar.gz` which are archives containing all example code for this and subsequent chapters.

Next, move to the directory containing the file `Hello.java`, and type, at a command line:

```
javac Hello.java
```

There should be a pause while the program is compiled, following which you will get a new command prompt. If compilation has been successful then the java compiler has generated the output file `Hello.class` from `Hello.java`. This file is stored in the same directory as `Hello.java`. Compilation will not produce any output on the screen if it is successful. If compilation is not successful, then the Java compiler will output an error message. There are two possible causes for this: either the installation did not succeed, or, if you decided to type the program in by hand, then you may have made a mistake. If you typed the program in then check your typing very carefully: a single misspelling or missed character is enough to stop the program from compiling correctly. The compiler error message should give you a good idea of where you mistyped. If you are using the program from the website, then the problem cannot be a mistype, so the problem must be that you did not install Java correctly. Reread the previous section, and, if necessary, talk to an expert on your particular system.

Once you have compiled the program, while still in the directory containing `Hello.java` and `Hello.class`, you should type:

```
java Hello
```

This runs the java byte-code interpreter over the `Hello.class` file that you generated in the previous step. Note that you do not type `java Hello.class` – the `.class` is omitted. If everything goes correctly, you should get the output

```
Hello world in Java
```

and then another command prompt. This tells you that the program has run successfully, has produced its output and then has terminated. Thus, in total, assuming that you are running under Windows and have copied the `Code` directory onto your `C:` drive, the screen will now show something like:

```
C:\Code\GetStart\Hello>javac Hello.java

C:\Code\GetStart\Hello>java Hello
Hello world in Java

C:\Code\GetStart\Hello>
```

Congratulations! You have successfully compiled and run your first Java program!

EXERCISES

1.1 Find out about your Java development environment. This book is too small to describe all popular systems. However, your chosen environment may well provide features that will prove very useful as your knowledge of the language increases. In particular, if you have a source-level debugger then it is worth making an effort to understand how it works – many bugs are located and understood only by stepping through a program under manual control. You can experiment with the small programs in the first few chapters as you learn about your debugger.

WHERE TO GO FROM HERE

At this point, you have learnt the basics of how to use the compiler and interpreter to run your programs. You now need to learn how to write programs. Java is very similar in basic syntax to C/C++, although at a larger scale it does have a substantially different structure, which is more similar to Smalltalk or Modula-3. As a result, this book provides two alternative routes into Java. If you do not know C or C++, then you should read the next chapter and then skip to Chapters 4 to 6. If you do know C or C++, then you should start with Chapter 3 and then move on to Chapters 4 to 6.

CHAPTER 2

Java from basics

2.1   Introduction

At the end of the previous chapter, we installed a Java development system and compiled and ran our first program. This chapter teaches you the basics of Java programming, so that you will be able to write that program and other more complicated examples by yourself. It requires no previous experience with any particular programming language, although some general competence with computers is taken for granted, such as familiarity with the ideas of a variable and a procedure/function. If you already know either C or C++, you should read the next chapter instead of this one since it covers the common ground between the languages rather more quickly and discusses their differences as well.

All substantial pieces of code are available from the accompanying website at

`http://www.jscieng.co.uk/Code/JavaBas/`.   Each program has its own
directory within `JavaBas` containing all of the files associated with that program.

Some people prefer to learn in a structured fashion, whilst others prefer to learn from
examples. We discuss Java syntax in the former fashion, building up from descriptions
of the different legal statements to a set of examples at the end. If you prefer the second
style of learning, you may want to refer to the example sections at the end of the chapter
as you read.

2.2   Class syntax and `.java` file format

Like many modern languages, for example C++ and Modula-3, Java is an **object oriented**
language. This enables programmers to write code in several new and powerful ways as
well as being able to write traditional, **procedural** code as found in languages such as
Fortran, C and Pascal. In object oriented programming, the subroutines, functions and
procedures that other languages use are replaced by a similar concept called **methods**,
each of which is associated with an object, which is known as a **class** in Java.

It is still possible to use Java to write procedural code. Because such code has a
simpler structure, in this chapter we concentrate on standard procedural programming.
We move on to discuss object oriented programming briefly in Section 4.3.3 and more
fully in Chapter 6, after you have already understood the basics of the language.

In order to get started we take two bits of program structure as given. These will be
discussed further at a later stage. The first part is the call `System.out.println` which
is a text output command. We can create a string for this command by enclosing the
text in double quotations marks, `"this is a string"`. We can also print variables
by specifying the variable name, and can join two strings together or join a variable to
a string using the '+' operator. Finally, we need to understand the overall structure of a
file.

A Java program is written as a collection of source files, each ending in `.java`. Until
Chapter 4, each program will consist of a single source file containing exactly one class
definition and the definitions for all methods and variables associated with that class.
The names of the file (before the `.java` extension) and of the class should be identical,
including their capitalization. Names for classes in Java are conventionally written in
lower case with an initial capital letter.

As an example, we consider the `.java` file for a class called `FirstClass`. This file
will be called `FirstClass.java` and its structure is:

```
public class FirstClass
{
  <optional class variable definitions>

  <class method definitions>
}
```

Note that we adopt the convention that any code in angle brackets `<like this>` is a
placeholder. You should remove the angle brackets and the description that they contain

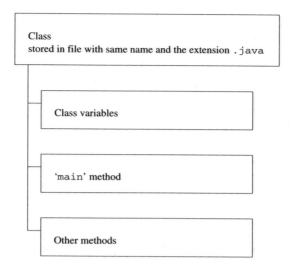

Figure 2.1 Structure of a simple class.

and write some appropriate code on your own in their place. We also use '. . .' to mark large regions of code which have been omitted.

When we run the java compiler, it converts each of our .java files into compiled .class files. Thus, for instance, in the first chapter, running javac Hello.java generated the compiled file Hello.class. Next, we execute the .class file over the interpreter by typing java Hello (the .class is omitted).

When the interpreter is given a .class file to execute, it looks for a class method called main within that file with the definition

```
public static void main(String[] argv)
{
    <some code>
}
```

and starts execution there. The structure of class methods and variables is discussed further later in this chapter (in Section 2.14), and for the time being it suffices to say that public static cannot be properly explained for another few chapters, but will be used consistently until then. You can think of it as acting to turn off object orientation (it is discussed in Section 4.3.3 and Chapter 6). The public before the class performs a similar function. void is the type of the value returned by the method main, and String[] argv is the type of the argument passed to it by the interpreter. This is an array of strings. It should be emphasized that this main method is required to have this structure in order for the interpreter to find it and start execution. Your other methods may have any names, return values and argument lists. Only the class in which execution starts needs to have a main method. Figure 2.1 depicts this structure in full.

Thus the full structure of the simplest Java program is

```
public class <classname>
```

```
{
    public static void main(String[] argv)
    {
        <some code>
    }
}
```

all of which should be stored in a file called `<classname>.java`. As you can see, this was the structure of the familiar 'Hello World' program from the last chapter. We can now move on to discuss the contents of the block labelled `<some code>`.

2.3 Lines of code

A line of text is defined as a string of characters ending in a carriage return. This is not the same as a line of code.

At the most simple level, the inside of a method consists of a series of lines of code. Each line performs a single, simple action, such as declaring a variable or performing a calculation. Lines are executed in series in the order in which they are written. Each line of code ends with a semicolon. Spacing, indentation and carriage returns are irrelevant to the concept of a line of code. You may split a line of code over several lines of text if it is very long.

The curly brackets which occur at the start and end of a method serve to group these lines into a single block. This grouping is the standard use for this type of bracket and makes any number of enclosed lines behave much like a single line. The use of `begin` and `end` in Pascal-like languages is equivalent to this.

At the next level of structure, we have a number of control statements, such as `if` statements, which are discussed in Section 2.11. These allow us to direct the program's execution. Such statements are not followed by semicolons. Instead the subsequent lines contain blocks of code for each of the cases that the statement distinguishes. In general, control statements will accept either a single line of code for each case (without enclosing curly brackets) or a single block of code (which uses curly brackets to group one or more lines into a single unit).

There are exceptions to this. For example, comments have a structure all of their own – one form of comment ends at the end of a line of text. In addition, a method must be followed by a block of code in curly brackets: it cannot have a single unbracketed line of code on the grounds that this does not need grouping. However, you will be able to spot these general principles in action again and again in the rest of this chapter.

Strings are the other important exception to our rules about lines of code. Any text enclosed by double quotation marks will be converted into a string by the compiler. Unlike other all other situations, the exact number of spaces in a gap is significant inside double quotation marks and will be reproduced exactly in the string. A string may not be specified over several lines. If it is too long to fit on a single line then you should use the ' + ' operator to join together several shorter strings:

```
System.out.println("A long string"
                 + "over several lines");
```

2.4   Reserved words

The following words are reserved for internal use in the Java language or for future expansion and may not be used for names of classes, variables or methods:

```
abstract, boolean, break, byte, byvalue, case, cast, catch,
char, class, const, continue, default, do, double, else, extends,
false, final, finally, float, for, future, generic, goto, if,
implements, import, inner, instanceof, int, interface, long,
native, new, null, operator, outer, package, private, protected,
public, rest, return, short, static, strictfp, super, switch,
synchronized, this, throw, throws, transient, true, try, var,
void, volatile, while, widefp
```

2.5   Comments

There are two sorts of comments in Java. The long form may last over several lines. It starts with /* and ends with */. The short form starts with // and lasts until the end of the current line of text.

```
/* This is a comment. It does not end here...
   but keeps on going until it reaches a */

// This is also a comment which ends at the end of the line
```

Comments may be placed on the same line as pieces of code (although a short form comment *preceding* a piece of code on the same line will cause the code not to be compiled!). Long form comments may not be nested within each other. In other words, the code

```
/* A long style comment /* Another trying to nest inside. */ */
```

will not compile correctly. You should use short style comments when embedding comments into code. These comments may be embedded inside long form comments, so this will enable you to comment out large block of code if you need to without worrying about ending up nesting long form comments. For example,

```
/* This comments out a large block of code...

   int i, j;
   i = 5;
   j = i + 1;  // Including a short form comment

   System.out.println(j);

   ... and ending here. */
```

Table 2.1   Basic data types.

`boolean`	logical truth	1 bit	`true` or `false`
`byte`	signed integer	8 bits	-128 to 127
`short`	signed integer	16 bits	$-32\,768$ to $32\,767$
`int`	signed integer	32 bits	$-2.1e9$ to $2.1e9$
`long`	signed integer	64 bits	$-9.2e18$ to $9.2e18$
`float`	IEEE 754 floating point	32 bits	$1.4e-45$ to $3.4e38$
`double`	IEEE 754 floating point	64 bits	$4.9e-324$ to $1.8e308$

2.6   Basic data types

Java offers a number of basic types for storing integers and floating point numbers. These are listed in Table 2.1. Note that the `boolean` data type is *not* an integer, in contrast to C/C++.

The `float` data type stores real numbers to eight significant figures of accuracy, whilst `double` stores them to 16. As we mention later, floating point calculations default to using `double`, so `float` is available mainly to offer you the chance to save memory. Scientific computing should usually be done entirely using `double`. At the time of writing (August 1998), there is a proposal underway to use the keywords `strictfp` and `widefp` to distinguish between standardized floating point arithmetic and faster arithmetic, done at machine precision. You will have to refer to Sun's website at `http://java.sun.com/` to discover the outcome.

Unlike virtually every other standard programming language, the ranges of the data types are guaranteed. Regardless of the machine architecture, all of the above will be available and will have the stated sizes. This is in contrast to Fortran, C or Pascal where changing compiler or platform may require code changes.

Variables are declared using the syntax

```
<variable type> <first variable's name>, <second name>, <others>;
```

The names chosen can contain lower and upper case letters, numerals and some special characters. They may not start with a numeral, and may be longer than one character. You may not have two variables of the same name and different types. For example,

```
int    i, long_name, d4;
long   l;
float  gh_L9;
```

are all legal declarations. Like C or Pascal, but unlike BASIC or early Fortrans, all variables must be declared before they are used. Class variables are declared at the class level, as indicated in our previous discussion of class-level structure. Discussion of these is deferred until Section 2.14. Local variables can be declared at any point in a method, but this is conventionally done at the start, after the initial opening bracket:

```
public static void main(String[] argv)
{
    // We now declare some variables
    int   i, long_name, d4;

    <some code>
}
```

Unlike most other languages, variables are automatically initialized to contain 0 for integers or 0.0 for floating point numbers at the point of declaration.

2.7 Handling numerical data

When performing numerical computations you will frequently want to include numbers in your code as the initial values for variables, values to be added or subtracted from variables at certain points or for many other reasons. Some simple examples of such occasions are:

```
x = 3.1;
r = 1.7 / (9 + x);
if (x > 1.9) ...
```

As you would expect, this is possible, and, as shown above, numbers can normally be typed directly into the program code. There are, however, some complications. The problems are all caused by the fact that when the compiler is compiling your code, it considers the right-hand side of the assignment before considering the left-hand side. This means that the compiler decides what data type the numbers on the right are, or what calculation is to be done, before finding out what data type the result should be in order to be assigned to the variable on the left-hand side.

This probably seems rather abstract. To give a more concrete example, consider the statement:

```
double d;
d = 1/3;
```

There are two operators using the symbol /. One represents integer division, giving the integer part, and the other is floating point division. Thus, in this case, the compiler considers the right-hand side of the assignment. It recognizes both 1 and 3 as integers, and so performs integer division, getting the result 0, the integer part of the division. Next, the compiler considers the left-hand side of the assignment. d is a double, so 0 is converted into the floating point number 0.0 and stored in d. Probably not the result that you were expecting!

This is one of the easiest mistakes to make in Java (or indeed any other language with C-like syntax). The solution is to alter the right-hand side to alert the compiler that a double is what is expected. Any of the following would do this:

```
d = 1.0 / 3;
d = 1 / 3.0;
d = ((double) 1) / 3;
```

The same problem also occurs when dividing integer variables. Here, we cannot add a decimal point, so only the last of the above solutions works. For example,

```
int i,j;

d = ((double) i) / j;
```

You might also consider writing

```
d = (1.0 * i) / j;
```

This would indeed work. However, the first version is better since there is a risk that in the second case the compiler will not spot the intention of the code and will explicitly perform the multiplication '1.0 * i', slowing your program down.

To understand the problem fully, we must consider how numbers are understood by the compiler. Integer and floating point values are distinguished by the presence of a decimal point. Hence 1 and 1.0 are very different indeed.

Integer values may be specified in decimal (base 10) as above, in octal (base 8) by use of a leading zero (i = 017 is 15 decimal for example) or in hexadecimal by use of a leading 0x or 0X. All such integer values are, by default, considered as being of the smallest data type from int downwards capable of storing them. Thus, for example, 5 is a byte, but 50000 is an int. If the letter L or l is added at the end of an integer value then it is treated as a long.

Floating point values are assumed to be of type double unless they have a trailing F or f, in which case they are of type float. They can be entered directly or in scientific notation, 3.01e+8 for example. There are also a few special values representing concepts such as infinity. These are discussed in Section 5.10.

Next, we note that as data is transferred from a byte to a short to an int to a long to a float to a double it can be maintained intact through each conversion, whilst any conversion in the opposite direction could cause data loss. For example float to long would lose any decimal part, and an int might store a value too large to be expressed as a byte.

As a result, the compiler will automatically **promote** numerical data from one type to a wider type without needing any prompting. For example, in

```
double d;
d = 1.0 / 3;
```

the compiler looks at the right-hand side, realizes that it cannot divide a double by an integer and automatically converts the integer into a double before the division. The division is then between two doubles, and so uses floating point arithmetic, as expected.

However, the compiler will not perform a conversion that could lose data. These must be explicitly performed by the user. The syntax is

```
<variable> = ( <new type> ) <number or variable>;
```

and the word **cast** is used to refer to user-specified type conversions like this. For example, casts are necessary in each of the following:

```
float f;
int i;


f = (float) 8.31;     // necessary as 8.31 is a double
i = (int) f;          // necessary as f is a float
```

Casts can also be performed in the opposite directions, as you can see if you now look back at the examples using `d = 1 / 3`, which you should now be able to understand.

Whilst on this topic, you should note two other examples:

```
float f;
long l;


f = 8.31F;
l = 1000000000000L;
```

In both cases, the appended letter is necessary. In the first case, it stops `8.31` from being a `double` and so needing casting. In the second case, `1000000000000` would, by default, be an `int`. Although this would successfully be promoted to a `long` for the assignment, there is still the problem that this number is simply too large to be an `int`, so the code will fail to compile unless it is explicitly flagged as a `long`.

This has probably been one of the hardest sections so far, containing a lot of technical detail. As a scientific programmer, you can avoid most of these problems by consistently using the types `double` and `int` for your floating point and integer variables respectively. You will still need to bear in mind the problems with dividing integers. In my view, this problem is a flaw in the language – if the operators for dividing integers and dividing floating point numbers were different then it would not occur. However, the Java designers chose to use the same syntax as C/C++ in order to help the large number of programmers who know these languages, and the problem was inevitable following this decision.

2.8   Initialization

You will frequently declare a variable and then immediately assign a value to it. As a result Java provides a shorthand syntax for this.

```
int i;
i = 5;
```

can also be written as

```
int i = 5;
```

All of the rules described in the previous section still apply, so, for example, in the statement

```
float f = 8.31F;
```

the F is necessary.

2.9   Constants

Constants are declared in exactly the same way as variables, with the extra keyword `final` in front, indicating that their value is final and will not change. Constants still have a type, just like variables, which the compiler uses to check that they are being used appropriately. Because their value cannot be changed, all constants must be initialized with a suitable value immediately on declaration. For example,

```
final int ITERATIONS = 5;
final float PI = 22F / 7;
```

As you can see it is traditional for constants to have names consisting entirely of capital letters.

2.10   Operators

Java comes with a full selection of operators. We have standard arithmetic, bit shifts, comparison operators and boolean operators. In all cases operator precedence is as you would expect from any other programming language (or the laws of mathematics!).

2.10.1   Arithmetic operators

The standard arithmetic operators, `+`, `-`, `*`, `/` and `%`, are all supported. `+` and `-` are available in both **unary** form ('`-9`', for example, where the operator takes one argument) and as `binary` operators ('`6 - 9`', where the operator takes two arguments). `/` represents division, and returns the whole part for integer divisions, whilst `%` returns the remainder. Note that, as in all other programming languages, integer division is slightly peculiar for negative numbers, rounding towards zero. Hence, `4 / 3` is equal to `1` and `4 % 3` is equal to `1`, which is correct. However, `(-4) / 3` is equal to `-1` and `(-4) % 3` is equal to `-1`, whereas it might be more mathematically natural for `(-4) / 3` to be equal to `-2` and `(-4) % 3` to be equal to `2`.

`++` and `--` are unary increment and decrement operators. Acting as **postfix** operators they are written after a variable name and perform their action on the variable after it has been used, whilst as **prefix** operators they are written before a variable name and perform their action on the variable before it is used. Hence, `i = j++;` is equivalent to `i = j; j = j + 1;`, whilst `i = ++j;` is equivalent to `j = j + 1; i = j;`. These operators can also be embedded in more complicated statements: `i = 17 * (j++) * i;` is equivalent to `i = 17 * j * i; j = j + 1;`.

There is no operator for raising numbers to powers. This is performed by the member function `pow` of the class `java.lang.Math` (see Section 5.2).

2.10.2   Equality operators

There are two conceptually different types of equalities: a kind which assigns a value 'let a be equal to 5' and a kind which makes a comparison 'check if a is equal to 5'.

Some languages, such as BASIC, do not make a distinction between these two. Java uses = for assignment and == for comparisons. Pascal users and some mathematicians, who are used to := for assignment and = for comparisons, should take care about this, whereas Fortran users, who are used to = for assignment and .EQ. for comparisons, will be less prone to make mistakes.

2.10.3 Comparison operators

<, <=, > and >= perform as expected. == is the logical comparison equality and != is the comparison operator for 'not equal to'. All comparison operators return a `boolean` value.

Note that when applied to objects, == and != test whether two references do or do not refer to the same object. To compare actual object values, you should use the method `equals`, as described in Section 4.3.3.

2.10.4 Logical operators

!, &, | and ^ perform logical NOT, AND, OR and XOR operations respectively on `boolean` arguments (such as the output from any comparison operator). && and || are also logical AND and OR, but do not evaluate the right-hand operand if the left-hand operand has already determined the result of the operation. The equivalent ^^ operator does not exist, since both arguments are always necessary to be able to determine the result.

```
// In this case the second argument will never be evaluated
if ((1 != 0) || (9 == 5)) ...
```

You are advised to use these faster forms of the operators unless the second part of your expression calls a method with some side-effect which means that the method must always be called.

As you can see from the above, logical operators are used to construct complicated conditions for `if` statements and other such constructs. The keywords `and` and `or`, as used in many other languages, do not exist in Java. As another example, to test that two conditions are both true, we would write

```
if ((1 != 0) && (i > 7)) ...
```

Note the heavy use of brackets in these expressions. As explained later, in Section 2.11.1, the `if` statement requires an additional layer of brackets on top of those needed in the logical expression.

2.10.5 Bitwise operators

~, &, | and ^ perform boolean NOT, AND, OR and XOR on the twos-complement binary representations of integer values (if you do not already understand these words, then you will not be using these operators anyway, so skip straight to the next section). << performs a bitwise left shift. There are two types of bitwise right shift: >> fills the new top bits with sign bits (that is, it behaves like division by two), whilst >>> fills the new top bits with zeros (that is, it treats the argument as a bit field).

Hence, 1 << 1 is equal to 2, -1 << 1 is equal to -2, 2 >> 1 is equal to 1, and -2 >> 1 is equal to -1. However, 2 >>> 1 is equal to 1 and -2 >>> 1 is some very large positive number, since, using short integers as an example, -2 is 1111 1111 1111 1101 in binary, so the right shift leaves 0111 1111 1111 1110, which is 32766. You should also note that >> behaves like division by two followed by rounding strictly downwards, not towards zero. For example, -3 >> 1 is equal to -2.

2.10.6 Assignment operators

The straightforward assignment operator = assigns the value on its right to the variable named on the left. Note, however, that when applied to classes, this operator sets the left-hand reference to refer to the same class as the right-hand reference. To duplicate the contents of an object, many classes provide a **constructor** from another object of the same type, as discussed later in Section 4.3.3.

In addition to this, Java provides a set of 'assignment and operation' operators. These are +=, -=, *=, /=, %=, &=, |=, ^=, <<=, >>= and >>>=. Each of these contains a standard Java operator (for example, '+' in '+=') as well as a '='. The combination takes two arguments: a variable to the left and an expression to the right. It performs its standard operation on the variable and expression and then stores the result in the variable. In other words, the following are equivalent:

```
<variable> <operator>= <expression>;
```

and

```
<variable> = <variable> <operator> <expression>;
```

For example, i += 1; is equivalent to i = i + 1;. These operators exist as a short-hand because programs often involve complicated data structures. Hence the variable specification may look more like Object1[Object2.method(i)].variable, in which case having to type this in twice would be both cumbersome and a source of bugs.

2.11 Flow control

A block of Java code, in a class method, consists of a list of operations separated by semicolons. For example,

```
// Declare integer variables a, b and c
  int a, b, c;

// Perform actions on them.
  a = 4;
  b = 5;
  c = a + b;
```

In the above example, the operations specified are performed strictly in sequence. However, in general programming we need to be able to control the flow of execution through our program in more varied ways than this.

2.11.1 The `if` statement

The `if` statement allows the programmer to perform a test, probably using the comparison operators described above, and then execute different pieces of code depending on the test's result. The full syntax is

```
if ( <test> )
{
   <actions to be performed if the test is true>
}
else
{
   <actions to be performed if the test is false>
}
```

and the `else` must follow directly after the closing curly bracket from the `if` – we may not insert statements between them. For example, if we wanted a variable b to be set to 5 if a was less than 7, and to be set to 6 otherwise, then we would write

```
if (a < 7)
{
   b = 5;
}
else
{
   b = 6;
}
```

The brackets around the test to be performed are essential. The `else` clause, however, is optional, and everything from that point onwards may be omitted if not needed. Unlike many other languages, Java never has a `then` keyword in `if` statements; `then` does not exist at all in the language. There is no `end if`, unlike Fortran and some versions of BASIC.

Note the use of curly brackets, { and }, to divide the code into blocks. This is characteristic of Java and corresponds to `begin` and `end` in Pascal and other such constructs. They act to group multiple lines of code into a single block. We have seen them before, grouping the line of code following a method definition, or grouping the whole of a class definition, and we will see them again in many structures. In a case like the above, where there is only one line of code in each section, the brackets are in fact optional, since the single line is a single block in any case. If, however, we wanted to perform several actions in a row based on the test then brackets would be needed to group them:

```
if (a < 7)
{
   b = 5;
```

```
    c = c + 1;
  }
else
{
  b = 6;
  c = c - 1;
}
```

It is good coding practice to use the brackets even if they are not necessary, since it makes your code structure clearer and stops them being left out when you later decide to add a second instruction. Note that the same point about bracketing is also true in the for, while and do ... while structures that follow.

Note that the and and or operators that exist in many other languages do not exist in Java. You should use && and ||, as discussed in Section 2.10.4. If you use these, then you must still enclose the entire test in another layer of brackets. For example,

```
if ((a < 7) && (b == 5))
{
  c = c + 1;
}
```

We should also note from this example that = and == are different operators with different uses. = performs assignments, like = in Fortran or := in Pascal, whilst == performs comparisons, like .EQ. in Fortran or = in Pascal. BASIC does not distinguish between these operators.

2.11.2 The ? operator

This operator behaves like an abbreviated if (...) ... else ... for use in assignments. The syntax is:

```
<test> ? <result if true> : <result if false>
```

Because it is less clear when used with large blocks of code, it should probably not be used in cases when a substantial block of code needs to be executed, such as those in the previous section. However, unlike 'if' statements, it has the advantage that if expressions are placed in the two <result> spaces then the value of the selected expression is returned and can be used in assignments or suchlike. This can provide useful brevity. Thus the first example from Section 2.11.1 can be written as

```
b = (a < 7) ? 5 : 6;
```

The test will be performed and the selected value will be returned from the ? : operator, following which it will be assigned to b.

This use is not limited to assignments. For example, we can write

```
System.out.println( (a<7) ? 5 : 6);
```

which will perform the test and then return one or the other value to println.

2.11.3 The `switch` statement

The `switch` statement provides the opportunity to make a choice between more than two possibilities. The syntax is

```
switch ( <variable or expression giving a value> )
{
  case <first value>:
    <first action>;
    break;

  case <second value>:
    <second action>;
    break;

  <as many more cases as you want>

  default:
    <default action>;
    break;
}
```

When a `switch` statement is executed, the expression at the start is evaluated. If there is a `case` statement for this value then execution jumps straight to that statement. If not, then execution jumps to the `default` statement. Following this jump, execution proceeds line by line, continuing straight through any further `case` or `default` statements, even if the actual value of the expression did not match these. When a `break` statement is reached execution jumps to the line after the curly bracket which ends the `switch` statement.

Note that the labels (`case` and `default`) are followed by colons, not semicolons. The `default` label is optional, and may be omitted, in which the default behaviour is to jump to the end of the statement.

The `switch` statement is actually more powerful than is shown above. The labels and `break` statements need not occur in matching pairs. The labels can appear anywhere in the code, and any `break` statement sends execution to the end of the `switch` statement. Thus, for example, you can write

```
switch ( <variable or expression> )
{
  case <first value>:
  case <second value>:
    <action for first or second case>;
    break;

  case <third value>:
    <action for third case only>
  case <fourth value>:
    <action for third or fourth case>;
    break;
}
```

Looking at this structure it is clear that the `switch` statement is actually implemented using something like `go to` from Fortran or `goto` from BASIC. The labels provide positions to which the `switch` can jump, and the `break` statement is simply a `goto` to the end of the `switch`. Whilst on this subject, it is worth mentioning that Java does not have a `goto` statement, since extensive use of this is considered bad programming practice in every language.

Unfortunately, the flexibility of the `switch` statement makes it very easy to produce incorrect code. For example, in the program

```
switch ( <variable or expression> )
{
  case <first value>:
    <first action>;

  case <second value>:
    <second action>;
    break;
}
```

the `break` statement after the first `case` has been forgotten. As a result, in the first case, the program will execute both the first and the second actions.

2.11.4 The `for` loop

The `for` loop is the most commonly used program construct for performing iterative loops. The structure is

```
for (<initial expr> ; <test expr> ; <update expr>)
{
  <code to be iterated>;
}
```

Given this code, the program sets up the iteration using the initial expression, and then repeatedly tests if the test expression is still true, runs the code and then executes the update expression. The test expression is checked the first time through, which means that if it was not true under the initial conditions then the code is never run at all.

This may sound quite complicated. You may want to look ahead to Section 2.11.5, which compares this with `for`. Meanwhile, as an example, I consider a simple loop, which prints out the numbers from 1 to 10. This is the sort of loop which would be written as

```
for i = 1 to 10 do
```

in the clearer syntax of a language such as Pascal, or as

```
do i=1, 10
```

in Fortran. Here, we can write it as

```
for (i=1 ; i<=10 ; i=i+1)
{
  System.out.println(i);
}
```

In fact, a more experienced Java programmer would almost certainly write it as

```
for (i=1 ; i<=10 ; i++)
```

using the ++ operator as discussed earlier. This is in fact the most common use of this operator and is just a standard shorthand.

So, why should the Java syntax (borrowed from C) be so much more convoluted? The answer is that it provides extra power. For example, we can easily list the powers of two up to 1024 using:

```
for (i=1 ; i<=1024 ; i*=2)
{
  System.out.println(i);
}
```

Note that the usage i*=2 is equivalent to i = i*2.

Finally, there are a few extra features of for. Firstly, within the initial and update expressions we can enter several commands, separated by commas. The test expression does not allow this: multiple conditions must be linked using && or ||. For example, we can write:

```
for (i=1, j=10 ; (i<imax) && (j>jmin) ; i++, j--)
```

Secondly, in the initial expression we can define new variables, which are local to our loop. This is most useful for examples like that above, where the loop counter has no use outside the loop. Hence we could write:

```
for (int i=1 ; i<=10 ; i++)
```

thus declaring the variable at the point of use. The variable i can now be used within the loop control expressions and inside the loop. However, it is local to the loop, and so is not visible outside it.

The final comment on for loops is that any of the control expressions may be left out. Hence for(;;) is perfectly valid Java and implements an infinite loop.

2.11.5   The while loop

The while command is much simpler than for. The syntax is:

```
while ( <test expression> )
{
  <code to be executed>;
}
```

and the program will repeat the code, testing first each time, until the test fails. Hence, to count to 10 again, we can write

```
i=1;

while (i<=10)
{
  System.out.println(i);
  i++;
}
```

Once again, the code will never get run if the test fails the first time through.

Finally it is interesting, and helpful to those who are still struggling a bit over `for`, to show how the two are more or less equivalent:

```
for (<initial expr> ; <test expr> ; <update expr>)
{
  <code to be iterated>;
}
```

is almost equivalent to

```
<initial expression>

while ( <test expression> )
{
  <code to be iterated>;
  <update expression>;
}
```

The only differences are that the `for` loop can declare local variables in the initial expression and can use the comma operator in the initial and increment expressions.

2.11.6   The do loop

This command is simply a `while` loop in which the test is carried out at the end of the loop as opposed to the beginning.

```
do
{
  <code to be iterated>;
}
while ( <test expression> );
```

The main difference to note is that the code is guaranteed to be run once, even if the initial conditions fail the test, because the test is not run until the end of the first loop.

2.12   Summary – basic syntax

Comments	`/* Multi line comment */` `// Single line comment`
Variable declaration	`<type> <name 1>, <name 2>;`
Variable initialization	`<type> <name> = <value>;`
Constant initialization	`final <type> <name> = <value>;`
Logic data types	`boolean`
Logic operators	`!, &, |, ^, &&, ||`
Integer data types	`byte, short, int, long`
Floating point data types	`float, double`
Arithmetic operators	`+, -, *, /, %, ++, --`
Bitwise operators	`~, &, |, ^, <<, >>, >>>`
Comparison operators	`<, <=, >, >=, ==, !=`
Assignment operator	`=`
Composite operators	`+=, -=, *=, /=, %=, &=, |=, ^=, <<=, >>=,` `>>>=`

Flow control	`if (...) ... else ...`
	`... ? ... : ...`
	`switch (...) { case ...: ...; break; }`
	`for (<init>; <test>; <updt>) { ...; }`
	`while (...) { ...; }`
	`do { ...; } while (...);`

2.13   Example – integration

At this point we have enough syntax to be able to write some simple programs. Our programs will be limited to one method – the `main` one – but this is probably still a sensible point to take a break from learning new syntax. The first program that we are going to write performs a simple numerical integration:

$$\int_{1.0}^{2.0} \frac{\mathrm{d}x}{1+x}$$

using the **trapezium rule** with 100 divisions.

The trapezium rule approximates the graph of the function to be integrated by a series of trapeziums, as shown in Figure 2.2. The area of each trapezium is obtained by multiplying its width by the average of the side heights, and then these areas are added together to generate an approximate value for the integral.

First of all, here is a pseudo-code version of the program which makes our algorithm clear:

```
The variable i is used to count the current division
The variable total is used to store the integral.
```

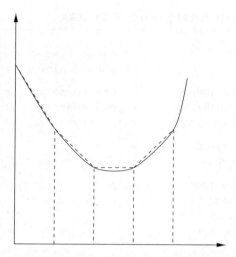

Figure 2.2   The trapezium rule.

```
total is initially set to 0

add the y coordinates at each end of the range to total

iterate the following, setting i to 1, 2, ... up to 99
  Set the variable x to 1 + i/100
  (x is the x coordinate of a division)
  Set the variable y to 1/(x + 1)
  (y is the y coordinate of the division)
  add 2 * y to total
  (middle values have twice the weighting of edges)

multiply the total by 0.005
(half of the step length)

print out total
```

Written in Java, this becomes

```
public class Integ
{
  public static void main(String[] argv)
  {
    double total, x, y;

    total = 0;

    // We are using the trapezium rule, so each end
    // point has a weighting of one.
```

```
total += 1 / (1 + 1.0);    // LH end, x = 1
total += 1 / (1 + 2.0);    // RH end, x = 2

// whilst each middle point has weight two

for (int i=1; i<=99; i++)
{
  x = 1 + i/100.0;
  y = 1 / (x + 1);

  total += 2 * y;
}

// Finally, we multiply by half the step size

total *= 0.005;

System.out.println(total);
    }
  }
```

Points worth noting in this program include the deliberate addition of decimal points to `1.0`, `2.0` and `100.0` in order to force the divisions to occur in floating point arithmetic. This was discussed earlier in Section 2.7. We also use the `+=` and `*=` operators as shorthand for `total = total + 2*y;` and `total = total * 0.005;`.

In addition, the class name starts with a capital letter, which is just a convention. Finally, the line `total = 0;` is not essential – variables are automatically initialized to standard values, and `0` is the standard value for a `double`. However, this line is included because the compiler issued a warning otherwise – it thought that the programmer had forgotten to initialize the variable before using it.

This program is called `Integ.java`, and is available from the website at `http://www.jscieng.co.uk/Code/JavaBas/Integ/`. As we noted in the first chapter, you may want to download the entire `Code` directory, available at `http://www.jscieng.co.uk/Code.tar.gz` or `http://www.jscieng.co.uk/Code.zip`. To compile the program, move to the appropriate directory at a command line and type '`javac Integ.java`'. There will not be any response to this command except for a pause before the command prompt reappears. However, the program has successfully compiled and a file `Integ.class` has been generated. To run the program type '`java Integ`'. Note that the `.class` is omitted.

In order to provide a reference point for those of you who know another language, we also include the program in Fortran and Pascal for comparison. Here it is in Fortran:

```
PROGRAM INTEG

DOUBLE PRECISION total, x, y
INTEGER i

total = 0
```

```
* We are using the trapezium rule, so each end
* point has a weighting of one.

      total = total + 1 / (1 + 1.0)
      total = total + 1 / (1 + 2.0)

* whilst each middle point has weight two

      DO 10 i = 1 , 99
        x = 1 + i/100.0
        y = 1 / (x + 1)

        total = total + 2*y
10    CONTINUE

* Finally, we multiply by half the step size

      total = total * 0.005

      PRINT *, total
      END
```

And now in Pascal (this code was produced using Borland's Turbo Pascal for Windows):

```
program Integ;
uses
  WinCrt;

var
  total, x, y : real;
  i : integer;

begin
  total := 0;

  { We are using the trapezium rule, so each end }
  { point has a weighting of one.                 }

  total := total + 1 / (1 + 1.0);   { LH end, x = 1 }
  total := total + 1 / (1 + 2.0);   { RH end, x = 2 }

  { whilst each middle point has weight two. }

  for i := 1 to 99 do
  begin
    x := 1 + i/100.0;
    y := 1 / (x + 1);

    total := total + 2*y;
  end;
```

```
{ Finally, we multiply by half the step size }

total := total * 0.005;

Writeln(total);
end.
```

Note that even in a program this simple the Pascal code is not entirely portable – the uses WinCrt at the top includes a library to handle text output into a window. This library is specific to this compiler and this operating system. Compare this situation to Java, where any compiler will compile exactly the same program on any platform and the .class file generated will run unchanged on any platform. At present this advantage may seem trivial; it is only one line of code, after all. However, the advantage of Java becomes very important when you try to do graphics. No other common language has a standard graphics library. Code written in any other language may have to be substantially rewritten to transfer between computers.

2.14   Methods, class variables and constants

Now that we have most of the basic syntax for the code that is written inside a method, we can start to consider the structure of the methods and variables themselves within a class. At the start of this chapter, we outlined the structure as being:

```
public class <classname>
{
  <class variable definitions>

  <class method definitions>
}
```

However, up to now all of our code and all variables have been located within the single method main.

As already mentioned, Java is object oriented, and so contains many possibilities at this point. Once again, we leave discussion of these to Section 4.3.3 and to Chapter 6. For the time being all variables, constants and methods declared at the class level must be preceded by the commands public static (as we have seen, this does not apply to variables and constants declared within methods).

Thus we can declare class variables and constants as:

```
public class <classname>
{
  // A class variable
  public static int i;

  // A class constant
  public static final double PI = 355.0 / 113;

  <method definitions>
}
```

The advantage of doing this is that these are visible from within all methods of the class (and indeed from outside too if the **fully qualified** name is used: see Section 4.2). These are equivalent to so-called **global** variables in traditional programming languages. By contrast, the variables declared in any method are said to be **local** to it. They are not visible from other methods. Indeed, two methods may both have local variables with the same name, and the two will not interfere with each other.

Extra class methods are declared as:

```
public class <classname>
{
  <some variables and constants>

  public static <return type> <method name>( <arg list> )
  {
    <the method's code>;

    return <return value>;
  }
}
```

The `<return type>` is some Java type, for example `int`, that the method returns after finishing its computations. `void` is a special return type signifying that no result is produced. The final line of the method should be a `return` statement, stating the value that is actually returned to the caller. No `return` statement is necessary if the method is declared as `void` (remember `main`).

The argument list for the method is listed in brackets after its name. This list consists of a sequence of what look like variable declarations, separated by commas, declaring the expected types of the parameters and the names by which they will be called inside the method. If the method does not take any arguments, then its argument list should be empty `()`, but cannot be omitted, unlike in Pascal (like `function`, but unlike `subroutine` for Fortran users). Thus, for example,

```
public static double squareroot(double x)
public static int multiply(int x, int y)
public static void pause()
```

would all be valid method declarations. Note that, unlike Pascal, if a method takes two arguments of the same type then it must name the type on both occasions.

The name given to a parameter in an argument list is a placeholder representing whatever value is **passed** to the method when it is called. During execution of the method, a local variable with the name given in the argument list is set to take the value passed to the method.

You should note that variables declared in a method or as parameters passed to a method are **local** to that method. This means that the association of the variable name with its value is valid only inside the method in which it is declared. Methods are not able to access local variables of another method. We can even use the same name for different local variables in several different methods and these will not affect each other because none of them is valid outside its own method.

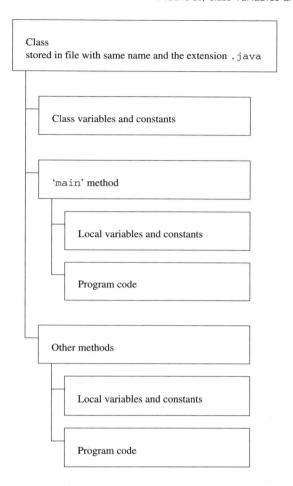

Figure 2.3   Structure of a more complicated class.

The `String[] argv` that you have seen for the `main` method is required as the argument list for that method only. You can pass any arguments you like to your other methods. Like variables, method names may be combinations of upper or lower case letters, numerals or underscores (but may not start with a numeral). A method may not change the value of its arguments. At this point, we can extend the diagram for the structure of a class that we drew earlier. The fuller diagram is shown in Figure 2.3.

Within a method, code is written exactly as we have done so far, except that the parameters are referred to by their declared names, and a `return` statement must be provided. For example, a method to compute the square of a number might look like:

```
public static double square(double x)
{
   return x*x;
}
```

You might want to compare this with the equivalent Fortran function:

```
DOUBLE PRECISION FUNCTION square(x)
DOUBLE PRECISION x

square = x * x

END
```

and the equivalent Pascal,

```
function square(x : double) : double;
begin
  square := x*x;
end;
```

Other methods can **call** this method by specifying its name, followed by appropriate arguments (which may be typed values, variables or calculations) in round brackets, separated by commas. The method call as a whole is syntactically equivalent to its return value, and so can be used in the right-hand side of an assignment or in many other constructs. For example,

```
double d = square(2);
double e;

if (1.44 == square(d))
{
  e = 1 / (1 + square(7.9 + d));
}
```

Note that we can pass a variable called 'd' or even the result of a calculation to the method – the parameter is only called 'x' internally. Also note that a method call always involves brackets after the name of the method. Even if the method is declared as

```
public static void pause()
```

you must call it using the syntax `pause();`. This is a difference from Fortran, Pascal and some other languages.

Java provides support for a programming technique called **method overloading**. This means that you may declare several versions of a method, all with the same name, but with different argument lists and return types. The compiler will be able to tell which version of the method to use by considering the types of the arguments that you pass to it. You may not, however, have several versions of a method that differ only in return type.

Having completed our survey of simple `public static` methods, there are three general points about class level program structure to be noted. Firstly, unlike some languages, such as Pascal, all methods in Java occur at the same level, directly under the class. Method declarations cannot be nested inside each other.

Secondly, you may notice that, given the existence of class variables, there is no necessity to pass parameters to any method, nor indeed to get a return value. All of your methods could be `void <method name>()` and they could read data from class variables and alter these to contain their output. Although possible, this is generally thought to be very bad programming practice. Ideally, a program should have very few or no class variables (although it can have many class constants). All required data should be passed to a method, and it should return its output as its result. This enables the programmer to be much clearer about the flow of data around the program, to be able to reuse the same method to operate on data from a different place and to avoid obscure bugs caused by interactions between two methods on a global variable which it was not obvious that either used.

Finally, unlike almost all languages, Java allows you to call and declare your methods in any order: you need not declare a method nearer the start of the program than the place where you first call it; the compiler will always manage to work out where the method is declared.

2.15   Example – integer powers

As an extended example of the use of methods, we include a sample program for raising a floating point number to an integer power. This is entirely illustrative – this method is available in the standard library (see Section 5.2). This program is available at `http://www.jscieng.co.uk/Code/JavaBas/Power/`.

The algorithm that we use is considerably better than the simplistic method of just multiplying the number by itself the appropriate number of times. Instead, we effectively split x^{2m+1} into $x * x^m * x^m$ and x^{2m} into $x^m * x^m$. We can then compute a much lower power and simply perform a few multiplications to get the desired result. Of course, we compute the lower powers by the same method (our algorithm is **recursive**, that is it calls itself), thus achieving a large saving in the number of multiplications used. There is no limit to the number of levels of recursion allowed except that each level requires additional memory to store the local variables for the new copy of the method, so you are limited by your system's total memory.

```java
public class Power
{
  // The method 'power' raises x to the power
  // of n.
  public static double power(double x, int n)
  {
    if (n == 1)
    {
      return x;
    }
    else
    {
      // Integer division rounds down
      double value = power(x, n / 2);

      if (n % 2 == 1)
```

```
        {
            return x * value * value;
        }
        else
        {
            return value * value;
        }
    }
}


// For our main method, just compute a power
// of two - the point of this example is in the
// preceding method.
public static void main(String[] argv)
{
    System.out.println(power(2,10));
}
}
```

It is interesting to note that this program is in fact incorrect: the method power will fail if n is negative or zero. This is an example of a standard problem in software engineering: when we designed this method, we clearly did not intend to support negative powers, since no attempt at all has been made to do so. In this sense, the method does fulfil its design criteria. However, at a later point it may well be used to compute a negative power, since the programmer will have forgotten exactly what they wrote. In general, when writing methods that will be kept as a toolbox and reused, it pays to make them as general as possible. See Section 4.2 for information on how to produce a class that acts as your toolbox.

2.16   Example – integration a second time

By now, you have covered enough Java to be able to write quite sophisticated programs. Chapter 4 discusses use of objects, arrays and other useful features, but the language as you currently understand it is already fairly powerful. To demonstrate this, we rewrite our previous integration program taking advantage of the extra knowledge that we now have. We move the endpoints and number of steps out into class constants so that these can easily be changed and the rest of the program will adapt. Similarly, we move the function to be integrated out into a method of its own. This program is available at http://www.jscieng.co.uk/Code/JavaBas/Integ2/.

```
public class Integ2
{
    // Constants define the endpoints of the integration
    // and the number of steps.
    public static final double LEFT = -4.5;
    public static final double RIGHT = 17.3;
```

```
    public static final int STEPS = 1000;


    // The method 'f' is the integrand
    public static double f(double x)
    {
      // Here we choose the function y = | x*x/3 + 4 |
      // We use a local variable z
      double z;

      z = x*x/3 + 4;

      if (z > 0)
        return z;
      else
        return -z;
    }


    // The method main does the integral
    public static void main(String[] argv)
    {
      double total = 0;
      double sectionwidth = RIGHT - LEFT;
      double stepwidth = sectionwidth / STEPS;
      double x, y;
      int i;

      // We are using the trapezium rule, so each end
      // point has a weighting of one.

      total += f(LEFT);
      total += f(RIGHT);

      // whilst each middle point has weight two.

      for (i=1 ; i < STEPS; i++)
      {
        x = LEFT + i*stepwidth;
        y = f(x);

        total += 2 * y;
      }

      // Finally, we multiply by half the step size

      total *= stepwidth / 2;

      System.out.println(total);
    }
}
```

You may be wondering how to pass a method as an argument to another method. This would allow us to write an integration method that took the function to be integrated as one of its arguments. Unfortunately, this is fairly hard. It is discussed in Section 6.6.4.

2.17   Example – limiting processes

This example takes a simple iteration scheme, here

$$x_{n+1} = \frac{x_n}{x_n + 1}$$

and repeatedly performs the iteration until the value seems to have settled down (as measured by taking the difference between consecutive terms). This program is available at `http://www.jscieng.co.uk/Code/JavaBas/Limit/`.

```java
public class Limit
{
  // Constants define number of iterations,
  // starting point and final error required.
  public static final int STEPS = 1000;
  public static final double START = 1.0;
  public static final double ERROR = 10e-6;


  // The method 'f' is to be iterated
  public static double f(double x)
  {
    return x / (x+1);
  }


  // The method 'main' does the iteration
  public static void main(String[] argv)
  {
    double current, last;
    int i=1;

    last = START;
    current = f(START);
    System.out.println(START);

    // Iterate until either we've done as many steps
    // as required or the convergence has become slow
    // enough that we may be near the limit of the series.
    while ((i <= STEPS) && (abs(current-last) > ERROR))
    {
      System.out.println(current);
      last = current;
      current = f(current);
```

```
      i++;
   }


   // Check whether it did converge and print
   // appropriate text.
   if ((i == STEPS) && (abs(current-last) > ERROR))
      System.out.println("No convergence");
   else
      System.out.println("Convergent to: " + current);
   }


   // The method 'abs' returns the absolute value
   // of a floating point number.
   public static double abs(double s)
   {
      if (s>0)
         return s;
      else
         return -s;
   }
}
```

This program teaches you two things. First of all, there are two quite complicated conditions, in the `if` and `while` statements. Java does not have `and` or `or` operators. Instead, you must use `&&` and `||`, as discussed in Section 2.10.4 earlier. Note that the entire condition must be enclosed in round brackets, that `==` is the equality operator for comparisons, unlike Pascal (`=` is the assignment operator, as in Fortran), and that we can call the method `abs` inside the condition.

Secondly, the program deliberately uses `abs` before it is declared. In this case this is artificial, but in general it is useful to know that Java allows you to declare and use your methods in any order, unlike most other languages.

You should also note the use of `+` to **concatenate** (join together) a number of arguments to `println` into one long string.

2.18 Example – computation of π

As a final example, we compute π by a method which is very inefficient but does require some interesting pieces of program structure. The method chosen is to form a grid of points within a square centred on the origin, aligned with the x and y axes and with a side length of 2. Within this square we consider the unit circle about the origin. The circle has area π, while the square has area 4. We count the number of grid points lying in the circle and use this to find the ratio of the areas and hence an approximation for π. To understand this, consider Figure 2.4.

In this diagram there are three points per unit distance, which makes $4 * 3^2$ in total in the grid. Counting these, there are 27 in the circle. The ratio between the areas should

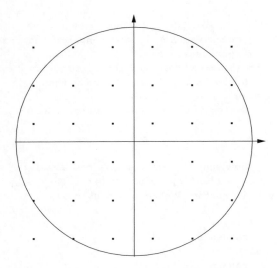

Figure 2.4 Computation of π.

be π:4, so we estimate π as $27/3^2$, i.e. 3 in this estimate. Once again, this example is entirely illustrative since π is available in the standard library (see Section 5.2).

This program is available at `http://www.jscieng.co.uk/Code/JavaBas/PIComputation/`.

```java
public class PIComputation
{
  // Constant number of grid squares per unit
  public static final int GRID = 100;

  // The constant PI to be computed
  public static final double PI = computePi();


  // The method 'inside' checks if the point x, y
  // lies inside a unit square centred on the origin.
  public static boolean inside(double x, double y)
  {
    // Use Pythagoras's theorem.
    if (x*x + y*y <= 1)
      return true;
    else
      return false;
  }


  // The method 'computePi' steps across the grid in the
```

```
// square |x|<=1, |y|<=1, counting the number of
// grid points inside a unit circle.
public static double computePi()
{
  int count = 0;
  double x, y;

  // Set up two loops to step across the grid.
  // We consider the middle point in each
  // grid square.
  for (int xstep=-GRID; xstep<GRID; xstep++)
  {
    // Calculate the x position
    x = (xstep + 0.5) / GRID;

    for (int ystep=-GRID; ystep<GRID; ystep++)
    {
      // Calculate the y position
      y = (ystep + 0.5) / GRID;

      // Count that point if it is inside
      if (inside(x,y))
        count++;
    }
  }

  // Finally, the area of the square should be 4,
  // whilst the area of the circle is Pi.
  // Divide by the number of squares per unit
  // area to compute Pi.

  return ((double)count) / (GRID*GRID);
}


// The main method just prints the constant.
public static void main(String[] argv)
{
  System.out.println(PI);
}
}
```

There are two points to note here. Firstly, we see that the constant PI can be initialized from a method. This is perfectly valid: the method does not use PI, and the compiler makes sure that the method computePi has been called and PI initialized before any other code, for example the main method, is run. What would be illegal is to declare PI as a constant and then to set its value in some later code, as opposed to in the initializer.

Secondly, the method computePi takes no arguments. Notice how this is declared and how, when we call it, the name must be followed by empty brackets, unlike in languages such as Pascal, which would omit these brackets entirely.

2.19   Mathematical functions

Section 5.2 discusses in detail how to include the standard libraries in your programs and what features they provide.

Although some of these features cannot be explained until that point, we jump briefly ahead to state that the standard functions sin, cos, tan, asin, acos, atan, exp, log, pow, sqrt, round, abs, max and min , and the constants PI and E all exist and are used with the syntax Math.<function>(<arguments>).

For example, we can write

```java
double x = 3.5;
double y = Math.sin(x);
double z = Math.pow(y, 3);
```

Refer to the section itself for further details on these functions and explanation of this notation.

EXERCISES

2.1 Spot 10 errors in the following program:

```java
class TimesTables
{
  public void main()
  {
    for (i=1; i<13; i++)
    {
      System.out.println("9 times " + i + " is " 9i);

      if (9*i = 99)
        System.out.println('which is one less than one hundred.')
    }
  }
}
```

2.2 What output is generated by the following program?

```java
public static boolean isPositive(int i)
{
  if (i > 0)
  {
    System.out.println("isPositive: success");
    return true;
  }
  else
  {/*
    System.out.println("isPositive: failure");
    */return false;
  }
}
```

```
public static void main(String[] argv)
{
  int a = 7;

  if ( (!((a>0) || isPositive(2))) || isPositive(-5))
    System.out.println("Tests passed");
}
```

2.3 What is the value of a at the end of the following?

```
int i = 3;
int j = 2;
double a = 1.0 + i/j + i/j;
```

2.4 What output is generated by the following program?

```
int a = 7;

switch (a)
{
  case 7:
    System.out.println("a is seven.");

  default:
    System.out.println("a is not seven.");
}
```

2.5 Why is no output produced in the following program?

```
double a = 3;

a /= 17;

if (5*a == 15.0/17)
  System.out.println("This line will not be printed!");
```

2.6 Write a program to differentiate a function of one variable numerically. The function should be stored in a method f and the differentiation can be done by moving a small distance either side of the point in question, measuring the change in the value of f, and applying the definition of gradient as rise over tread.

WHERE TO GO FROM HERE

You now understand the basics of programming in Java. The next chapter covers exactly the same ground from a different point of view, which means that you should not need to read it. You should go straight on to read Chapters 4 to 6.

CHAPTER 3

Java for C programmers

3.1   Introduction

This is an alternative to Chapter 2 and is designed to give those who already know C or C++ a faster route into the language. It covers the same ground, but does so more quickly and includes additional material pointing out the similarities and differences between these three languages.

This chapter requires a good knowledge of C/C++ and will frequently omit explanation of a topic, simply stating that the behaviour is unchanged. Some of you may not have this level of knowledge, so we use similar section headings to those of Chapter 2. If you get stuck then you should usually be able to read the section in Chapter 2 with the same name which will provide a fuller explanation and more examples.

In addition, the discussion of the differences will sometimes get very technical. You can ignore these discussions if you did not know about the feature of C/C++ in the first place. C programmers can ignore mentions of C++. We do not discuss object oriented programming here; this is done later in Section 4.3.3 and in Chapter 6. Therefore, most of the extra knowledge that C++ programmers have is irrelevant for the purposes of this chapter.

Finally, all examples are available from the accompanying website at `http://www.jscieng.co.uk/Code/JavaForC/`. You may also be interested in looking at the longer examples at the end of the previous chapter, which are available in the directory `JavaBas`.

3.2   Overview

Java was deliberately designed to use much of the same syntax as C/C++. This was intended to make it more accessible, since the vast majority of commercial programming is currently done in these languages. It is, however, important to realize that the language is actually fairly different on a large scale (it is much more similar to Smalltalk or Modula-3 in terms of structure). Hence the syntax for structures like `for` loops is the same, but the memory management, for instance, is totally different. Despite the fact that Java and C++ are object oriented and C is not, C is arguably the closer language to Java since a larger fraction of the behaviour survives. Java objects behave somewhat differently from those in C++.

3.2.1   Similarities

As a very simple example, just to point out how similar the languages are in terms of small-scale syntax, here is a simple program, as presented in the previous chapter, which performs the numerical integration:

$$\int_{1.0}^{2.0} \frac{\mathrm{d}x}{1+x}$$

using the **trapezium rule** with 100 divisions.

The trapezium rule approximates the graph of the function to be integrated by a series of trapeziums, as shown in Figure 3.1. The area of each trapezium is obtained by multiplying its width by the average of the side heights, and then these areas are added together to generate an approximate value for the integral.

The C version, `Integ.c`, is:

```
#include <stdio.h>

int main(int argc, char* argv[])
{
    double total, x, y;
    int i;

    total = 0;

    // We are using the trapezium rule, so each end
    // point has a weighting of one.

    total += 1 / (1 + 1.0);   // LH end, x = 1
    total += 1 / (1 + 2.0);   // RH end, x = 2
```

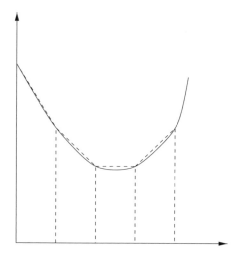

Figure 3.1 The trapezium rule.

```
// whilst each middle point has weight two

for (i=1; i<=99; i++)
{
  x = 1 + i/100.0;
  y = 1 / (x + 1);

  total += 2 * y;
}

// Finally, we multiply by half the step size

total *= 0.005;

printf("%.16f\n", total);
}
```

whilst the Java version, Integ.java, is:

```
public class Integ
{
  public static void main(String[] argv)
  {
    double total, x, y;

    total = 0;

    // We are using the trapezium rule, so each end
    // point has a weighting of one.
```

```
      total += 1 / (1 + 1.0);   // LH end, x = 1
      total += 1 / (1 + 2.0);   // RH end, x = 2

      // whilst each middle point has weight two

      for (int i=1; i<=99; i++)
      {
        x = 1 + i/100.0;
        y = 1 / (x + 1);

        total += 2 * y;
      }

      // Finally, we multiply by half the step size

      total *= 0.005;

      System.out.println(total);
    }
  }
```

Both versions of the code are available at `http://www.jscieng.co.uk/Code/JavaForC/Integ/`.

As you can see, the code in the body of the program is identical. The structure surrounding it is quite different, demonstrating the different large-scale syntax, whilst the different text output calls indicates how different the standard libraries are. The Java program can declare the integer i inside the `for` loop, which would be valid in C++, but not in C.

As a performance comparison, the Java program ran almost exactly three times slower than the C program on my system (JDK 1.1.1 under Linux; to allow an accurate timing of the speed, I performed the integral 10 000 times with 1000 divisions to slow the programs down). This is pretty good for an interpreted language. Also, as noted in Section 1.4, we can expect substantial increases in Java performance with the arrival of optimizing compilers and JIT compiling interpreters. Java technology is currently fast enough for many applications and it seems that Java will soon be almost as fast as any other language.

3.2.2 Fundamental differences

The example in the previous subsection gave a good idea of the level of similarity between the languages on a small scale. Continuing, we now list some of the structural differences at a larger scale.

Memory management

Pointers do not exist in Java. To many of you this will seem like an astonishing omission, so we take a little space to explain Java's equivalent structure, **references**.

In traditional languages such as C/C++, the programmer is entirely responsible for memory management. The commands `malloc` in C or `new` in C++ allocate an area of memory and return a **pointer** which stores the address of that memory. The programmer can perform whatever actions they choose, including performing arithmetic on the pointer to get to known locations within the memory allocated. However, the programmer must also keep track of when memory goes out of use and deallocate it using `free` in C or `dispose` in C++.

In Java, there is also a `new` command, which allocates an area of memory but returns a **reference** to the memory. References are much more restrictive than pointers. For example, **reference arithmetic** does not exist, and it is impossible to extract the actual address of the memory from a reference. However, this produces a benefit in that the interpreter can keep track of your memory use and will automatically deallocate memory when no more references refer to it. This is called **garbage collection**. The benefits are that the programmer need not think about memory so much and also that a typical C/C++ programming error, in which random memory is overwritten because of faulty handling of pointers, is impossible.

Preprocessor

There is no preprocessor in Java. This means you can no longer `#define` macros. In fact, macros do not exist. Similarly, conditional compilation using `#ifdef` or `#if` does not work, and `#include` does not exist (although, of course, an equivalent command, `import`, does). See Section 4.4.3 for a more extended discussion of these topics.

Standard libraries

These are totally different in Java. Hence strings, text input and output, and file input and output, are all handled very differently. Strings are handled using objects, not with pointers. The Java standard library is significantly more wide ranging than that of either C or C++. It includes most standard operating system features, such as graphical user interface commands, networking and threads. The result is that you can write a much larger selection of programs whilst maintaining portability. Standardized graphics is probably the most important issue for a scientific programmer, since even drawing a simple graph normally requires learning a different set of commands for every operating system or even compiler. See Chapter 5 for more information.

Large projects

C/C++ provide a dual structure of **header files** (`.h`) in which you declare functions and variables, and **implementation files** (`.c`) in which the actual code is written. The header files are textually included using `#include`. In addition, extra syntax is needed to handle issues such as referring to a function which is written later in the same program file.

Java provides a significantly better solution in which everything is written exactly once. `.java` files contain the implementation only. Other files which want to refer to them use `import`, which does not perform textual inclusion. The compiler is clever enough both to be able to work out what variables and functions the implementation is defining and to handle code referring forwards to functions which have not yet been mentioned. This is discussed in Section 4.2.

Type safety

Java is totally type safe. This is significantly stronger than either ANSI C or C++. What this means in practice is that you are not allowed to perform arbitrary casts between data types. For example, in C pointers can be cast to integers to extract the address that they refer to. In Java such casts are illegal. Similarly, variable length argument lists (such as that for `printf`) are not allowed. These restrictions allow the compiler to catch a higher fraction of simple programming errors, as opposed to a situation in which such errors are also valid code.

3.3   Class syntax and `.java` file format

Now that you have some understanding of how the languages compare, we move on to discuss Java syntax in much more detail. The first topic to cover is the overall structure of a program.

Like many modern languages, for example C++ and Modula-3, Java is an **object oriented** language. This enables programmers to write code in several new and powerful ways as well as being able to write traditional, **procedural** code as found in languages such as C. In object oriented programming, the functions that other languages use are replaced by a similar concept called **methods**, each of which is associated with an object, which is known as a **class** in Java.

It is still possible to use Java to write procedural code. Because such code has a simpler structure, in this chapter we concentrate on standard procedural programming. We move on to discuss object oriented programming briefly in Section 4.3.3 and more fully in Chapter 6 after you have already understood the basics of the language.

In order to get started, we take two bits of program structure as given. These will be discussed further at a later stage. The first part is the call `System.out.println` which is a text output command. As in C/C++, we can create a string for this command by enclosing the text in double quotation marks: `"this is a string"`. We can also print variables by specifying the variable name. Unlike C/C++ we can join two strings together or join a variable to a string using the '+' operator.

Finally, we need to understand the overall structure of a file. A Java program is written as a collection of source files, each ending in `.java`. Until Chapter 4, each program will consist of a single source file containing exactly one class definition and the definitions for all methods and variables associated with that class. The names of the file (before the `.java` extension) and of the class should be identical, including their capitalization. Names for classes in Java are conventionally written in lower case with an initial capital letter.

As an example, we consider the `.java` file for a class called `FirstClass`. This file will be called `FirstClass.java` and its structure is:

```
public class FirstClass
{
  <optional class variable definitions>
```

```
    <class method definitions>
}
```

Note that we adopt the convention that any code in angle brackets <like this> is a placeholder. You should remove the angle brackets and the description that they contain and write some appropriate code on your own in their place. We also use '. . .' to mark large regions of code which have been omitted.

When we run the java compiler, it converts each of our .java files into compiled .class files. Thus, for instance, in the first chapter, running javac Hello.java generated the compiled file Hello.class. Next, we execute the .class file over the interpreter by typing java Hello (the .class is omitted).

As already mentioned, Java is object oriented, and so contains many possibilities at this point. Once again, we leave discussion of these to Section 4.3.3 and to Chapter 6. For the time being, all variables, constants and methods declared at the class level must be preceded by the commands public static. As we have seen, this does not apply to variables and constants declared within methods.

Other than this, class variable and method definitions are exactly as they would be in ANSI C. Remember that methods correspond to functions in C; class variables correspond to global variables. The syntax for class variables is:

```
public static <variable type> <first name>, <second>, <others>;
```

while that for methods is:

```
public static <return type> <method name>( <arg list> )
```

which should be followed immediately by the actual code for the method.

As you saw at the start of this chapter, this code is written as in C/C++, ending in a return statement if the return type is not void. public static is not used inside the method. Similarly, calling methods is the same as in C – the method name is written followed by the list of arguments in round brackets. There is one difference: you should note that if a method does not take any arguments, then its argument list should be empty: (). The alternative form (void) is not allowed.

When a C/C++ program is run, execution starts at a method called main with a standard declaration. Similarly, when the Java interpreter is given a .class file to execute, it looks for a class method called main with the definition

```
public static void main(String[] argv)
{
    <some code>
}
```

and starts execution there. String[] argv is the type of the argument passed to it by the interpreter. This is an array of strings. It should be emphasized that this main method is required to have this structure in order for the interpreter to find it and start execution. Your other methods may have any names, return values and argument lists. Only the class in which execution starts needs to have a main method. Figure 3.2 depicts this structure in full.

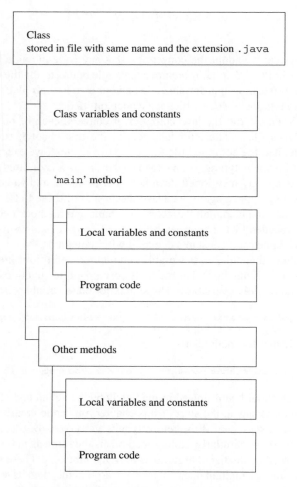

Figure 3.2 Structure of a class.

Finally, you should note that Java provides a facility called **method overloading**, which is also present in C++. This allows you to define several versions of a method, all with the same name, but with different argument lists and return types. The compiler will be able to tell which version to use by considering the types of the arguments that you pass to it. You may not, however, have several versions of a method that differ only in return type. This is the closest feature that Java provides to variable length arguments in C. It is also the closest to default values for arguments in C++. For example, if we wanted to write a method taking two values, the second of which was 5 by default, then we would write:

```
public static int calculate(int x, int y)
{
    <code for the general case>
```

```
      }

      public static int calculate(int x)
      {
        return calculate(x, 5);
      }
```

3.4   Example – computation of e

At this point we include a simple program to demonstrate the structures that we have just explained. The program that we are going to write computes e, the base of natural logarithms, using its series expansion

$$e = \frac{1}{0!} + \frac{1}{1!} + \frac{1}{2!} + \frac{1}{3!} + ... = \sum_{n=0}^{\infty} \frac{1}{n!}$$

We note that each term can be computed easily if the previous term is already known, so we use a method `nextTerm` to do this as opposed to calculating each factorial from scratch. `nextTerm` is actually short enough to be written out inside `computeE` but we write it as a separate method to demonstrate the lessons of the previous section.

```
      public class EComputation
      {
        // The number of terms to be added up.
        public static final int TERMS = 20;

        // The constant E to be computed
        public static final double E = computeE();


        // The method 'nextTerm' computes a term
        // in the expansion given the previous term
        // and the index of the term to be computed.
        public static double nextTerm(double prev,
                                       int index)
        {
          return prev/index;
        }


        // The method 'computeE' sums the series.
        public static double computeE()
        {
          double res = 1;
          double term = 1;

          for (int i=1; i<TERMS; i++)
          {
```

```
            term = nextTerm(term, i);
            res += term;
        }

        return res;
    }


    // The main method just prints the constant.
    public static void main(String[] argv)
    {
        System.out.println(E);
    }
}
```

This program is called EComputation.java and is available from the website at http://www.jscieng.co.uk/Code/JavaForC/EComputation/. As we noted in the first chapter, you may want to download the entire Code directory, available at http://www.jscieng.co.uk/Code.tar.gz or http://www.jscieng.co.uk/Code.zip. To compile the program, move to the appropriate directory at a command line and type 'javac EComputation.java'. There will not be any response to this command except for a pause before the command prompt reappears. However, the program has successfully compiled and a file EComputation.class has been generated. To run the program type 'java EComputation'. Note that the .class is omitted.

Note that the constant E can be initialized from a method. This is perfectly valid: the method does not use E, and the compiler makes sure that the methods computeE has been called and E initialized before any other code, for example the main method, is run. What would be illegal is to declare E as a constant and then to set its value in some later code, as opposed to in the initializer.

3.5   Reserved words

The following words are reserved for internal use in the Java language or for future expansion and may not be used for names of classes, variables or methods:

abstract, boolean, break, byte, byvalue, case, cast, catch, char, class, const, continue, default, do, double, else, extends, false, final, finally, float, for, future, generic, goto, if, implements, import, inner, instanceof, int, interface, long, native, new, null, operator, outer, package, private, protected, public, rest, return, short, static, strictfp, super, switch, synchronized, this, throw, throws, transient, true, try, var, void, volatile, while, widefp

Table 3.1 Basic data types.

`boolean`	logical truth	1 bit	`true` or `false`
`byte`	signed integer	8 bits	−128 to 127
`short`	signed integer	16 bits	−32 768 to 32 767
`int`	signed integer	32 bits	−2.1e9 to 2.1e9
`long`	signed integer	64 bits	−9.2e18 to 9.2e18
`float`	IEEE 754 floating point	32 bits	1.4e−45 to 3.4e38
`double`	IEEE 754 floating point	64 bits	4.9e−324 to 1.8e308

3.6 Comments

There are two sorts of comments in Java. The long form of comment is exactly the same as in C. It may last over several lines, starts with /* and ends with */. The short form of comment is that used in C++. It starts with // and lasts until the end of the current line of text:

```
/* This is a comment. It does not end here...
   but keeps on going until it reaches a */

// This is also a comment which ends at the end of the line
```

Comments may be placed on the same line as pieces of code (although you must remember that a short form comment *preceding* a piece of code on the same line will cause the code not to be compiled!). Long form comments may not be nested within each other. In other words, the code

```
/* A long style comment /* Another trying to nest inside. */ */
```

will not compile correctly. You should use short style comments when embedding comments into code. These comments may be embedded inside long form comments, so this will enable you to comment out a large block of code if you need to without worrying about ending up nesting long form comments.

3.7 Basic data types

Java offers a number of basic types for storing integers and floating point numbers. These are listed in Table 3.1. Note that the `boolean` data type is *not* an integer, in contrast to C/C++.

The `float` data type stores real numbers to eight significant figures of accuracy, whilst `double` stores them to 16. As we mention later, floating point calculations default to using `double`, so `float` is available mainly to offer you the chance to save memory. Scientific computing should usually be done entirely using `double`. At the time of writing (August 1998), there is a proposal underway to use the keywords `strictfp` and `widefp` to distinguish between standardized floating point arithmetic and faster arithmetic, done at machine precision. You will have to refer to Sun's website at `http://java.sun.com/` to discover the outcome.

These look much the same as the types provided by C/C++. However, unlike these languages, the ranges of the data types are guaranteed. Regardless of the machine architecture, all of the above will be available and will have the stated sizes. `unsigned` data types do not exist.

Local variables are declared in exactly the same way as in C, as we have seen in the examples (class variables are prefixed with `public static`). As in C, we can provide initializing expressions at the point of declaration, such as

```
int count = 0;
```

and these can be method calls if desired. In addition, Java provides a piece of syntax copied from C++. This allows us to insert a variable declaration line into the program at any point, as well as just at the top of the method. Hence, for example, we can write

```
int count;

<some code>

double d;

<more code>
```

Integer and floating point numerical values are entered exactly as in C. You should already know that C-style syntax causes some fairly serious problems in this area, especially in the case of division:

```
double d = 1/3;
```

will evaluate to set `d=0.0` in both Java and C, because integer division is applied to the integers on the right-hand side, giving the integer part of the result. This can be corrected by typing

```
double d = 1.0 / 3;
```

If you are in any way unsure about this problem, then please read Section 2.7.

3.8   Constants

As we have already mentioned, `#define` does not exist in Java, so constants are implemented differently from C. In addition, for some reason the designers chose not to use the `const` syntax from C++.

Instead, Java implements constants using the keyword `final`, which is inserted into what looks like a standard variable declaration in front of the data type:

```
final int STEPS = 50;
```

Constants can also be declared at the class level, in which case this should be preceded by `public static` as normal. Note that a constant must be initialized immediately, as above. After the declaration its value is fixed. You may initialize constants with expressions to be computed, even those involving method calls, and these will be performed before the program starts.

Typed constants, like those in Java, provide an advantage over textual substitution as provided by `#define` in C, since they enable the compiler to check that the constant is being used appropriately.

3.9   Operators

The standard C operators `+`, `-`, `*`, `/`, `%`, `++`, `--`, `<`, `<=`, `>`, `>=`, `==`, `!=`, `!`, `&`, `|`, `^`, `&&`, `||`, `<<`, `=`, `+=`, `-=`, `*=`, `/=`, `%=`, `&=`, `|=`, `^=` and `<<=` are all provided and perform exactly the same function as in C, except that the comparison operators return true `boolean` values as opposed to integers.

In C, the rightward bit shift `>>` is partially undefined: it is unspecified whether the new top bits are filled with zeros or the integer value is sign extended. Java needs to define this because of its greater portability. As a result, two sets of rightward bit shifts are provided: `>>` (and `>>=`) perform sign extension, whilst `>>>` (and `>>>=`) fill the new top bits with zeros.

The '+' operator is overloaded to perform concatenation of strings. Any text written in double quotation marks (`"`) is automatically a string, as in C, and + is capable of converting all other standard data types into strings. Hence we can write commands like:

```
double value;
System.out.println("The value is: " + value);
```

Finally, the `*` operator is used in C/C++ for declaring and dereferencing pointers. Java does not contain pointers and uses references instead. The syntax for references differs from that for pointers and does not use `*`. This syntax is discussed in the next chapter. However, `=` and `==` do behave with references as they would with pointers. They are concerned with equality of the references — that is, whether the references refer to the same object — as opposed to whether the objects referred to are equal.

3.10   Flow control

`if (...) ... else ...`, `? :`, `switch`, `for`, `while` and `do ... while` all behave exactly as they do in C.

You should note that, unlike C/C++, there is a `boolean` data type which is not the same as `int`. `if`, `?`, `for` and `while` all take a `boolean` argument in the obvious place. This means that

```
int i = 0;

if (i)
```

is no longer valid! You will have to write

```
if (i != 0}
```

There is one additional feature of `for` loops, which is borrowed from C++. This is that variables may be declared inside the `for` expression. Hence, for example, in C you would write:

```
int i;

for (i=0; i<10; i++)
{
  <code>
}
```

whereas in Java or C++ you can write:

```
for (int i=0; i<10; i++)
{
  <code>
}
```

3.11 Constructed data types

In C, you can construct a new data type using the keyword `struct`. In C++, `struct` still works, but `class` is preferred. Similarly, Java provides support for this through its object orientation and the keyword `class`. The following are equivalent.

In C:

```
struct Complex
{
  double realpart;
  double imagpart;
};
```

In C++:

```
class Complex
{
public:
  double realpart;
  double imagpart;
};
```

and in Java:

```
public class Complex
{
  public double realpart;
  public double imagpart;
}
```

This is discussed much more fully in Section 4.3.3 and in Chapter 6. Note that such declarations involve multiple classes, which are also discussed in the next chapter, and so may require additional `.java` files. Classes must be manipulated by reference, unlike in C++ and unlike `struct` in C.

Java does not support `typedef`, bit fields, `union` or `enum`. The last of these is somewhat surprising given that Java is a strongly typed language. However, the standard is to store enumerated values in an `int` and to define each of the possible values as a class constant.

3.12 Mathematical functions

Section 5.2 discusses in detail how to include the standard libraries in your programs and what features they provide.

Although some of these features cannot be explained until that point, we jump briefly ahead to state that the standard functions `sin`, `cos`, `tan`, `asin`, `acos`, `atan`, `exp`, `log`, `pow`, `sqrt`, `round`, `abs`, `max` and `min` and the constants `PI` and `E` all exist and are used with the syntax `Math.<function>(<arguments>)`.

For example, we can write

```
double x = 3.5;
double y = Math.sin(x);
double z = Math.pow(y, 3);
```

Refer to Section 5.2 itself for further details on these functions and explanation of this notation.

3.13 Other differences from C

- `goto` does not exist. The equivalent functionality is provided by a combination of labelled `break` and `continue` and exceptions. Both of these are discussed in Section 4.4.

- In C you can pass a pointer to a value as an argument to allow a function to change the value. In Java, references provide the same functionality (see Section 4.3).

- In C, the name of a function, without round brackets after it to call the function, is treated as a **function pointer**. This can be stored in a variable and then later called. This enables you to write functions that take other functions as arguments. For example, you can write a function that integrates a function passed to it over a given range.

- In Java, function pointers do not exist. The equivalent mechanism is implemented using object inheritance and `interface`, as discussed in Section 6.6.4.

- `void` cannot be used to specify an empty argument list. This must be done with a pair of empty brackets.

- There is no **void reference**, equivalent to `void *` pointers in C. A reference to a `java.lang.Object` comes fairly close to this, since all object types are descended from this object.

- There is no `sizeof` operator.

- There is a special value, `null`, for references which do not point anywhere, but this is not equivalent to `0`. `nil` and `NULL` do not exist.

- `if` statements do not allow checking for `null` references using the syntax `if (ref)`; instead, you must write `if (ref != null)`.

- The comma operator that is used in C to perform several actions on the same line of code does not exist in Java. It is provided in the one special case of `for` loops to allow multiple statements within the initial expression or the increment expression. However, it cannot be used in any other circumstances.

- Strings in C are represented as an array of characters. In Java, they are stored using objects of the type `String`. Text placed in double quotation marks is automatically converted into an object of this type.

3.14 Additional differences from C++

In addition to the differences from C that are listed above, Java differs from C++ in the following ways.

3.14.1 General

- Operator overloading does not exist. This is definitely a shame, since it would allow us to handle mathematical structures such as matrices and vectors in a much nicer way. However, it was deliberately omitted for simplicity of syntax. Visual Numerics are campaigning to introduce some limited overloading for the JNL (see Chapter 8).

- Templates do not exist either, for the same reason. Java without templates is more capable than C++ without templates, since in Java all objects are automatically descended from `java.lang.Object`, and all data types can be made into objects. Thus, you can write generalized structures such as lists to accept `java.lang.Object`, and they will be able to accept anything.

- Name mangling: Java does support method overloading, though the implementation of this is internal to the compiler and does not cause method names to be modified in a way that is accessible to the programmer.

- `const` does not exist. `final` replaces this for declaring constants, but there is no equivalent to `const` for declaring arguments to methods which may not be changed.

- Default arguments for methods do not exist. However, you may produce a similar effect using method overloading, as discussed in Section 3.3.

3.14.2 Object orientation

- All class member functions are `virtual`. Non-`virtual` member functions do not exist in any form. The slight speed advantage that non-`virtual` functions gain by not having to be looked up in the virtual function table is possible under some circumstances using the keyword `final` (discussed in Section 6.6.2).

- Destructors do not exist. The idea of a destructor is somewhat problematic in Java since objects are deleted by the garbage collector, so the exact timing of their deletion is unpredictable. In addition, the standard use of a destructor is to deallocate some memory that was allocated for the class in its constructor. This is no longer necessary, since this memory will be garbage collected after the class is gone. However, if you must find something equivalent to destructors , then an inferior mechanism, called **finalizers** , is available. These are inferior since they do not automatically chain. This mechanism is discussed in Section 6.5.

- Multiple inheritance does not exist. This greatly simplifies the language. It is only possible to inherit actual code from one class, but classes may also inherit virtual functions from abstract base classes, called **interfaces**. This is discussed further in Section 6.6.3.

- Access control is performed differently. There are four classes of control in Java: `public`, the default, `protected` and `private`. These correspond only roughly to the C++ commands. Classes may be only `public` or default, and they may change the access controls only on classes from which they inherit to make them more public. Access control modifiers are placed in front of every variable or method, as opposed to delimiting sections of the declaration. The concept of a `friend` is partially implemented with the extra levels, but does not explicitly exist. This is discussed in Section 6.4.

- In C++ you can create objects using `new` or can declare them as local variables, in which case the storage is deleted when the function is finished. In Java all objects are created with `new` and handled by reference.

- C++ lets you define automatic conversions of objects into other objects or other data types. This cannot be done in Java.

- In C++, during an object's construction the virtual function table is repeatedly rewritten. For example, if a class A is descended from B, then the virtual function table for A is not used until after the chaining of B's constructor has finished. The automatic call to B's constructor runs with the virtual function table for an object of type B. Hence, for example, you may not call pure virtual functions in a constructor, even if the subclasses implement them. In Java, by contrast, the final virtual function table is used right from the beginning. This means that you can call such functions in constructors. The potential drawback is that functions defined in A may try to use data set up in A's constructor. If you accidently call such a function from B's constructor, then it may fail since A's constructor has not yet run.

- In C++ all variables in a class definition exist once for every instance of the class, and all member functions act on these. Other code and global variables are written outside the class definition. In Java, all code is written inside a class definition. Object oriented code is declared without the keyword `static`, whilst code and variables which would not be part of a class in C++ are declared as `static`.

- The `::` operator does not exist. The class declaration and definition are combined and the code is written inside there.

- Constructors which take no arguments must still be explicitly called by putting a pair of empty brackets in the `new` statement. For example, we would write `new`

```
Complex(); above.
```

- A constructor calls its superclass constructors in the first line of its code, as opposed to before its main block of code starts.
- The class declaration/definition is not followed by a semicolon.

EXERCISES

This chapter has brought you to a similar standard to that reached at the end of Chapter 2. Hence, all of the exercises at the end of that chapter would now be appropriate. In addition, the following exercises concentrate on the differences between C/C++ and Java. The later ones are specific to C++.

3.1 What is wrong with the following program fragment?

```
int remainder;

for (int i=1; i<=100; i++)
{
   remainder = i % 7;

   if (!remainder)
      System.out.println(i + "divides by seven.");
}
```

3.2 What is wrong with this function declaration?

```
public static int random(void)
```

3.3 Java objects do not have destructors; C++ objects do. Why is this feature less necessary in Java?

3.4 We define the following class:

```
public class Complex
{
   public double realpart;
   public double imagpart;
};
```

Indicate one mistake in the definition. Why does the following line fail?

```
Complex c = new Complex;
```

WHERE TO GO FROM HERE

You now understand the basics of programming in Java. The previous chapter covered exactly the same ground as this one and, as a C/C++ programmer, you were advised to read this instead. However, you are now able to understand all of the example code in that chapter and may decide to go back and look at it. Chapters 4 to 6 describe the remainder of the language.

CHAPTER 4

Advanced Java

4.1 Introduction

This chapter follows on from either Chapter 2 or Chapter 3 and teaches more advanced syntax. Although I believe that all topics covered in this and all subsequent chapters are interesting and relevant to the scientific programmer, we have already covered a sufficient volume of material to enable you to write worthwhile programs. Given this situation, it is only fair to indicate the interdependencies in the remainder of the book so that those who wish to hurry straight to specific sections may do so. This is done in Figure 4.1.

I would urge you to master this chapter and Section 5.2, which will bring you to a level approximating to standard Pascal. Beyond that, the choice is yours, although I should mention that if you do not explore object orientation and the graphical and Internet features of the language (both of which can be done using the JSGL) then you will be missing out on much that Java has to offer.

Finally, before beginning this chapter, you are reminded that all of the substantial programs in it are available at `http://www.jscieng.co.uk/Code/AdvJava/`.

4.2 Working with multiple classes

So far, all of the programs that you have written have consisted of a single class stored in a single `.java` file. Java does, of course, allow you to extend this to work with projects containing many classes. For instance, you might want to write a standard toolbox class of your own, containing your commonly used methods, and then use this class in all of your programs. In addition, the language provides quite large standard libraries, and these are used in exactly the same way as extra classes of your own would be.

Unfortunately the syntax used to work with multiple classes is fairly complicated and the benefits of this complexity are not immediately obvious. However, it is necessary to

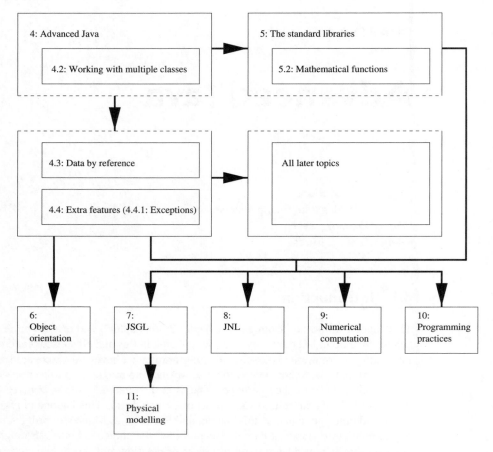

Figure 4.1 Dependencies in Chapters 4–11.

understand this syntax before we can move on to discuss objects or the standard libraries, so we cover it in its full depth in this section.

4.2.1 Packages

In large projects, you may provide some structure for your classes by dividing them into several groups. Java provides support for this through the concept of **packages**. Every class belongs to some package, and every package can be generated from one or more .java files each containing one or more classes. The packages are structured in a hierarchical fashion – each package may have lower level packages – and are referred to using textual lower case names, with the parts of the name separated by decimal points. A class in a lower level package is not also considered to be in that package's parent package.

Packaging is achieved by inserting a new top line into each .java file. Each file may contain several classes, all of which will be put into the package named in the top line. Only one of the classes in a `.java` file may be declared `public` because the `.java` file is named after its public class. Only public classes may be used by classes from other packages. Ordinary classes may be used by all classes in their package, whether or not these are in the same `.java` file. The syntax is:

```
package <package name>;

public class <class name>
{
    <class structure as normal>
}

class <optional extra classes>
{
    <class structure as normal>
}
```

All of our classes so far have had a `main` method. This is not a requirement of class structure. It provides a starting point for execution of the program. Therefore, in a large project, including many classes, only one of these need have a `main` method, and that is where execution will start. The class containing the `main` method must be public.

Up until this point, we have omitted the package line, which meant that all of our classes were in an unnamed top-level package. This is allowed for experimentation, testing and brevity. However, you should learn the package syntax in order to be able to write larger structured programs and to be able to use the standard libraries.

To refer to a class, you use its fully qualified name, which is produced by writing the package name in front of the class name. Class names conventionally start with a capital letter, which enables you to see where the package name ends. A package may not contain a class with a fully qualified name which is also used as a lower level package's name. This means that there is no possibility of confusion.

Figure 4.2 gives an example of packaging of classes. Note that the class `animal.cat.Claw` will not be able to refer to `animal.bird.Wing`, since this class is not public and is in a different package.

Because Java has a major role as an Internet language, a standard naming scheme has been suggested for packages to ensure that different developers do not produce code that conflicts with each other. The scheme is for package names to start with the reversal of your organization's Internet Domain Name, and then for the organization to allocate space within this. For example, Microsoft owns the domain name `microsoft.com`. Under this convention, all of their packages would be within `com.microsoft` and they could organize any further subdivision themselves. For example, a spreadsheet might be written using packages within `com.microsoft.spreadsheet`. This book does not name packages according to this scheme, mainly for brevity. You should probably do so if you write software for wide distribution.

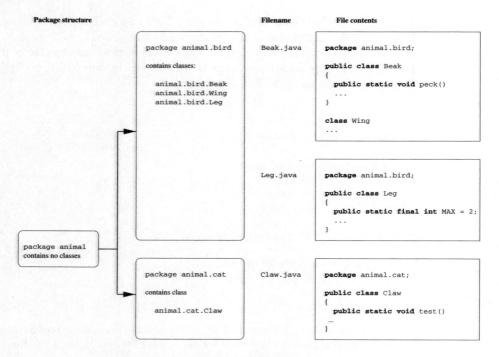

Figure 4.2   Packaging of classes.

4.2.2   Importing packages

To refer to another class's class variables, constants or methods, we can prefix the fully qualified name of the class in front of the required item. For example, in Figure 4.2 Leg defines a constant called MAX and any other class can refer to this by the name animal.bird.Leg.MAX. Similarly, Claw contains the method test and another class can refer to this as animal.cat.Claw.test.

This syntax is somewhat awkward, so Java provides several shorthands. Firstly, any class can refer to any other within the same package using its unqualified name. For example, Leg could refer to the method peck of the class Beak, which is in the same package, using the name Beak.peck. Claw, however, cannot do this since it is not in the same package.

The second shorthand is the import statement. This can be written at the top of a .java file, and allows the programmer to specify certain classes which will be able to be used without full qualification within that .java file. There are two forms, both shown below (see later for a description of the '*' form).

```
package <package name of class>;
import <package1>.<specific class>;
import <package2>.*;

public class <class name>
```

```
{
  <class structure as normal>
}
```

A `.java` file may contain multiple `import` statements in order that its code may refer to several different classes without full qualification. `import` statements affect only the `.java` file in which they are written – they must be repeated in any other files in which the programmer wants to be able to make easy reference to the classes.

For example, if `Beak.java` contained the line

```
import animal.cat.Claw;
```

then it would be able to use the `test` method of the class `Claw` as `Claw.test`. The `*` form imports all of the files in a package, so if `Claw.java` contained the line

```
import animal.bird.*;
```

then it would be able to use both `Leg.MAX` and `Beak.peck` without further qualification. Note that we cannot use `*` to specify a range of packages (for example '`import animal.*.*;`') and also that, since a parent package does not include the classes in its lower level packages, '`import animal;`' does not include the classes from the package `animal.bird`.

At this point, we can discuss the call `System.out.println`, which we have used extensively. The most important parts of the Java standard library are stored in the package `java.lang`. This includes a class `System` with the method `out.println`. We could refer to this as `java.lang.System.out.println`, but the Java compiler automatically behaves as if our `.java` files included the line `import java.lang.*`, and so we can refer to it by the shorter form.

Note that unlike in C/C++, there is no concept of header files. Similarly, unlike in some versions of Pascal there is no division into `interface` and `implementation` sections. This makes the programmer's job easier since all code is stored in one place.

4.2.3 Compiling large projects

Now that we are handling large projects with several `.java` files to be compiled, a number of new issues appear. We need to consider which order to compile them in (for instance, what happens if one file references another?) and probably want to automate the whole procedure to stop it from becoming very boring.

Fortunately, Java provides two useful features at this point. Firstly, an optional argument to the compiler will allow it to work with `.java` and `.class` files that are in a hierarchical directory structure corresponding to their package structure. The '`-d <base directory>`' option turns this mode on and specifies a **base directory**. This is the directory which will contain the start of the hierarchical directory structure. In the situation shown in Figure 4.2, the base directory would contain a directory called `animal`, which would contain subdirectories `bird` and `cat`, each containing the `.class` files for that package.

Secondly, assuming that the above option is in force, the `-depend` option means that compiling the single file containing the `main` method will automatically cause the compiler to work out whether any of the other files need recompiling and to recompile them if they do. This works even if the files that have been changed are not directly referred to in the file with the `main` method. Note that this option is automatically selected in some recent versions of `javac`. These versions will give an error message if it is used at the command line and you may safely remove it if you see such a message.

As always, `javac` also takes the name of the `.java` file containing the `main` method as the last argument. Thus the compilation command looks like:

```
javac -depend -d <base directory> <.java file incl. main>
```

If you always issue this command from the base directory, then you can enter '.' for the base directory, but will need to specify the main `.java` file's location – it will probably be somewhere inside the hierarchical directory structure.

Just as Java is capable of using methods before they have been defined, when this method of compilation is used the compiler is capable of handling situations where two files both use the other and many other such cases. You do not need to specify an order for compilation of the files, and what's more there does not even need to be a simple linear order in which they build on each other.

The fact that Java is capable of working out which files need recompilation is symptomatic of a more general distinction from other standard languages. Languages such as C and Pascal are generally statically linked. This means that all of the compiled code is joined together in a monolithic block. Java is dynamically linked: the `.class` files contain structural information about their methods, enabling their references into each other to be resolved during execution. This is a more modern programming mechanism and means, for example, that a single `.class` file can be replaced by a more modern version of itself and the other `.class` files in the program will still manage to interlink with it.

If you ever want to recompile the entire project from scratch (for instance, if the compiler seems to have failed to spot which files need recompilation), then this can be achieved by deleting all of the `.class` files before running `javac`. You could do this by hand, but it could become very boring and time consuming. Under Windows, it would be better done using the 'Find Files...' command (right click on the base directory) to find all `.class` files for you. Under UNIX, typing

```
rm `find . -name "*.class"`
```

in the base directory will find and delete all of these files.

As an example, the minimization project that is discussed in Section 4.2.4 uses three classes: `Minimize` and `Function` from a package `minimize.partone` and `Region` from a package `minimize.parttwo`. We create a base directory `Minimize` to contain the whole project.

Next, corresponding to the package structure, we place the files `Minimize.java` and `Function.java` inside a directory `partone` inside a directory `minimize` inside the `Minimize` base directory. The file `Region.java` goes inside a directory `parttwo` inside the directory `minimize` inside the base directory. The directory structure is shown in Figure 4.3.

At this point, moving to the base directory and issuing the command

```
javac -depend -d . minimize\partone\Minimize.java
```

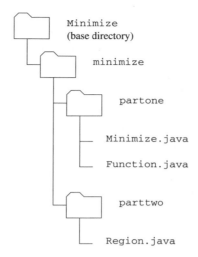

Figure 4.3 Directory structure for minimization project.

under Windows, or

```
javac -depend -d . minimize/partone/Minimize.java
```

under UNIX will cause the compiler to compile all of the files in the project and place the `.class` files into their correct places in the hierarchical directory structure. Note the spaces around the '.' in both cases and remove `-depend` if this causes an error message.

Better still, if we change a single file, say `Region.java`, issuing exactly the same command from the base directory will first detect which files need to be compiled and will then recompile only those files that have changed or that use something which has changed.

Having all of this functionality built into the compiler means that utilities such as `make` under UNIX are effectively redundant. The only useful automation that we can provide is to store the compilation command in a batch file/shell script, since it is rather long to type repeatedly. Note that you can also use batch files/shell scripts in a similar way for single file projects, but that it is probably not worth the effort in that case.

Under Windows, we create a file `compile.bat` in a text editor, containing the line:

```
javac -depend -d . minimize\partone\Minimize.java
```

and save this file in the base directory. From this point, typing 'compile' in this directory will run this batch file.

Under UNIX, we can write a shell script containing the equivalent compilation command (with the opposite kind of slash for directory separators). We then use `chmod a+x <script name>` to make it runnable. Alternatively, we can write a `makefile` containing the lines:

```
all :
    javac -depend -d . minimize/partone/Minimize.java
```

and run this by typing 'make' in the base directory. Note that the indentation must be provided by a tab and that it is important not to specify Minimize.class as the target in the makefile, since compilation can in fact affect any of the classes that have changed.

4.2.4   Example – minimizing over a region

At this point, we consider an example program which finds the minimum of a function over a region. This was the program that we discussed in the last subsection. It is rather artificially split into three classes in order to display the structures you have just learnt. The class Function contains a single method, evaluate, to compute the function at any point, inside or outside the region. The class Region contains a method isInside which returns whether a given point is inside the region. The class Minimize contains the main method which steps across a square extending one unit in both directions from the origin, taking STEPS steps per unit travelled, evaluating the function at every grid point, checking if it lies inside the region, and updating the minimum if it does. All of the code for this example is available at http://www.jscieng.co.uk/Code/AdvJava/Minimize/.

Stored in Function.java, we have:

```
package minimize.partone;

public class Function
{
  // This is the function whose value we are
  // trying to minimize.
  public static double evaluate(double x, double y)
  {
    return (x-0.5)*(x-0.5) + 3*y*(y-1);
  }
}
```

Stored in Region.java, we have:

```
package minimize.parttwo;

public class Region
{
  // isInside returns if a point is inside the
  // region or not.
  public static boolean isInside(double x, double y)
  {
    if (x*x + y*y < 1.0/4)
      return true;
    else
      return false;
  }
}
```

Finally, Minimize.java contains:

```
package minimize.partone;

// Import minimize.parttwo so we can use Region
import minimize.parttwo.*;

public class Minimize
{
  // Define the fineness of the grid with
  // which we step across the region
  public static final int STEPS = 500;


  // The main method.
  public static void main(String[] argv)
  {
    double lowest, x, y;

    // Set lowest to an unachievably high value
    lowest = Double.POSITIVE_INFINITY;

    // and then step across the grid, updating
    // lowest every time we find a lower point
    // which is inside the region.
    for (x = -1 ; x <= 1 ; x += 1.0/STEPS)
      for (y = -1; y <= 1; y += 1.0/STEPS)
      {
        if ((Function.evaluate(x,y) < lowest)
            && Region.isInside(x,y))
        {
          lowest = Function.evaluate(x,y);
        }
      }

    System.out.println(lowest);
  }
}
```

Once you have successfully compiled this program code, which is best done as described in the previous subsection, the program can be run by typing

```
java minimize.partone.Minimize
```

at a command line whilst in the base directory of the .class files' directory structure (if you compiled with 'javac -d .', then this will be the same directory in which you issued this command). This is exactly like running a single file program: the command java starts the interpreter, and the argument specifies the class containing the main method at which execution should start. The fully qualified name of this class is used to enable the interpreter to find it within the .class files' directory structure.

There are several points to be noted about the above program. Firstly, the for loops may be nested within each other and need not use an integer as their control variable. In addition, since an entire `for` loop counts as a single block, the outer loop need not place curly brackets about the inner loop. Secondly, the `main` method contains a complicated `if` statement: note that the return type of `Region.isInside` is `boolean` and so can be used directly without adding a comparison operator. Finally, when initially setting `lowest`, we use the value `Double.POSITIVE_INFINITY` to ensure that any other value will be lower. The special values for real numbers are discussed in Section 5.10.

4.2.5 Summary – multiple classes

- **The** `.java` **file** contains one or more class definitions. Only one may be public. The `.java` file is named after this class.
- **The** `package` **statement** places all classes defined in a `.java` file into the named package.
- **Fully qualified name** consists of `<package name>.<class name>`. Allows classes to refer to those in other packages. They can omit `<package name>` for classes in their own package.
- `public`: Only `public` classes may be referred to from outside their package.
- **Class variables and methods** are accessed via their class's fully qualified name as `<class name>.<variable or method>`.
- **The** `import` **statement** allows you to refer to classes from other packages without full qualification.
- **Compilation:** '`javac -depend -d . <hierarchical directories>/<file>.java`'
- **Execution:** '`java <fully qualified name of class with main method>`'

4.3   Data by reference

Until now, all of the data that we have dealt with has been stored in **primitive data types**: integers, floating point numbers or booleans. In addition to these, Java allows the programmer to create and use more complicated data types, built up from these primitives. These data types are referred to as **reference data types** because they are handled **by reference**. Primitive data types are handled **by value**, which means that the actual values are stored in the variables and passed to methods. By contrast, the data for reference data types is stored in some other area of memory and we handle it using **references**, which record the position of the data itself. This is done because these data types can become very large and so it could take substantial amounts of processor time to move or copy the actual data.

The two reference types that we will consider are arrays and objects. An array consists of a large, fixed size list of identical data types (such as a vector or matrix), whilst an object contains specified, named pieces of data which may be of any type (such as a structure for storing both an eigenvalue and its eigenvector, or perhaps a data type that contains both an integer storing the integer part of a number and a floating point variable storing the rest of it). Objects behave like `struct` in C, `class` in C++, `record` in Pascal or `object` in Modula-3. There is no equivalent structure in FORTRAN 77, whose users have to maintain synchronized parallel arrays for each type of data to be stored. We will consider arrays first because they are simpler and we can use them to explain the general behaviour of reference types.

It is important to understand reference types – you cannot just assume that they behave like data handled by value. For example, the following code fragment creates an array and then performs some simple operations on it (the exact syntax used is explained later in the section):

```
double[] a = { 1, 2, 3 };
double[] b = a;
b[0] = 7;
System.out.println(a[0]);
```

If you treat this as if it were handled by value, then you would expect b to become a copy of a, the copy stored in b to be altered and then the `println` to output 1. However, it actually outputs 7 because b is set to refer to the same data at a, not to a copy of it, so altering b alters a too.

4.3.1 Arrays

Note that the size of an array is fixed. To get a similar data structure with the ability to resize, consider the class `java.util.Vector`, described later in Section 5.11.

The JNL contains many methods for handling vectors and matrices and performing standard operations on them. These are documented in Section 8.4. However, you will have to finish this section before you understand enough to be able to use the JNL.

A reference to an array is declared in Java using either of the syntaxes

```
<data type>[] <variable name>;
```

```
<data type> <variable name>[];
```

The first of these is probably preferable; the second preserves compatibility with C/C++ but can be confusing in complicated statements as the definition of the data type is spread across both ends of the line of code.

These do not actually create an array, but merely declare that the type of a variable is a reference to an array. To actually create an array we use one of two constructions. Either we can use `new`, followed by the data type and the size of the array in square brackets, to obtain an array initialized to zero, or we can enter the starting values for the members of the array, enclosed in curly brackets. In both cases, we use an assignment to make the reference refer to the array. Thus either of the following is legal:

```
int[] table;
table = {1, 2, 4, 8, 16, 32};
```

```
double[] vector;
vector = new double[5];
```

In addition, in either case we may perform the creation of the reference and the creation of the array that it refers to on the same line of code:

```
int[] table = {1, 2, 4, 8, 16, 32};
double[] vector = new double[5];
```

If we use the starting value syntax, then the values may be arbitrary expressions, such as method calls, unlike in C/C++.

Once our array has been created, we refer to elements using the syntax

```
<array reference name>[<element number>]
```

Elements in the array are numbered from zero, and must start with zero (unlike in Fortran or Pascal whose users can choose the starting index, which is 1 by default). If we created the array using the size syntax, then the final element is at [size-1], not [size]. An array element can be used precisely like a normal variable in assignment, tests and other operations. For example

```
int[] table = new int[6];

table[0] = 1;

for (int i=1; i<6; i++)
  table[i] = 2 * table[i-1];
```

will create the same array that we declared using the starting value syntax above.

We can also create multidimensional arrays. The reference variable is simply declared using extra square brackets to enumerate the expected number of dimensions:

```
double[][][] cubevalues;
```

is a three-dimensional array, for example. Once again, we can create the actual array using new or a set of starting values. The one complication is that the multidimensional array is implemented as an array of references to subarrays. This means that the subarrays need not actually be the same size, so we can create two-dimensional arrays which are not rectangular.

For instance, we create rectangular arrays by:

```
double[][] squarevalues = { {1.0, 2.7, 3.4},
                            {7.6, 0.0, 3.2},
                            {1.8, 6.3, 2.4} };

// This new call creates array and subarrays.
int[][] squaretable = new int[5][5];
```

Note how the starting value syntax makes it clear that this is an array of arrays. However, we can also create non-rectangular arrays in which the component subarrays are not all the same size. For instance:

```
double[] bit = {1.8, 6.3};

double[][] values = { {1.0, 2.7, 3.4},
                      {7.6},
                      bit };
```

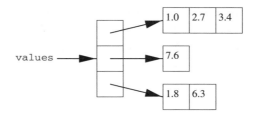

Figure 4.4 The array 'values'.

```
// This new call only creates an array
// of null references.
int[][] table = new int[5][];
table[0] = new int[3];
table[1] = new int[2];
```

Once again, the way in which we can put the one-dimensional array bit inside the two-dimensional array values, or the way in which we can create the component subarrays of table independently, emphasizes that this really is an array of references to subarrays. The structure of the array values is shown in Figure 4.4, in which arrows denote references.

These multidimensional arrays' elements are treated just as those for simple arrays are. We use extra sets of square brackets to index each additional dimension.

Finally, unlike many other languages, in Java the interpreter checks that all uses of the array stay within its declared size. If you step outside this range, the interpreter will throw an ArrayIndexOutOfBoundsException (see Section 4.4.1 for exception handling). Arrays are not accessed using pointers, unlike in C/C++, which makes this possible and also prevents the programmer from performing pointer arithmetic with positions in the array. The programmer can find out the size of an array by adding .length onto the end of the variable's name. For example, to clear an array:

```
for (int i=0; i<array.length; i++)
    array[i] = 0;
```

This syntax using .length is very much like that which we will use with objects later in this chapter.

4.3.2 References

Since we now know how to create one sort of reference type, we can enter a more general discussion of operating on data using references. As discussed above, the idea is that you create the actual data structure somewhere in memory using new, but that you use a reference to get at the data. The reference must be declared as a variable. Next, data storage can be allocated using new or a set of starting values, and then the reference can be set to refer to that data. Alternatively, we can use the '=' operator to set a reference to refer to the same data as another existing reference.

References can be passed to methods, returned from methods, and manipulated much as normal variables. For example, the following is valid:

```
public static int thirdElement(int[] array)
{
  return array[2];  // The array starts at zero.
}

public static void main(String[] argv)
{
  int[] numbers = {1, 5, 7, 9, 13};

  System.out.println(thirdElement(numbers));
}
```

Note that the array `numbers` is passed by reference. This stops the data from having to be copied. The local variable `array` in `thirdElement` is simply set to refer to the same bit of memory as `numbers`. This is much faster than copying arrays, which could be very large. This discussion explains another, potentially unexpected property of references. Normally, a method may not change the values of its arguments. This is also true for references: the method may not change where the reference passed to it refers to. However, it may change the value of data that is referred to. Thus

```
public static void change(int value)
{
  value = 3;
}
```

is incorrect, as is

```
public static void change(int[] values)
{
  values = {1, 2, 3, 5};
}
```

However, the following is legal:

```
public static void changeThird(int[] values)
{
  values[2] = 7;
}
```

If we actually wanted to change the value of all of the elements of the array, then since the reference is fixed to refer to one particular array, we must change each element in turn:

```
public static void change(int[] values)
{
  int[] newvalues = {1, 2, 3, 5};

  for (int i=0; i<4; i++)
    values[i] = newvalues[i];
}
```

Thus variables passed by reference behave like `var` parameters in Pascal or those passed as pointers in C or references in C++ (in Fortran it is undefined whether variables are passed by value or by reference). There is no equivalent of the `const` syntax provided by C++ to stop data that references refer to from being changed. Passing by reference can be useful: for instance a method might need to return several values, and the extra parts could be returned via reference parameters. However, it is also potentially dangerous in distorting the obvious program flow. There is no simple way to pass primitive data types by reference in a way that lets them be changed by a method.

References are not pointers, which many other languages such as Pascal, C and C++ use. However, they behave in a very similar way, except that there is no way for the programmer to find out the actual address of the data in memory, and therefore pointer arithmetic cannot be performed. This is a security feature in Java to prevent programs loaded from the Internet from accessing data which they should not. It is also useful since it makes it harder to write incorrect programs. Pointers do not exist at all in Java, and references are the nearest equivalent. If you have used C/C++, you should note that the '`.`' operator that we use to dereference objects later in the chapter is much more like '`->`' in these languages than their '`.`' operator.

Another useful feature that references provide and pointers do not is **garbage collection**. The Java interpreter will automatically detect when some data is no longer referred to by any references and will then delete it. This contrasts with traditional languages in which the programmer must explicitly dispose of all memory that they allocate and makes programming both easier and more bug-free.

There is one potentially surprising feature of references: the standard assignment and comparison operators perform their actions on the reference, not on the actual data.

For example, in the code

```
double[] one = {7.6, 5.4, 3.21};
double[] two = {7.6, 5.4, 3.21};
double[] three;

if (one == two)
    three = two;
```

the comparison `==` does not compare the actual data in the arrays. Instead it compares whether the two references `one` and `two` refer to the same array. Similarly, the assignment `=` does not make a copy of `two`'s array in `three`, but instead changes `three` to refer to the same array as `two`. If we consider an extreme case, we can see that arrays containing a single integer behave very differently from an `int` variable.

Because of this, extra functions are provided to perform actions on the values referred to by the references. For objects, constructors from the same type are used to copy the actual data and there is an `equals` method (both are discussed in the next subsection), whilst for arrays the class `java.lang.System` provides a method `arrayCopy`. Because of the standard implicit `import java.lang.*;`, this can be referred to as `System.arrayCopy`, and the syntax is:

```
System.arrayCopy(<source array>, <source start pos>,
                 <dest array>, <dest start pos>,
                 <no of elements to copy>);
```

Finally, there is one special value, `null`, for references. This value means that a reference does not currently refer to anything. If you create a reference variable, then it is set to `null` until you assign it something to refer to. You may perform comparisons with `null`, or even assign `null` to reference variables in order to stop them from referring to some piece of memory so that the interpreter will know that this memory is no longer being used and can be garbage collected. You may not attempt to use an element of a `null` array reference or access an object via a `null` reference. Either of these actions will result in a `NullPointerException` being thrown (see Section 4.4.1).

C/C++ users should note that, unlike `nil` or `NULL`, `null` is not equal to `0`. In addition, there is no shorthand for testing references in `if` statements:

```
if (ref) ...
```

is illegal in Java. You must write

```
if (ref != null) ...
```

4.3.3 Manipulating objects

As discussed earlier, we use references to manipulate objects. An object is a non-primitive data type which contains several named components. It is like a `struct` in C, a `class` in C++, a `record` in Pascal or an `object` in Modula-3. There is no equivalent structure in FORTRAN 77 whose users have to maintain synchronized parallel arrays for each type of data to be stored. Object orientation is a large topic and Chapter 6 provides much more detail on the syntax and concepts involved. However, for now we discuss this in enough detail to be able to use objects defined by other people, the JNL or the standard libraries.

An object in Java is produced from a class declaration in which the variables of the class are not static. For example, if we write

```
public class Complex
{
  public double realpart;
  public double imagpart;
}
```

omitting the word 'static' which has been in front of all previous variable and method declarations, then we have declared a data type called `Complex` which contains two parts called `realpart` and `imagpart`, both of which are of the type `double`.

This data type can be used in all situations in which primitive types can be used. We create a reference capable of referring to this data type with

```
Complex <variable name>;
```

and can then create the object for it to refer to (called an **instance** of the class) with `new Complex()`. Note the brackets at the end of this statement: unlike in C++, these are essential.

The two parts of the object are referred to by appending `.realpart` and `.imagpart` to the name of the variable referring to it. We cannot use `Complex.realpart` or `Complex.imagpart` – these variables only exist in instances of the class.

Hence we can now write code such as

```
public static void main(String[] argv)
{
  Complex a;

  a = new Complex();

  a.realpart = 1.0;
  a.imagpart = 3.4;
}
```

We can pass `Complex` objects to methods and get them back as return values. For example, the following method multiplies two complex numbers and returns the result:

```
public static Complex multiply(Complex a, Complex b)
{
  Complex ans = new Complex();

  ans.realpart = a.realpart * b.realpart;
  ans.realpart -= a.imagpart * b.imagpart;

  ans.imagpart = a.realpart * b.imagpart;
  ans.imagpart += a.imagpart * b.realpart;

  return ans;
}
```

If this was as far as objects went, then they would offer no improvement over `struct` or `record` in C and Pascal respectively. However, we are also able to define non-static methods. The way in which these are written is the major topic of Chapter 6. However, for the time being we note that such methods are intimately connected with their object. The method cannot be called using normal syntax (appending the method name to the class name), but is called by appending `.<methodname>(<argument list>)` to the end of a variable referring to an object of the correct type. The method will normally act to modify that object using the arguments that are passed to the method.

For example, we might consider writing a method to multiply a complex number by a scalar. Using a static method, this would be written as:

```
public static Complex scalarMultiply(Complex c, double s)
{
  Complex ans = new Complex();

  ans.realpart = c.realpart * s;
  ans.imagpart = c.imagpart * s;

  return ans;
}
```

and we could perform a multiplication in which an object was altered in place using code like

```
c = scalarMultiply(c, 2.7);
```

However, we can also write the method in a non-static manner. In this case, it implicitly acts to change the `Complex` object with which it is called. The equivalent method would be declared as (writing the actual code for this method involves new syntax and is the topic of Chapter 6):

```
public void scalarMultiply(double s)
```

and would be called using

```
c.scalarMultiply(2.7);
```

Note that the declaration omits the word '`static`', which has been used in every method declaration to date, and that the `Complex` argument, which gets altered in place, is entirely implicit. Nevertheless, the actions of the two calls are entirely equivalent.

Because of the problems with `==` for reference types, a special non-static method `equals` is provided. This takes an object as an argument and returns whether it is equal in value to the current one. Hence the expressions which you might think were written as:

```
if (a == b) ...
```

are in fact written for objects as

```
if (a.equals(b)) ...
```

This special method is optional – the language provides only a very basic version that is equivalent to `==` and classes must implement an improved version themselves. However, if such a method exists then it will have this name. It will exist for most well-written classes (such as those in the standard libraries). You will have to write it yourself for any classes that you produce.

Similarly, to correspond to `=`, objects often use a constructor (see next paragraph) from another object of the same sort to create copies. This is entirely optional on the part of the class's designer.

As a final (for now) enhancement, special non-static methods, called **constructors**, may be written which allow the programmer to specify some initial setup information when creating an object using a `new` statement. Constructors are declared as methods with no return type and the same name as the class of which they are part. We pass the setup information to the constructor in an argument list enclosed in round brackets following the `new` statement. You will notice that until now these brackets have existed, but have been empty. This corresponds to a default constructor, taking no arguments, which the compiler writes for us if we do not provide one. You can rewrite this constructor yourself if you wish.

For example, the `Complex` class might provide a constructor from two floating point numbers: the real and imaginary parts. This would be declared as:

```
public Complex(double a, double b)
{
    ...
}
```

We could now write either

```
Complex a = new Complex();
a.realpart = 1.0;
a.imagpart = 3.7;
```

or

```
Complex b = new Complex(1.0, 3.7);
```

If a class provides a constructor from an object of the same class, then this will create an exact copy of that object, and can be used like = would be for primitive types:

```
Complex a = new Complex(1.7, 5.6);
Complex b = new Complex(a);
```

would create a new object containing the same data as a if there was such a constructor for `Complex` objects.

You should note that classes may have both static and non-static variables and methods. The two behave completely independently, with static parts being called just as we have done in all previous chapters. Non-static variables or functions may not be used except in conjunction with an object; the `<class name>.<method name>` syntax used for their static equivalents will not work.

Note that, as will be discussed in Chapter 6, non-static variables in complicated classes should probably be accessed indirectly via non-static methods of the class (**accessor methods**) rather than directly as `<object>.<variable>`. This second approach is considered bad program design.

4.3.4 Summary – references

- **References** are used to manipulate all non-primitive data types. They contain an address in memory at which the actual data is stored.
- **Creation:** A standard variable declaration creates a `null` reference. Data for it to refer to must then be created using `new` or the starting value syntax for arrays. Alternatively, you can use the operator '=' to make it refer to the same data as an existing reference.
- `null` is the value of a reference which is not attached to any data.
- **Comparison:** The operator '==' tests whether two references refer to the same bit of memory. It does not compare the data that they refer to.
- **Destruction:** Garbage collection automatically deallocates areas of memory when they are no longer referred to.
- **Passing by:** Data passed by reference may be altered. Only the choice of memory location for the reference to refer to may not be changed.
- **Arrays** are declared using `<type>[] <name>;` and are manipulated by reference. They are created by `new <type>[<size>];` or by listing the elements enclosed by curly brackets. They are indexed from zero.
- `<array>.length` returns the number of elements in an array. This is one more than the index of the last element.

- **Objects** are defined by classes with non-static variables or methods and are manipulated by reference. Each instance of the class can store data in its non-static variables. Non-static methods are called via an instance of the class and can use that instance's data.

- **Usage:** `<reference>.<non-static variable>` for variables, `<reference>.<non-static method>(<arguments>)` for methods.

- **Creation:** An instance of a class is created by `new <class name>()`.

- **Constructors** are special non-static methods which allow parameters for an object's creation to be passed during a `new` call.

- `<reference>.equals(<reference>)` performs a comparison of the objects' data as opposed to the references. You must write this method for your own objects.

4.4 Extra features

4.4.1 Exceptions

Exceptions have already been mentioned a few times in this book but never properly explained. An exception is a modern idea in programming (present in C++ and Modula-3, absent from FORTRAN 77, C and Pascal). They allow a program to handle recovery from errors in a syntactically nice manner.

The idea is that when an error occurs, an exception is **thrown**. This is done with the command `throw`:

```
throw <exception object>;
```

For example, if `MyException` is a type of exception, then we can write:

```
throw new MyException();
```

At the point when the exception is thrown, execution of the program stops. The exception exits the current method, exits the method that called that one and so forth until something **catches** it. The structure for doing this is:

```
try
{
  <code to be executed, may throw exceptions>
}
catch (<Exception type> <name>)
{
  <code for when an exception of this type>
  <is caught>
}
finally
{
  <code to be executed after the try block>
  <regardless of if an exception is thrown>
}
```

For example, if we write

```
try
{
  System.out.println("One");

  switch (failure)
  {
    case 0:
      break;

    case 1:
      throw new MyException();

    case 2:
      throw new OtherException();
  }

  System.out.println("Two");
}
catch(MyException e)
{
  System.out.println("Three");
}
finally
{
  System.out.println("Four");
}
```

then if `failure=0`, `One`, `Two` and `Four` are written. If `failure=1` then `One`, `Three` and `Four` are written. If `failure=2` then `One` and `Four` are written and the exception is still uncaught and exits the current method. You may write multiple `catch` blocks to catch several types of exception.

There are two other bits of syntax:

```
public class <exception name> extends Exception
{
}
```

declares a new type of exception that you can throw, whilst any method which may cause an exception to be thrown within it and does not catch this must have

```
throws <exception 1 name>, <exception 2 name>
```

included at the end of its first line. For example

```
public static void main(String[] argv) throws MyException
```

Note that, according to the concept of **inheritance** (discussed in Section 6.3), all exception types are subclasses of `java.lang.Exception`. They also have their own inheritance structure beyond this: for example, `java.io.IOException` has several, more specific, descendants. You should refer to the online documentation for further information about types of exceptions, but should also note that a `catch` clause will catch the specified type and all of its descendants. This means that, for example, catching `java.io.IOException` will catch all of the types of IO exception.

Having discussed all of the syntax, you may wonder why exceptions should be considered interesting. First of all, the standard libraries use them to signal abnormal conditions, as you will see in the next chapter. In fact, we have previously mentioned a few incidences: integer division by zero throws an `ArithmeticException`, illegal array indices throw an `ArrayIndexOutOfBoundsException`, and dereferencing `null` references throws a `NullPointerException`. Thinking about this in retrospect, you may wonder why you did not need to write `catch` clauses for these, or at least declare them in a `throws` statement. The answer is that a subgroup of exceptions, the subclasses of `RuntimeException`, are deemed to be too common to enforce these rules, although they behave normally in all other respects. All of the above exceptions fall into this group. Others that we define ourself or meet later will not.

The second reason why exceptions should be considered is that they are genuinely useful. Imagine writing a large program, with many methods which call each other in a complicated way. Now consider that some method needs to handle an error condition. You could decide that some special return value would signal the error and then write an `if` statement. However, you would then need to pass this return value on through several other methods in the call chain until you reached back to a method able to handle the error. With exceptions, the inner method throws the exception, and execution automatically jumps through all of the intermediate methods back to the outer method without any extra coding.

4.4.2 Break **and** continue

As we have already mentioned, Java does not provide a `goto` statement because use of `goto` is considered bad programming practice. The closest equivalents are the `break` and `continue` statements. You have already seen `break` in `switch` statements and the general case is similar.

When written inside a `for`, `while`, `do` or `switch` statement, `break` immediately exits the statement and continues execution from just after it.

When written inside a `for`, `while` or `do` statement, `continue` immediately stops execution of the current repetition of the loop and continues with the next repetition.

These features are just as seen in C/C++. However there are two additions. Firstly, we can use labels to jump out more than one level. A label consists of `<label name>:` written at the start of the first line of the loop. For example, we can write:

```
outer_loop: for (int i=1; i<10; i++)
              for (int j=1; j<10; j++)
              {
                if (j>i)
                  continue outer_loop;
              }
```

in order to jump out of the inner loop entirely and proceed to the next iteration of the outer loop.

Secondly, `break` and `continue` behave as if they were implemented using exception throwing and catching. The result is that any `finally` clauses which they would seem to skip over are in fact executed!

4.4.3 Preprocessor

Some programmers, especially those who have come from C/C++, may be wondering about the apparent absence of a preprocessor which runs over the program code before it is compiled.

The answer is that Java does not have a preprocessor. There are three typical uses for one, and we will now discuss the equivalent Java syntax.

Firstly, C/C++ programmers use the preprocessor to `#include` header files. Java does not have header files and uses the `import` statement instead. This is a much superior solution since the programmer does not need to maintain two sets of files and it allows for dynamic linking.

Secondly, C/C++ programmers use commands like `#ifdef` to perform conditional compilation of code, enabling the same code to be compiled for different platforms or purposes. The fact that Java is totally portable removes the first of these reasons. The second problem is solved because a good compiler is capable of eliminating code which will never be used. For example,

```
public static final boolean TRACE = true;

public static void main(String[] argv)
{
  if (TRACE)
    System.out.println("Program stating up ...");

  ...
}
```

will not contain an `if` statement in the compiled code since the decision is guaranteed.

The final use is for defining macros (`#define` in C/C++). This is not present in Java and there is no good substitute for it. The argument that **inlining** of macros speeds up a program is not valid with good modern compiler technology, which will inline small methods in any case. However, the syntactical shorthand that a good macro can provide is simply not possible. The ability of a macro to work with many types of data can be mimicked using `java.lang.Object` and inheritance (see Chapter 6).

4.4.4 `javadoc`

One of the most interesting, and yet consistently underreported, features of Java is the ability to write your documentation and code at the same time. The mechanism behind this is that the JDK supplies a program called `javadoc` which will run over your source code, extracting information from a special category of comments and producing documentation in HTML (the mark-up language used on the web). All of the online documentation for Java's Standard Class Library was produced this way, as was that for the JNL (the documentation for each is available in a subdirectory of the installation).

The idea of combining code and documentation is that it makes it much more likely that the documentation will reflect the current state of the code: the programmer can see the documentation as they write the code and so is much more likely to remember to change all the relevant parts. This idea is not new. For example, Donald Knuth, author of the TeX typesetting package (in which this book was written) and of *The Art of Computer Programming* (Knuth, 1981), wrote TeX using a language called Web, which included both Pascal code and TeX documentation. However, Java is the first mainstream language to provide this facility.

Comments in the special format are called **doc comments** and start with `/**` as opposed to `/*` for standard comments. They should be placed immediately before class, class variable or class method definitions. The structure is:

```
/**
 * General comments to be placed in the documentation.
 * May contain HTML tags, but should not contain
 * structural tags like <H2> and <HR>.
 */
```

Note that the structuring of the comment matters. If you repeatedly stop and restart the comment over multiple lines, like

```
/********************************************************/
/* General comments to be placed in the documentation. */
/* May contain HTML tags, but should not contain        */
/* structural tags like <H2> and <HR>.                  */
/********************************************************/
```

then `javadoc` fails to understand it. In front of a class definition we may add the special tags:

```
@author <author name>
@version <version name>
```

In front of a method we may add:

```
@param <parameter name> <description>
@return <description>
@exception <full class name of exception> <description>
```

And we may always use:

```
@see <full class name>
@see <full class name>#<method name>
```

As an example, we include a fully documented version of the initial 'Hello' program, available at `http://www.jscieng.co.uk/Code/AdvJava/DocHello/`.

```
/**
 * This is a fully documented <TT>Hello World</TT> program.
 * Use 'javadoc' on it to generate the HTML documentation.
 *
 * @author Richard J. Davies
```

```
 * @version 1.0
 */
public class DocHello
{
  /**
   * This is the message used by the main method
   *
   * @see DocHello#main
   */
  public static final String message = "Hello world";


  /**
   * This is the main method which actually
   * prints the message on screen
   *
   * @param argv Required argument for interpreter
   * @return nothing
   */
  public static void main(String[] argv)
  {
    System.out.println(message);
  }
}
```

The `makefile` contains a command to make the documentation. This is done by running `javadoc` with the options:

```
javadoc -d <destination for files> -author -version <file.java>
```

JDK 1.0
JDK 1.1   Note that under JDK 1.1 or later, `javadoc` generates documentation for `public` and `protected` classes and their `public` and `protected` methods, variables and constants. Under JDK 1.0, it generates documentation only for `public` classes. See the online documentation for more information. The exact structure of the documentation files generated also changed between JDK 1.1 and 1.2. This will not be a problem as long as all of your documentation is produced by the same version of `javadoc`.

The HTML generated refers to a set of standard images. You should copy the entire directory `images` from the directory `api` in the directory `docs` in your installation of the JDK and put the copy wherever you told `javadoc` to generate the documentation.

Your documentation is now ready to view using any web browser.

EXERCISES

4.1 Find three mistakes in the following:
      A file `Five.java` contains:

```
package d;
```

```
public class Five
{
  public static void main(String[] argv)
  {
    e.Seven.iterate();
  }
}

public class Six
{
  public static int calculate()
  ...
}
```

Another file `Seven.java` contains:

```
package e;
import d.Five;

class Seven
{
  public static void iterate()
  {
    int a = Six.calculate();
    ...
  }
}
```

4.2 What directory structure would you use to store the above files, and how would you compile and run the program?

4.3 Find three mistakes in the following code:

```
int[] table;

for (int i=1; i<=5; i++)
  table[i] = 7*i + 5;

int[] table2 = { 12, 19, 26, 33, 40 };

if (table == table2)
  System.out.println("Good, they're meant to be the same");
```

4.4 Translate the following C/C++ code into Java:

```
int *i = (int *) malloc(5 * sizeof(int));
int *index = i;

while (index - i < 5)
{
  *index = 0;
```

```
    index++
}
```

4.5 Explain the difference between the static and non-static variables and methods below, paying attention to how they are used, how many instances of them can exist and which variables the methods can use.

```java
public class TwoParts
{
  public static int varone;
  public int vartwo;

  public static int methodone();
  public int methodtwo();
}
```

4.6 Find three errors in the following program fragment. HouseholdObject is a class, implementing a non-static method isBreakable. We have an exception BreakableObjects that we throw when we get into problems because an instance of a HouseholdObject tests as breakable where we cannot handle this.

```java
public static void preprocess(HouseholdObject o)
              throws BreakableObjects;
{
  // We cannot handle breakable things.
  if (o.isBreakable())
    throw BreakableObjects;
  else
  {
    // Continue preprocessing
    ...
  }
}

public static void process(HouseholdObject o)
{
  preprocess(o);

  // Perform additional operations
  ..
}


public static void main(String[] argv)
{
  HouseholdObject[] l;

  // Generate the objects for somewhere.
  // We assume that none will test true for
  // is breakable.
```

```
try
{
  for (int i=0; i<=l.length; i++)
    process(l[i]);
}
catch (BreakableObjects b)
{
  // Handle if something was breakable after all
  ...
}
finally
{
  // Code to be run in either case
  ...
}
}
```

WHERE TO GO FROM HERE

You now understand all of the Java syntax that will be taught in this book, excluding that concerned with object orientation. As such, all subsequent chapters, excluding Chapter 6, are intended either as references for various libraries or as discussions of areas of scientific programming.

You are now free to pick and choose your own course. The diagram at the start of this chapter summarizes the interdependencies in the remainder of the book – you are advised to consult it to help with your decisions.

CHAPTER 5

The standard libraries

5.1   Introduction

This chapter provides a reference to those parts of the Java standard libraries that are relevant to the scientific programmer. To understand most of these you will need to have read all of Chapter 4, although only Section 4.2 is necessary to understand Section 5.2.

You should note that this chapter is much less tutorial than anything before it. For some parts of the library it goes little further than listing class declarations. You should study these carefully, noting which methods are static and which are non-static so that you will know the appropriate syntax for calling them.

The standard libraries consist of all packages whose names start with 'java'. The .class files for these are archived inside the JDK directory. Similarly, source code is archived in the JDK directory in the file src.jar and documentation is available in the subdirectory docs. The libraries are automatically included by the compiler, so you will not need to use this knowledge directly. However, advanced users may be interested in reading the source code or documentation. In order to read the source code, you will need to expand the archive at the command line with the command 'jar xf src.jar'.

Finally, as always, sample code from this chapter is available from the companion website at `http://www.jscieng.co.uk/Code/StdLib/`.

5.2 Mathematical functions

The standard libraries contain support for mathematics in two ways. Firstly, a class `java.lang.Math` provides standard functions such as `sin` and `cos`. Secondly, under JDK 1.1 or later, a package `java.math` provides two classes `BigDecimal` and `BigInteger` for handling arbitrary precision arithmetic. These classes are discussed later in this chapter.

We now present a simplified declaration for the class `java.lang.Math`. All of the code to implement the methods has been left out, as have some program structures irrelevant to the scope of this book. What remains is sufficient to summarize what methods are available and how they should be called.

Note that you do not need to do anything special to use the standard libraries; they are available by default. The actual `.class` files for the libraries are archived inside the JDK directory.

```java
package java.lang;

public class Math
{
  // Standard Mathematical constants
  public static final double E = 2.7182818284590452354;
  public static final double PI = 3.14159265358979323846;

  // Trigonometric functions
  public static double sin(double a);
  public static double cos(double a);
  public static double tan(double a);

  // Inverse trigonometric functions
  public static double asin(double a);
  public static double acos(double a);
  public static double atan(double a);

  // Computes atan(b/a) : polar coordinate of (a,b)
  public static double atan2(double a, double b);

  // Exponential and natural logarithm
  public static double exp(double a);
  public static double log(double a);

  // Raise a to the power of b
  public static double pow(double a, double b)
               throws ArithmeticException;

  // Square root
  public static double sqrt(double a);
```

```
// Remainder as specified in IEEE 754
// If n is the integer closest to the
// quotient f1/f2 then return
// f1 - n * f2. If two values for n are
// equally close, then the even value is
// used.
public static double IEEEremainder(double f1, double f2);

// Nearest integers above and below
public static double ceil(double a);
public static double floor(double a);

// Nearest integer
public static double rint(double a);

// Round to nearest integer value
public static int round(float a);
public static long round(double a);

// Produce a random number uniformly
// distributed in 0.0 to 1.0
public static double random();

// Absolute (positive) values
public static int abs(int a);
public static long abs(long a);
public static float abs(float a);
public static double abs(double a);

// Maximums
public static int max(int a, int b);
public static long max(long a, long b);
public static float max(float a, float b);
public static double max(double a, double b);

// Minimums
public static int min(int a, int b);
public static long min(long a, long b);
public static float min(float a, float b);
public static double min(double a, double b);
}
```

As you can see, the class `java.lang.Math` contains only `public static` constants and methods. We use these as described in the last chapter. For example, `cos` is accessible as `java.lang.Math.cos`, or, since all programs contain an implicit `import java.lang.*`, we can just write `Math.cos`. Unfortunately, there is no way to remove the 'Math.' and just write `cos`, so an example method call looks like

```
double x = 1.3;
double y = Math.cos(x);
```

Method overloading, as discussed in Section 2.14, is used to provide multiple versions of abs, min and max in order that these can be used with all data types. Note that Math.pow can throw an ArithmeticException. ArithmeticException is a subclass of RuntimeException, and so need not be handled explicitly (see Section 4.4.1).

The algorithms used in java.lang.Math are guaranteed to produce the same results as those from netlib's *Freely Distributable Math Library* (fdlibm, available at http://netlib.att.com/). Where that library contains several versions of an algorithm, that conforming with IEEE 754 has been used.

Finally, although other elementary functions, such as cosh, are not available in the Java standard library, the JNL implements many of these. See Section 8.2 for these elementary functions.

5.3 Example – Buffon's needle

We can now write a program that uses these standard mathematical functions. The program computes π by consideration of the statistical problem of Buffon's needle.

In this problem, a needle of unit length is thrown repeatedly onto a table covered by parallel lines a unit distance apart. The experimental setup is shown in Figure 5.1. The probability that the needle lands crossing a line is $2/\pi$, and we compute π by performing the experiment a large number of times to measure this probability.

In our computer simulation of the experiment, it is somewhat tricky to choose a random direction for the needle to land in without using π. We achieve this as shown in Figure 5.2.

The code for this example is available at http://www.jscieng.co.uk/Code/StdLib/Buffon/.

```java
public class Buffon
{
    // The number of times that we throw the needle
    public static final int THROWS = 1000;

    // This method returns if a point lies inside
    // the unit circle at the origin, but is not
    // actually the origin.
    public static boolean inCircle(double x, double y)
    {
        if ((x*x + y*y < 1) && !(x==0 && y==0))
            return true;
        else
            return false;
    }

    // Throw the needle once and return if it
    // crosses a line.
    public static boolean checkCross()
    {
        double x1, y1, x2, y2;
```

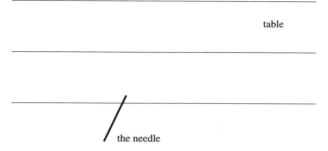

the needle

Figure 5.1   Buffon's needle.

```
double dist;

// Position one end randomly
x1 = Math.random();
y1 = Math.random();


// Pick another point in the unit circle to
// get the needle direction
do
{
  x2 = Math.random();
  y2 = Math.random();
}
while (!inCircle(x2, y2));

// Renormalize the direction into a unit
// vector
dist = Math.sqrt(x2*x2 + y2*y2);
x2 /= dist;
y2 /= dist;

// Add the first end's position to get
// the second end's position.
x2 += x1;
y2 += y1;

// Return whether the two ends are on
// different sides of a line
if (Math.round(x1) != Math.round(x2))
  return true;
else
  return false;
}
```

Pick a random point for one end of the needle.

Consider a circle of unit radius about this point
and pick a second random point in this circle.

Normalize displacement between two points
to get a unit vector.

This is the random position of the needle.

Figure 5.2   Choosing a random direction.

```
// This method calls checkCross to throw
// the needle THROWS times and counts the
// number that cross.
public static void main(String[] argv)
{
  int count = 0;

  // Do the throwing and counting
  for (int i=0; i<THROWS; i++)
  {
    if (checkCross())
      count++;
  }

  // The fraction that cross should be 2 / Pi
  System.out.println("Pi is " + Math.PI);
  System.out.println("Our estimate: ");
  System.out.println(THROWS * 2.0 / count);
 }
}
```

The method Math.random provides a relatively crude means of obtaining random numbers. A greater variety of features are available from the class `java.util.Random`, which is discussed in Section 5.11.

5.4 Arbitrary precision integers

The object types in the standard library that are probably most interesting to the scientific programmer are the classes `BigInteger` and `BigDecimal`, both of which are in the package `java.math`. These provide arbitrary precision arithmetic. Unfortunately, they were not present in JDK 1.0; they were added in JDK 1.1. At the time of writing (August 1998) some major web browsers are not fully JDK 1.1 compliant, so you should not use these classes in any programs that you intend to put on the web (see Section 5.13). However, there is nothing to stop you from using them in stand-alone programs, like those that we have discussed so far.

First of all, we consider `BigInteger`. Objects of this class represent integers. However, unlike the data types `long`, `int`, `short` and `byte`, there are no bounds on the range of integers that a `BigInteger` can store. The class supports all standard arithmetic operations via methods such as `add` and `multiply` (Java does not support operator overloading, so we cannot use '+' or '*' with classes). It also supports bitwise operations, which function as if the `BigInteger` were represented in twos-complement form (if you do not already understand these words, then you will not be using these operators anyway). Methods are provided to compute GCDs, work in modular arithmetic, generate primes and test for primality. This is the class that you should use for serious work in number theory.

We now move on to discuss two concepts that are needed to use the class. In several places in the class a 'sign bit' is referred to. This is an integer whose value is -1 if the `BigInteger` is negative, 0 if it is zero or $+1$ if it is positive.

In addition, an integer called '`certainty`' is used. This is used in probabilistic tests for primality of large numbers. If an integer tests prime with a `certainty` value c, then probability of primality is

$$1 - \frac{1}{2^c}$$

A `certainty` value is used in one of the constructors to construct a random number that is probably prime and is also used in `isProbablePrime` to test a number that has been created by some other means.

A simplified declaration for this class is reproduced below. This is in a similar style to that which we used for `java.lang.Math`. Many methods can throw an `ArithmeticException`, for instance if division by zero occurs, and the correspondingly large number of `throws` clauses have been omitted for clarity. Note that `ArithmeticException` is a subclass of `RuntimeException` and so need not be handled explicitly.

```
package java.math;

public class BigInteger
{
```

```
//// Constructors for the class
// Firstly from a twos-complement representation
public BigInteger(byte[] val)
        throws NumberFormatException;
// Or sign bit and twos-complement
public BigInteger(int signum, byte[] magnitude)
        throws NumberFormatException;
// Or a string and base for the number
// (bases up to 36 accepted using letters
// as the extra digits).
public BigInteger(String val, int radix)
        throws NumberFormatException;
// Or a string base 10
public BigInteger(String val)
        throws NumberFormatException;
// To get a random number of numBits length. An object
// of type java.util.Random is used.
public BigInteger(int numBits, java.util.Random rndSrc)
        throws IllegalArgumentException;
// To get a random, probably prime, number of bitLength.
public BigInteger(int bitLength, int certainty,
                    java.util.Random rnd);
// This method is not a constructor, but is used
// to generate BigIntegers from integers.
public static BigInteger valueOf(long val);

//// Standard arithmetic operations
public BigInteger add(BigInteger val);
public BigInteger subtract(BigInteger val);
public BigInteger multiply(BigInteger val);
public BigInteger divide(BigInteger val);
public BigInteger remainder(BigInteger val);
// The array returned is quotient, then remainder
public BigInteger[] divideAndRemainder(BigInteger val);
public BigInteger pow(int exponent);
public BigInteger abs();
public BigInteger negate();

//// Comparison operators
// return -1 if val is bigger, 0 if equal, 1 if val smaller
public int compareTo(BigInteger val);
public boolean equals(Object x);

//// Max and min of two values
public BigInteger min(BigInteger val);
public BigInteger max(BigInteger val);

//// Modular arithmetic
public BigInteger mod(BigInteger m);
public BigInteger modPow(BigInteger exponent, BigInteger m);
```

```java
// The inverse multiplies to 1 mod m.
public BigInteger modInverse(BigInteger m);

//// Special operations
// Find the GCD with another BigInteger
public BigInteger gcd(BigInteger val);
// Check primality
public boolean isProbablePrime(int certainty);

//// Logical operations on twos-complement form
public BigInteger and(BigInteger val);
public BigInteger or(BigInteger val);
public BigInteger xor(BigInteger val);
public BigInteger not();
public BigInteger andNot(BigInteger val);

//// Bit shifts and bitwise operations
public BigInteger shiftLeft(int n);
public BigInteger shiftRight(int n);
public boolean testBit(int n);
public BigInteger setBit(int n);
public BigInteger clearBit(int n);
public BigInteger flipBit(int n);

//// Getting at twos-complement representation
// Return the sign bit
public int signum();
// Return the twos-complement form
public byte[] toByteArray();
// return rightmost set bit (-1 if number is zero).
public int getLowestSetBit();
// return number of bits excluding sign bit.
public int bitLength();
// Return number of bits differing from sign bit
// Useful for implementing sets.
public int bitCount();

//// Conversions to other data types
// To a string of arbitrary base (up to 36)
public String toString(int radix);
// to a string base 10
public String toString();
public int intValue();
public long longValue();
public float floatValue();
public double doubleValue();

//// Generation of a hash code. This is a number
// used to reference the object when it is stored
// in a hash table.
```

```
    public int hashcode();
}
```

This was certainly a complicated definition to handle, especially since you have only just learnt about objects. However, you should be able to see that there is a static method, `valueOf`, which you would use in constructions such as:

```
BigInteger b = BigInteger.valueOf(45732);
```

In this code the `b` is declared as a reference to a `BigInteger` and then the static method `valueof` is used to get a reference to a `BigInteger` containing `45732`. Finally the reference `b` is assigned to refer to that new object.

Apart from this, all member functions are non-static and so should be used like:

```
BigInteger a, b, c;
a = new BigInteger("437");
b = new BigInteger("4E", 16);


c = a.add(b);


System.out.println(c.toString());
```

Note that creating a `BigInteger` from an integer is done using `valueOf`, whilst doing so from a string is done using a constructor.

In the above example we declared three variables as references to objects of type `BigInteger`. All three started referring to nothing, and thus were `null`. We then used the constructors to create two `BigInteger` objects for the first two references to refer to. Next we used the non-static method `add` to add these values and set `c` to refer to the resulting object. Finally, we used the method `toString` to convert the value of that object into a string to be printed out.

Those amongst you who have followed everything very carefully should be wondering where the actual data is stored: `BigInteger` appears not to declare any variables, static or non-static. In fact, it does declare non-static variables, so each instance does contain some data. However, these are not public and so are not directly accessible to the user. See Section 6.4 for a further discussion of `public`.

5.5   Example – RSA encryption

JDK 1.0

At this point we take a break to write a more extended example using `BigInteger`. The program implements RSA encryption, to which this data type is ideally suited. RSA is the famous public key encryption algorithm based on large prime numbers which is used by the program PGP and all good intelligence agencies (using primes several hundred digits long). The name is derived from the first letters of the names of Rivest, Shamir and Aldeman, the three US computer scientists who proposed it. The algorithm follows:

- Two large distinct primes, p and q, are generated. Their product N is calculated, as is P, which is equal to (p-1)(q-1). Finally, we choose a number e, coprime to P (two numbers are **coprime** if their highest common factor is one).

- Next we publish N and e (we keep p, q and P secret).
- Someone who wants to send us a message, which is coprime to N, encodes it by raising the message to the power of e modulo N.
- To decode this we compute the inverse, d, of e modulo P. Raising the encoded message to the power of d modulo N recovers the message.

It is thought that any other method of decoding would be equivalent to finding this inverse d. To do this requires knowledge of P which can only be obtained by methods equivalent to factorizing N, the product of the primes. This is thought to be very hard for sufficiently large primes.

The program code is available at `http://www.jscieng.co.uk/Code/StdLib/RSA/` and is as follows:

```java
import java.math.BigInteger;
import java.util.Random;
import java.io.*;

public class RSA
{
  // The bit length of our large primes.
  public static final int SIZE = 512;


  // This method prompts the user for a message,
  // encrypts it using N and e and returns the ciphertext.
  public static BigInteger encodeMessage(BigInteger N,
                                         BigInteger e)
                     throws IOException
  {
    // Get a message to encrypt. It should be
    // smaller than N and coprime to it.
    String input;
    BigInteger message;

    do
    {
      System.out.println("Enter a message "
                    +"(less than N and coprime to it):");
      input = (new BufferedReader(
            new InputStreamReader(System.in))).readLine();
      message = new BigInteger(input);
    }
    while ((message.compareTo(N) != -1)
          || (message.gcd(N).compareTo(BigInteger.valueOf(1)) != 0));
    System.out.println();

    // Encrypt the message
    BigInteger ciphertext = message.modPow(e, N);
    System.out.println("Encoded :" + ciphertext.toString());
```

```java
        System.out.println("Bet you cannot crack this "
                        +"using N and e alone");
        System.out.println();

        // Return the ciphertext
        return ciphertext;
    }


    // Generate keys, get encrypted message and decrypt it.
    public static void main(String[] argv) throws IOException
    {
        BigInteger p, q, N, P, e, ciphertext, d, plaintext;
        String input;

        // Generate two distinct large prime numbers p, q
        p = new BigInteger(SIZE, 10, new Random());
        do
        {
            q = new BigInteger(SIZE, 10, new Random());
        }
        while (q.compareTo(p) == 0);

        // Calculate their product
        N = p.multiply(q);

        // And calculate P = (p-1)(q-1)
        P = p.subtract(BigInteger.valueOf(1));
        P = P.multiply(q.subtract(BigInteger.valueOf(1)));

        // Next choose e, coprime to and less than P
        do
        {
            e = new BigInteger(2*SIZE, new Random());
        }
        while ((e.compareTo(P) != -1)
                || (e.gcd(P).compareTo(BigInteger.valueOf(1)) != 0));

        // Publish N and e
        System.out.println("N is " + N.toString());
        System.out.println("e is " + e.toString());
        System.out.println();

        // Get a message from the user, encrypted using N and e.
        ciphertext = encodeMessage(N, e);

        // Compute d, the inverse of e mod P
        d = e.modInverse(P);
        System.out.println("d is " + d.toString());
```

```
    // Decrypt the message
    plaintext = ciphertext.modPow(d, N);
    System.out.println("Decoded :" + plaintext.toString());
  }
}
```

In order to write this program we had to use text input and the class `java.util.Random`. These are discussed later in this chapter (in Sections 5.8 and 5.11 respectively). Excluding these bits of code, you should be able to understand all of the rest of the program, which is a workout for the methods of `BigInteger`. Note how we use the constructor to get prime numbers, but use the static method `valueOf` to convert integers to `BigInteger` objects. We also use the arithmetic methods and `compareTo`.

There are two important and new points to note. Firstly we note that having used the new command to create an object we do not have to assign a reference variable to refer to it. Other actions are possible. For example, the constructor calls require a `Random` object to be passed. We have no other interest in this object, so we create it in the argument list and never need give it a name. A similar structure occurs when we read the user's message.

Secondly, we note that we can use objects immediately, without assigning a name to them. The first case where this occurs is when we use the `readLine` method of the `BufferedReader` that we have created immediately after creating it. Similarly, the line `M.gcd(N).compareTo` actually calls `gcd` first, which returns a result, and then calls the `compareTo` method of that result.

5.6   Arbitrary precision floating point numbers

JDK 1.0

As well as providing the `BigInteger` class, JDK 1.1 or later provide a class `BigDecimal` for handling arbitrary precision floating point arithmetic.

Before moving on to the class declaration, we need to discuss how the precision of a `BigInteger` is handled. Firstly, a `BigDecimal` internally consists of a `BigInteger` and a non-negative integer, the `scale`, which stores the number of decimal digits to the right of the decimal point. In other words,

$$\text{value} = \frac{\text{integer value}}{10^{\text{scale}}}$$

Secondly, the `scale` for `BigDecimal` objects is not set globally. Instead, each object stores its own `scale` and, when two objects combine, they act to preserve the greatest possible precision at all times. The result is that when you perform some operations, such as a multiplication, the stored precision may increase to contain the extra digits. For example, adding two `BigDecimal` objects with `scale` 10 will produce one with `scale` 10, but multiplying them would produce one with `scale` 20.

However, certain operations, such as division, may add an infinite number of new digits if the result has a non-terminating binary expansion. In addition, you may wish to cut the `scale` back explicitly if you are not interested in all of the digits that are being stored.

Because of this, when you perform a division or change the `scale`, you must specify a rounding mode, which is used to determine the direction in which any extra digits that you do not want are rounded. The modes are all defined as class constants.

A simplified class declaration is as follows. Note that all exceptions used are subclasses of `RuntimeException` and so need not be handled explicitly.

```java
package java.math;

public class BigDecimal
{
    //// Constructors for the class
    public BigDecimal(String val)
            throws NumberFormatException;
    public BigDecimal(double val)
            throws NumberFormatException;
    public BigDecimal(BigInteger val);
    // specify integer value and scale
    public BigDecimal(BigInteger val, int scale)
            throws NumberFormatException;
    // These methods are not constructors, but are
    // used to generate BigDecimals from integers.
    public static BigDecimal valueOf(long val, int scale)
                throws NumberFormatException;
    public static BigDecimal valueOf(long val);

    //// The constants defining rounding types.
    // Increment digit before any fractional part
    public final static int ROUND_UP =          0;
    // Discard fractional parts
    public final static int ROUND_DOWN =         1;
    // ROUND_UP for positive, ROUND_DOWN for negative
    public final static int ROUND_CEILING =      2;
    // ROUND_DOWN for positive, ROUND_UP for negative
    public final static int ROUND_FLOOR =        3;
    // round to nearest, with 0.5 fraction ROUND_UP
    public final static int ROUND_HALF_UP =      4;
    // round to nearest, with 0.5 fraction ROUND_DOWN
    public final static int ROUND_HALF_DOWN =    5;
    // round to nearest, with 0.5 fraction rounding
    // to whichever of the nearest values is even
    public final static int ROUND_HALF_EVEN =    6;
    // Programmer assertion that rounding will not
    // be needed. An ArithmeticException
    // is thrown if it is.
    public final static int ROUND_UNNECESSARY = 7;

    //// Standard arithmetic operations
    public BigDecimal add(BigDecimal val);
    public BigDecimal subtract(BigDecimal val);
    public BigDecimal multiply(BigDecimal val);
```

```java
// Perform division, returning output of the given scale
public BigDecimal divide(BigDecimal val,
                     int scale, int roundingMode)
      throws ArithmeticException, IllegalArgumentException;
// Perform division, returning output
// of the same scale as ourself.
public BigDecimal divide(BigDecimal val, int roundingMode)
      throws ArithmeticException, IllegalArgumentException;
public BigDecimal abs();
public BigDecimal negate();


//// Comparison operators
// return -1 if val is bigger, 0 equal, 1 if val smaller
public int compareTo(BigDecimal val);
public boolean equals(Object x);


//// Max and min of two values
public BigDecimal min(BigDecimal val);
public BigDecimal max(BigDecimal val);


//// Decimal point shifts (no data loss)
public BigDecimal movePointLeft(int n);
public BigDecimal movePointRight(int n);


//// Getting at the number and scale
// return the sign bit
public int signum();
// return the scale
public int scale();
// return the unscaled value. JDK 1.2 or later only
public BigInteger unscaledValue();
// Change the scale as specified, with specified
// rounding if necessary.
public BigDecimal setScale(int scale, int roundingMode)
      throws ArithmeticException, IllegalArgumentException;
// Change the scale, assumes no rounding is necessary,
// throws exception if it is.
public BigDecimal setScale(int scale)
      throws ArithmeticException, IllegalArgumentException;


//// Conversions to other data types
public String toString();
public BigInteger toBigInteger();
public int intValue();
public long longValue();
public float floatValue();
public double doubleValue();


//// Generation of a hash code. This is a number
// used to reference the object when it is stored
```

```
          // in a hash table.
       public int hashCode();
   }
```

JDK 1.1

This class declaration is similar enough in structure to that for the `BigInteger` class that you should need no further help to use it.

5.7 Strings

Support for strings is provided via the class `java.lang.String` and an additional primitive data type, `char`. All textual information in Java is stored as Unicode: a two-byte per character encoding which can store many worldwide scripts as well as standard English characters and letters. The entire ASCII character set is a subset of Unicode. However, Unicode is implemented completely transparently and you need never notice that it is there.

Unlike in many other languages, such as C/C++, strings in Java do not consist of a simple array of characters. Instead, `String` is a class, so strings are objects, handled by reference. Java provides several special pieces of syntax to make this more convenient.

First of all, any text enclosed in double quotation marks, such as `"Some text"`, is automatically converted into a `String` object by the compiler. The behaviour is very much as if this was a constructor call for a `String` object. The special characters '\n' are used to show a carriage return and '\t' is used as a tab. To get a backslash in a string, you must use '\\'.

Secondly, any character enclosed in single quotation marks, such as `'a'`, is automatically converted into a `char` by the compiler.

Finally, Java provides an operator, '+', which will concatenate a string with any other data type, in either order. For example,

```
String r = "First bit" + "Second bit";
String s = "Text " + 1;
String t = 1.7 + " Text";
BigInteger b = BigInteger.valueOf(1534);
String u = b + " Text";
```

Together these mean that you can append anything that you want onto a string simply by listing the components, strings or otherwise, separated by + operators.

Note that this usage of '+' will only work if at least one of its arguments is already a string:

```
int a = 5;
int b = 7;
System.out.println(a + b);
```

will output 12. In order to output the two numbers, you must write:

```
System.out.println(a + " " + b);
```

It is also worth knowing *how* this works. The class `String` provides a method `valueOf` which has versions to convert any data type into a string. The + operator simply calls this to convert any arguments which are not already strings. Internally, the `valueOf` method is actually implemented using the data type's own `toString` method: corresponding to every primitive data type, there is a class containing this method as a static method. For instance, `Double.toString` converts a `double` to a `String`. These classes are discussed further later on, in Section 5.10. Similarly, all object types must define a non-static method `toString`, which returns a string representation of the object.

To convert the other way, we can use the constructors from a `String` to create a `BigInteger` or a `BigDecimal` which takes its value from the string. We use the static methods

```
Integer.parseInt(<string>)
```

under any JDK version or

```
Double.parseDouble(<string>)
```

JDK 1.1

under JDK 1.2 or later, but

```
Double.valueOf(<string>).doubleValue()
```

under earlier versions to convert strings into integers and floating point numbers, respectively. These are discussed in Section 5.10.

Since strings are objects, manipulated by reference, == tests whether the references refer to the same string. Use `equals` or `compareTo` to compare values of strings.

We can now give a simplified declaration for the class `String`. Note that `StringIndexOutOfBoundsException` is a subclass of `RuntimeException` and so need not be handled explicitly.

```
package java.lang;

public class String
{
  //// Constructors for the class
  public String();
  // Copy an existing string
  public String(String value);
  // Copy (some subrange of) a char array
  public String(char value[]);
  public String(char value[], int offset, int count)
        throws StringIndexOutOfBoundsException;
  // Copy (some subrange of) a byte array with the
  // named encoding (such as ASCII).
  public String(byte bytes[]);
  public String(byte bytes[], String enc)
        throws UnsupportedEncodingException;
  public String(byte bytes[], int offset, int length);
  public String(byte bytes[], int offset, int length,
              String enc)
```

```
                        throws UnsupportedEncodingException;
// From a StringBuffer
public String(StringBuffer buffer);

//// Comparison operators
public boolean equals(Object anObject);
public boolean equalsIgnoreCase(String anotherString);
// Compare strings lexigraphically, returning less than
// 0 if anotherString is greater, 0 if equal, >0 otherwise
public int compareTo(String anotherString);
public boolean regionMatches(int toffset, String other,
                             int ooffset, int len);
public boolean regionMatches(boolean ignoreCase, int toffset,
                         String other, int ooffset, int len);
public boolean startsWith(String prefix);
public boolean startsWith(String prefix, int toffset);
public boolean endsWith(String suffix);

//// Finding substrings
public int indexOf(int ch);
public int indexOf(int ch, int fromIndex);
public int lastIndexOf(int ch);
public int lastIndexOf(int ch, int fromIndex);
public int indexOf(String str);
public int indexOf(String str, int fromIndex);
public int lastIndexOf(String str);
public int lastIndexOf(String str, int fromIndex);

//// Extracting substrings
public String substring(int beginIndex)
      throws StringIndexOutOfBoundsException;
public String substring(int beginIndex, int endIndex)
      throws StringIndexOutOfBoundsException;

//// Operations to change the string
public String concat(String str);
public String replace(char oldChar, char newChar);
public String toLowerCase( Locale locale );
public String toLowerCase();
public String toUpperCase( Locale locale );
public String toUpperCase();
// Trim removes any leading or trailing spaces
public String trim();

//// Getting at the data
public int length();
public char charAt(int index)
      throws StringIndexOutOfBoundsException;
public void getChars(int srcBegin, int srcEnd,
                     char dst[], int dstBegin)
```

```
        throws StringIndexOutOfBoundsException;
public byte[] getBytes(String enc)
        throws UnsupportedEncodingException;
public byte[] getBytes();

//// Conversions to other data types
public String toString();
public char[] toCharArray();

//// Conversions from other data types
public static String valueOf(Object obj);
// The char[] valueOf uses the given array in the String
public static String valueOf(char data[]);
public static String valueOf(char data[],
                          int offset, int count);
// Whilst the copyValueOf copies it
public static String copyValueOf(char data[],
                          int offset, int count);
public static String copyValueOf(char data[]);
public static String valueOf(boolean b);
public static String valueOf(char c);
public static String valueOf(int i);
public static String valueOf(long l);
public static String valueOf(float f);
public static String valueOf(double d);

//// Generation of a hash code. This is a number
// used to reference the object when it is stored
// in a hash table
public int hashCode();

//// Memory reduction. Calling intern on a string forces it
// to share storage with any other strings of the same value.
public String intern();
}
```

Users whose needs are not satisfied by these features should note that the class `java.lang.StringBuffer` provides further functionality. In addition, the package `java.io` contains classes such as `StreamTokenizer` which can be helpful. However, these will not be described in this book. You should read the online documentation that comes with the JDK.

5.8 Text input and output

The Java syntax for handling input and output is very complicated, although also very powerful. A basic overview is that it is based on the concept of **streams**. A stream is an object which is capable of either receiving or emitting a succession of other objects. Thus, the most simple streams are ones which receive a succession of characters and

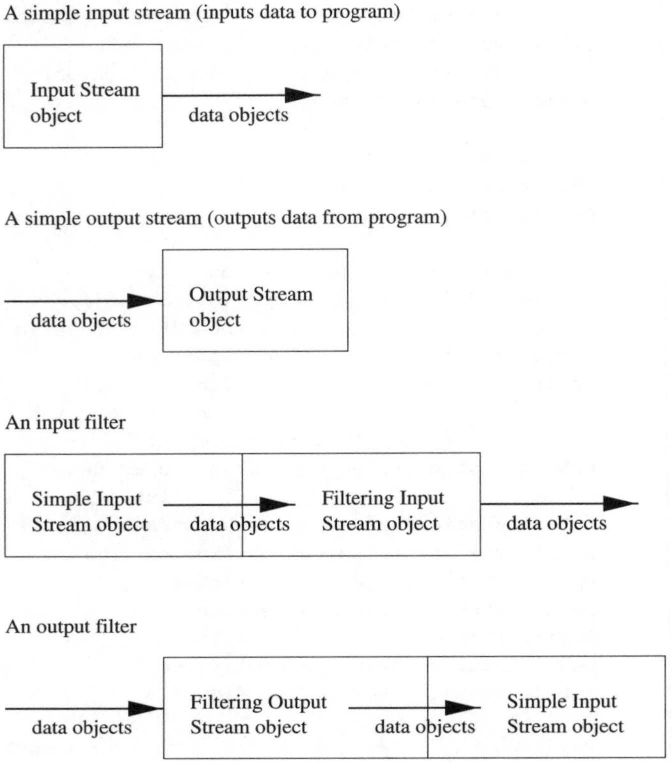

A simple input stream (inputs data to program)

A simple output stream (outputs data from program)

An input filter

An output filter

Figure 5.3 Streams.

print them on the screen or which emit characters as they are typed at the keyboard.

In addition, we can create more complicated streams which act as filters. They connect to a simple stream to provide a source of data and then output the data in a processed form. For instance, we can have a stream which connects to the output of a character stream, as described above, and produces output in which the characters have been gathered together into words. Figure 5.3 depicts filtering.

All of the classes to handle streams are grouped into a package called `java.io`. There is a lot of code here, so we shall not attempt to describe it in any detail. However, you can read the online documentation if you are interested.

The class `java.lang.System` contains two class variables called `in` and `out` which are, respectively, a stream that receives the characters that you type and a stream that prints to the screen. We use these two streams in what follows.

`out` is an object of type `java.io.PrintStream`. It provides several versions of the methods `print` and `println`, which use `toString` methods, as described in the previous section, to be able to print any type of primitive data or any object. The difference between the calls is that `println` moves output onto a new line after finishing. Hence, for output we write

```
System.out.println("First bit" + "Second bit");
System.out.println("Text " + 1);
BigInteger b = BigInteger.valueOf(1534);
System.out.println(b + " Text");
```

Input is more complicated, and differs with JDK version. Under JDK 1.1 or later, we write

```
BufferedReader b = new BufferedReader(
                    new InputStreamReader(System.in));
String s = b.readLine();
```

If the input is actually a value, we can then convert the string into another data type, as discussed in the previous section.

JDK 1.0   Under JDK 1.0, the corresponding statement is:

```
DataInputStream d = new DataInputStream(System.in);
String s = d.readLine();
```

Whichever case you choose, you might want to consider making the `BufferedReader` or `DataInputStream` a class variable for one of your classes, with the above as its initializer. This way you will be able to use it in several places without this unpleasant syntax recurring. You are also warned that either method may throw a `java.io.IOException`.

Looking at either version of the code we can see filtering, as discussed at the beginning of this section. For example, in JDK 1.1 or later, the `BufferedReader` is connected to the `InputStreamReader`, which is connected to `System.in`. Each input filter is passed the simpler input stream that it will receive objects from in its constructor.

See the RSA encoding example in Section 5.5 for an example of simple text input and output.

Note that a nicer method of handling text is provided by the scientific graphics library, the JSGL, provided with this book. The library creates a scrollable window into which text output is written and also provides simpler input and a means of saving the output to disk. This is discussed further in Chapter 7.

5.9   File input and output

File input and output is very similar to text input and output. Once again, we use streams, and all of the classes used are in the package `java.io`. To get an output stream to a file, we write:

```
PrintWriter q = new PrintWriter(
                    new FileOutputStream("file2.out"), true);
q.println("Hello there file2.out");
```

JDK 1.0   under JDK 1.1 or later, or, under JDK 1.0:

```
PrintStream p = new PrintStream(
                    new FileOutputStream("file1.out"));
p.println("Hello there file1.out");
```

Both `PrintStream` and `PrintWriter` provide `print` and `println`, as discussed in the previous section.

To get an input stream we write:

```
BufferedReader b = new BufferedReader(
                    new InputStreamReader(
                    new FileInputStream("file4.in")));
System.out.println(b.readLine());
```

JDK 1.0 under JDK 1.1 or later, or, under JDK 1.0:

```
DataInputStream d = new DataInputStream(
                    new FileInputStream("file3.in"));
System.out.println(d.readLine());
```

You need not worry about closing the files that you have read from or written to at the end of your program: this will happen automatically when the program exits. Once again, either reading or writing may throw a `java.io.IOException` or a `FileNotFoundException`.

It is interesting to see how close this code is to that for reading and writing to the screen. The same sort of filtering of streams occurs. As a result, when we change from the screen to files we must change some of the streams (those that connect to the hardware), but most of the others are performing processing such as collecting characters into lines and can remain unchanged.

Finally, an example program, available at `http://www.jscieng.co.uk/Code/StdLib/Files/`, demonstrates both types of file input and output mentioned **JDK 1.0** above. The code is as follows:

JDK 1.1

```
import java.io.*;

public class Files
{
  // Note that the method must throw the two exceptions
  // if it does not handle them.
  public static void main(String[] argv) throws IOException,
                                        FileNotFoundException
  {
    // Open an output file using methods supported by JDK 1.1
    // or later.
    PrintWriter q = new PrintWriter(
                    new FileOutputStream("file2.out"), true);
    // Write one line of text to it
    q.println("Hello there file2.out");

    // Open an output file the JDK 1.0 way.
    PrintStream p = new PrintStream(
                    new FileOutputStream("file1.out"));
    // Write one line of text to it
    p.println("Hello there file1.out");
```

```
// Open an input file using methods supported by JDK 1.1
// or later.
BufferedReader b = new BufferedReader(
    new InputStreamReader(new FileInputStream("file4.in")));

// Read the first line and print it out
System.out.println(b.readLine());

// Read the second line and ignore it
b.readLine();

// Read the third line and convert it to a double.
// Note that this method is only supported under JDK 1.2
// or later.
// You must use Double.valueOf(s).doubleValue() under earlier
// versions
String s = b.readLine();
double x = Double.parseDouble(s);
System.out.println("The double is: " + x);

// Read the fourth line and convert it to an integer
s = b.readLine();
int i = Integer.parseInt(s);
System.out.println("The integer is: " + i);

// Open an input file the JDK 1.0 way.
DataInputStream d = new DataInputStream(
                new FileInputStream("file3.in"));
// Read one line of text from it
System.out.println(d.readLine());
    }
}
```

5.10   Classes from `java.lang`

In addition to those classes that we have already discussed, the package `java.lang` contains simple classes corresponding to each of the primitive data types. These are not primarily intended to store values; the primitive type itself does this. Instead the classes serve as a place to keep some utility functions, such as conversion from strings, that are associated with the primitive type.

There is one additional use of these classes: certain operations require objects to work upon. For example, only objects may be stored in the standard lists described in the next subsection. These classes allow you to convert primitive data types into objects in order to do this.

The first class to be considered is `java.lang.Object`. This is not a class from which you will ever want to create an instance. However, through the mechanism of **inheritance** (discussed in Section 6.3), this defines a minimal set of standard methods for all classes. It is worth just looking to see what you can expect.

```java
package java.lang;

public class Object
{
  //// Comparison of objects
  // since == compares references
  public boolean equals(Object obj);

  // Duplication of current object
  protected Object clone()
            throws CloneNotSupportedException,
                   OutOfMemoryError;

  //// Conversion to String for '+' and printing
  public String toString();

  //// Generation of hash code for hash tables
  public int hashCode();

  //// Finalizer, discussed in next chapter
  protected void finalize()
            throws Throwable;
}
```

By means of **inheritance** all new classes that you write will come with a basic version of these methods. However, if you do define a new class then you should probably write your own versions of some of these methods to extend them to fit the class behaviour more accurately. The exact specifications are further discussed in Section 6.5. You should find that sensible versions of these methods have been written for most standard library classes.

Next we consider the class java.lang.Number. Once again you will never want to create an object of this type yourself (and indeed you cannot). However, by a similar use of **inheritance**, this defines the standard set of methods for the classes corresponding to primitive numerical data types.

JDK 1.0

```java
package java.lang;

public class Number
{
  //// Conversions from the object
  // to primitive types.
  // byte and short are JDK 1.1 or later only
  public byte byteValue();
  public short shortValue();
  public int intValue();
  public long longValue();
  public float floatValue();
  public double doubleValue();
}
```

Finally, we get on to the actual classes for these primitive types. I will not list declarations for all of these, as they are very similar. The classes are called `Byte`, `Short`, `Integer`, `Long`, `Float` and `Double`. `Byte` and `Short` are only available under

JDK 1.0   JDK 1.1 or later.

All of these classes implement all of the standard methods from `java.lang.Object` and `java.lang.Number`. All types have constructors from their primitive data type or from a string, a method `valueOf` which creates an object from a string containing a value, a method `toString` which creates a string from a primitive value, and class constants `MAX_VALUE` and `MIN_VALUE`.

In addition each integer type adds a method `parse<primitivename>` which returns the relevant primitive data type containing the same value as a string, a method `decode` which spots the base that a number in a string is using (via the standard prefixes such as `0x`) and converts it into an object, and a set of static methods `to<XXX>String` for converting the primitive data type into strings of different bases.

As an example, the `Integer` type is defined below. Note that `NumberFormatException` is a subclass of `RuntimeException` and so need not be handled explicitly.

```
package java.lang;

public class Integer;
{
  //// Standard from java.lang.Object
  public boolean equals(Object obj);
  public String toString();
  public int hashCode();

  //// Standard from java.lang.Number
  public byte byteValue();
  public short shortValue();
  public int intValue();
  public long longValue();
  public float floatValue();
  public double doubleValue();

  //// Constructors
  public Integer(int value);
  public Integer(String s)
        throws NumberFormatException;

  //// valueOf creates object from string
  public static Integer valueOf(String s)
              throws NumberFormatException;
  public static Integer valueOf(String s, int radix)
              throws NumberFormatException;

  //// Creating strings from primitives
  public static String toString(int i);
  public static String toString(int i, int radix);
```

```
//// class constants describe size
public static final int MIN_VALUE = 0x80000000;
public static final int MAX_VALUE = 0x7fffffff;

//// Creating primitives from strings
public static int parseInt(String s)
        throws NumberFormatException;
public static int parseInt(String s, int radix)
        throws NumberFormatException;

//// Creating objects from strings in arbitrary bases
// JDK 1.1 or later only for Integer and Short
// JDK 1.2 or later only for Long
public static Integer decode(String nm)
        throws NumberFormatException;

//// Converting primitive to string in arbitrary bases
// JDK 1.1 or later only, and Integer/Long only
public static String toHexString(int i);
public static String toOctalString(int i);
public static String toBinaryString(int i);
}
```

JDK 1.0
JDK 1.1

The classes for floating point types are similar. Each class has constructors, valueOf, toString, MIN_VALUE and MAX_VALUE as above. In addition, three new constants, NEGATIVE_INFINITY, NaN and POSITIVE_INFINITY, are defined, as are tests for these and functions performing bitwise conversion between the floating point type and the integer type that uses the same amount of memory: between int and float and between long and double.

As an example, the Double type is defined below. Again, NumberFormatException need not be handled explicitly.

```
package java.lang;

public class Double;
{
    //// Standard from java.lang.Object
    public boolean equals(Object obj);
    public String toString();
    public int hashCode();

    //// Standard from java.lang.Number
    public byte byteValue();
    public short shortValue();
    public int intValue();
    public long longValue();
    public float floatValue();
    public double doubleValue();
```

```
//// Constructors
public Double(double value);
public Double(String s)
        throws NumberFormatException;

//// valueOf creates object from string
public static Double valueOf(String s)
            throws NumberFormatException;

//// Creating strings from primitives
public static String toString(double d);

//// Class constants describe size
public static final double MAX_VALUE
                = 1.79769313486231570e+308;
public static final double MIN_VALUE
                = 4.94065645841246544e-324;

//// Creating primitives from strings
// JDK 1.2 or later only
public static double parseDouble(String s);

//// New constants for special values
public static final double POSITIVE_INFINITY = 1.0 / 0.0;
public static final double NEGATIVE_INFINITY = -1.0 / 0.0;
public static final double NaN = 0.0d / 0.0;

//// Tests for special values
static public boolean isNaN(double v);
static public boolean isInfinite(double v);
public boolean isNaN();
public boolean isInfinite();

//// Bitwise conversion to other data type
public static native long doubleToLongBits(double value);
public static native double longBitsToDouble(long bits);
}
```

JDK 1.1

These classes may seem very complicated. However, essentially there are only two uses for them. The first is to convert strings into values (the conversion back is generally done automatically in the `println` statement or by '+'). For an integer, we write:

```
int i = Integer.parseInt("341");
```

using the static method to convert directly. The equivalent methods exist for all integer types. For real types, we can write:

```
double d = Double.parseDouble("5.37");
```

JDK 1.1

under JDK 1.2 or later and the equivalent methods exist for all floating point types. Unfortunately, under earlier JDK versions, we must write:

```
double d = Double.valueOf("5.37").doubleValue();
```

This is rather more complicated. In the first stage we create a `Double` object from the string, then, in the second stage, we convert the answer into the primitive type. Again, the equivalent methods exist for all floating point types.

In either case, if the string cannot be converted into a number then a `NumberFormatException` is thrown.

The second use for these classes is to convert an integer into an object on those occasions when an object is required. For example, we might do this in order to store the integer in a list (see `java.util.Vector` in the next section).

There are two apparent uses for these classes which are not appropriate. The first is in converting between data types. This is not worthwhile, although it is possible. Conversions are much better performed by casts:

```
double d = 8.31;

int i = (int) d;
```

There are also a number of conversion methods in the class `java.lang.Math`, which we discussed earlier.

The second apparent use is to be able to pass an argument to a method which the method can change: the equivalent of `var` parameters in Pascal or passing a pointer to an argument in C/C++. This is valid in theory: arguments passed by reference can have their values changed, as we saw in Section 4.3.2. However, none of these classes allows their value to be changed *in situ*: in all cases you must create a new object with the new value, so this approach is useless.

Finally, to end our discussion of the `java.lang` package, two similar classes, `Boolean` and `Character`, exist to correspond to the primitive types `boolean` and `char`. Their use is very similar to the above, so we shall just give the declarations.

For `java.lang.Boolean`:

```
package java.lang;

public class Boolean;
{
  //// Standard from java.lang.Object
  public boolean equals(Object obj);
  public String toString();
  public int hashCode();

  //// Constructors
  public Boolean(boolean value);
  public Boolean(String s);

  //// Constants defining values for object
  public static final Boolean TRUE = new Boolean(true);
  public static final Boolean FALSE = new Boolean(false);

  //// Getting at the value of the object
```

```
    public boolean booleanValue();

    //// valueOf creates object from string
    public static Boolean valueOf(String s);
}
```

For `java.lang.Character`:

```
    package java.lang;

    public class Character
    {
        //// Standard from java.lang.Object
        public boolean equals(Object obj);
        public String toString();
        public int hashCode();

        //// Constructors
        public Character(char value);

        //// Constants showing min and max bases
        // for number stored in strings.
        public static final int MIN_RADIX = 2;
        public static final int MAX_RADIX = 36;

        //// Simple tests
        public static boolean isLowerCase(char ch);
        public static boolean isUpperCase(char ch);
        public static boolean isDigit(char ch);
        public static boolean isLetter(char ch);
        public static boolean isLetterOrDigit(char ch);
        public static boolean isSpace(char ch);
        public static boolean isSpaceChar(char ch);
        public static boolean isWhitespace(char ch);

        //// Case conversions
        public static char toLowerCase(char ch);
        public static char toUpperCase(char ch);

        //// Getting at the value of the object
        public char charValue();
    }
```

Note that the `Character` class is actually substantially bigger than this and supports Unicode lettering, which has the ability to display characters from most human scripts. These features are not documented in this book. Read the online documentation if you are interested.

5.11   Classes from `java.util`

Continuing with our tour of the standard library, we enter the package `java.util`, which includes the final four classes that are of interest to a scientific programmer.

The first is `java.util.Random`. This class provides the most sophisticated source of random numbers in the standard libraries. We have already encountered `java.lang.Math.random`, which creates a random `double` between 0.0 and 1.0. This class offers several more options. It was used by two of the `BigInteger` constructors in Section 5.4.

```java
package java.util;

public class Random
{
    //// Constructors
    public Random();
    public Random(long seed);

    //// Setting the seed.
    public void setSeed(long seed);

    //// Getting random numbers
    // Fill a whole array with random bytes
    public void nextBytes(byte[] bytes);
    public int nextInt();
    public long nextLong();
    // Floating point values are uniformly
    // distributed between 0.0 and 1.0
    public float nextFloat();
    public double nextDouble();
    // Gaussian values have a mean of 0.0
    // and a standard deviation of 1.0
    public double nextGaussian();
}
```

The random number generation proceeds using a 48-bit seed, which is used to generate a random number and then updated to be able to generate the one after that. The seed is stored in a hidden variable of the class. The class is used by creating an object of this type (which contains the current seed value) and then requesting random numbers from it. The object internally updates its seed each time it produces a random number.

The initial seed can be specified in the constructor or can be set using `setSeed`. Use one of these options to obtain the same 'random' numbers every time the program is run. If the other constructor, without an argument, is used then the initial seed is set to the current time when the program runs. This guarantees different random numbers on every occasion.

As an example, we can produce a list of random integers with:

```java
Random r = new Random();
```

```
for (int i=1; i<30; i++)
   System.out.println(r.nextInt());
```

Certain methods, for example two of the constructors for `BigInteger`, require a source of randomness, and request an object of type `Random` as an argument. In the RSA encoding examples, we handled this with

```
p = new BigInteger(SIZE, 10, new Random());
```

by creating the object and passing the reference directly to the constructor. We could also write

```
Random r = new Random();
p = new BigInteger(SIZE, 10, r);
```

and use the same random source again. This is especially relevant when we consider creating our own random number generators. Using **inheritance** of objects (described in Section 6.3), we could make our own object behave like a `Random` object, and thus be able to pass it to methods such as the `BigInteger` constructor. This is done as an example in Section 6.3.3.

The algorithm that `Random` uses is taken from *The Art of Computer Programming* (Knuth, 1981), Volume 2, Section 3.2.1. The algorithm used to generate the Gaussian values is in Section 3.4.1.

The final three useful classes from `java.util` are `Stack`, `Hashtable` and `Vector`. These implement general data structures for storing objects. The first two are self explanatory. `Vector` is badly named from the point of view of scientific programming. It implements an array of variable size.

The declaration of `Stack` is written below. Note that `EmptyStackException` need not be handled explicitly.

```
package java.util;

public class Stack
{
   // Add an element to the stack
   // returns the argument
   public Object push(Object item);
   // Get the element off the top of the stack
   public Object pop()
         throws EmptyStackException;
   // Return a reference to the top element
   // but leave it on top of the stack
   public Object peek()
         throws EmptyStackException;
   // Test if the stack is empty
   public boolean empty();
   // Return the distance of an element from
   // the top of the stack. -1 if not found.
   public int search(Object o);
}
```

Next, a hash table is a table storing associations between **keys** and **values**. The associations must be one-to-one. For example, you could use a hash table to store a relationship between the oldest child of a family and the mother. Every mother has exactly one oldest child and every oldest child has exactly one mother.

In the case of the Java class `Hashtable`, both keys and values can be arbitrary object types. The method `hashCode`, which you will have seen earlier in `java.lang.Object` and several other classes, is used to index the objects. If you choose to store one of your own classes in a hash table, then you should write a method called `hashCode` which generates an integer value for the object. The value should be constant over time for any object which is not changed, and should be the same for pairs of objects which the `equals` method shows are equal. However, it should ideally differ for all other pairs of objects. At the least, you should try to achieve a good spread of values.

The declaration of `Hashtable` that we give is somewhat simplified, but usable. Note that `NullPointerException` and `IllegalArgumentException` need not be handled explicitly. See the online documentation for a fuller version:

```
package java.util;

public class Hashtable
{
  //// Constructors
  // The table dynamically grows to take more entries as
  // needed. The fraction of entries filled is kept less than
  // loadFactor (0.0 to 1.0). A lower load factor wastes
  // memory but provides quicker access.
  public Hashtable();
  public Hashtable(int initialCapacity);
  public Hashtable(int initialCapacity, float loadFactor)
        throws IllegalArgumentException;

  //// Standard method from java.lang.Object
  public String toString();

  //// Return a new copy of the hashtable
  public Object clone();

  //// Finding out about the hashtable
  // The number of keys
  public int size();
  public boolean isEmpty();
  public boolean contains(Object value)
        throws NullPointerException;
  public boolean containsKey(Object key);

  //// Access to keys and values
  // Return value for a key. null if no such key
  public Object get(Object key);
  // Add a key/value pair
  public Object put(Object key, Object value)
```

```
        throws NullPointerException;
   // Remove key/value pair and return the value.
   // Returns null if no such key
   public Object remove(Object key);
   // Clear the hashtable
   public void clear();
}
```

Finally, `Vector`. This class implements a resizable array which automatically resizes as you add and remove data. Arbitrary objects may be stored in it, and each is associated with an index, which is its distance from the front of the array.

Once again, we can simplify the declaration a little. By noting that `ArrayIndexOutOfBoundsException` and `NoSuchElementException` need not be handled explicitly. The full version is available in the online documentation.

```
package java.util;

public class Vector
{
  //// Constructors
  public Vector();
  public Vector(int initialCapacity);
  public Vector(int initialCapacity, int capacityIncrement);

  //// Standard method from java.lang.Object
  public String toString();

  //// Return a new copy of the Vector
  public Object clone();

  //// Adding, removing and looking at elements.
  // Add an element at the end of the Vector
  public void addElement(Object obj);
  // Insert the element, shifting those after it up.
  public void insertElementAt(Object obj, int index)
         throws ArrayIndexOutOfBoundsException;
  // Remove the element, shifting those after it down.
  public void removeElementAt(int index)
         throws ArrayIndexOutOfBoundsException;
  // Remove the first occurrence of this element
  public boolean removeElement(Object obj);
  // Empty the Vector
  public void removeAllElements();
  // Return the element at an index without removing it
  public Object elementAt(int index)
         throws ArrayIndexOutOfBoundsException;
  // Set the given element
  public void setElementAt(Object obj, int index)
         throws ArrayIndexOutOfBoundsException;
  public Object firstElement()
```

```
              throws NoSuchElementException;
    public Object lastElement()
              throws NoSuchElementException;
    // Copy into an array, which must be big enough.
    public void copyInto(Object anArray[]);

    //// Finding out about the Vector
    public boolean isEmpty();
    public boolean contains(Object elem);
    // First occurrence
    public int indexOf(Object elem);
    // First occurrence starting at index
    public int indexOf(Object elem, int index);
    // Last occurrence
    public int lastIndexOf(Object elem);
    // Last occurrence starting at index
    public int lastIndexOf(Object elem, int index);

    //// Managing storage
    // Number of elements in vector
    public int size();
    // Number for which storage is allocated
    public int capacity();
    // Reduce storage to hold elements exactly
    public void trimToSize();
    // Increase storage to be able to hold at least
    // minCapacity elements.
    public void ensureCapacity(int minCapacity);
    // Set the number of elements. If this is an
    // increase, the new elements are null. If a
    // decrease, the tail is removed.
    public void setSize(int newSize);
}
```

5.12 Simple graphics

Chapter 7 presents a library written for this book which allows you to use both text and graphics in a simple environment, with the text being mapped into a window and the graphics being internally buffered.

Until we reach that chapter, we can write simple graphical programs with a single output window using just the standard libraries. The scope of this book does not include extensive explanation of the graphics and windowing libraries, so our program is split into unexplained support code and a small section of user-editable code.

In summary, the support code interfaces with the libraries so that a method called paint is called every time that the window needs updating, including when it is first created. If you write your code inside the paint method, then your graphics will appear in the window and will update correctly when the window is redrawn. Text input and output works as normal at the command line from which the program was started. However, there is a problem that switching between windows may cause the graphics window to try to start updating again, even if it is currently inside the `paint` method. Because of this, you should not use text input from inside the `paint` method, although you can use output to log data. If you need to let the user type in a few initial parameters for your program then you should put this code at the start of the `main` method, and store the returned values in `public static` class variables which your program can refer to during updates.

Finally we can discuss the graphics commands. `paint` is passed a `Graphics` object. This has two methods: `drawString`, which inserts some text into the graphics window at a specified position, and `drawLine`, which joins two points in the graphics window. The declarations are:

```java
public void drawString(String s, int x, int y);
public void drawLine(int x1, int y1, int x2, int y2);
```

In both cases, the points are specified in screen pixels. You should note that (0,0) is at the top left of the window, with the positive *x*-axis pointing right and the positive *y*-axis pointing down. These are not normal scientific axes. The point specified in `drawString` is the bottom left point of the text.

Now for the program, which is available at `http://www.jscieng.co.uk/Code/StdLib/Graph/`. This draws a graph of the function `f` with an *x* range from 0 to 1 and the same *y* range. The code is as follows:

```java
import java.awt.*;


// Declare a button that quits when pressed
class FinishButton extends Button
{
  // Constructor taking button name.
  public FinishButton(String s)
  {
    super(s);
  }


  // Catch events referring to the button
  public boolean action(Event e, Object what)
  {
    if (e.target == this)
    {
      // Close the window and exit
      Graph.closeWindow();
      System.exit(0);
      return true;
    }
    else
      return false;
```

```
        }
    }

    // Declare a class capable of being drawn to
    public class Graph extends Canvas
    {
        // Create the window object as a static class variable.
        private static Frame window = new Frame("Drawing");

        // Declare the button to quit the program.
        private static Button finish = new FinishButton("Finish");

        // Accessor method for the window variable.
        public static void closeWindow()
        {
            window.dispose();
        }

    // ********** COPY EVERYTHING BEFORE HERE **********


        // Steps is the number of points plotted on the graph
        public static final int STEPS = 100;
        // Graphsize is the size of the window for the graph
        public static final int GRAPHSIZE = 300;


        // f is the function which gets drawn
        public static double f(double x)
        {
            return x*x + 0.2 * Math.sin(8*x);
        }


        // The paint method is where you should write your
        // code to draw the graph.
        public void paint(Graphics g)
        {
            // Add a title and status message on the command line.
            g.drawString("A graph", 40, 40);
            System.out.println("Drawing graph...");

            // Step through the points
            for (int i=1; i<=STEPS; i++)
            {
                // Compute the previous point
                double oldX = (i-1) / ((double) STEPS);
                double oldY = f(oldX);
```

```
      // And the current point
      double newX = i / ((double) STEPS);
      double newY = f(newX);

      // Convert these values into screen coordinates
      int goX = (int) (GRAPHSIZE*oldX);
      int goY = GRAPHSIZE - (int) (GRAPHSIZE*oldY);
      int gnX = (int) (GRAPHSIZE*newX);
      int gnY = GRAPHSIZE - (int) (GRAPHSIZE*newY);

      // And draw the line segment
      g.drawLine(goX, goY, gnX, gnY);
    }
  }


// ********** COPY EVERYTHING AFTER HERE **********

  // main method starts up the window
  public static void main(String[] argv)
  {

// ********** PERFORM SETUP INPUT/OUTPUT HERE **********

    // The window and button were created statically

    // Create a graph object
    Graph g = new Graph();

    // Set the size of the graph
    g.resize(GRAPHSIZE, GRAPHSIZE);

    // Add graph and button to the window
    window.add("Center", g);
    window.add("South", finish);

    // Set the window up and show it
    window.pack();
    window.setResizable(false);
    window.toFront();
    window.show();
  }
}
```

Note how we inverted the graph in the calculation of goY and gnY to handle the fact that the origin is at the top left.

Figure 5.4 shows the program running under Windows 95. Note that, unlike any other popular language, in Java the graphics libraries are part of the standard. As a result this program will run unchanged on any computer that supports Java. This is very unusual for graphical code.

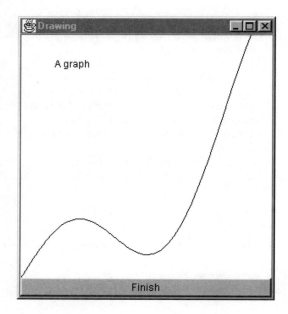

Figure 5.4 The `graph` application.

5.13   The Internet

If you had heard of Java before you started reading this book, then it was almost certainly in the context of the web (a worldwide system of interlinked pages of information – talk to somebody urgently if you had not heard of this!).

By now, you should be convinced that Java is a general programming language just as powerful as any other. In fact, since the standard libraries contain virtually everything that most operating systems do and are the same on all platforms, and the language supports modern features such as garbage collection, object orientation and threading, Java is one of the most powerful programming languages in existence at the moment (although not the fastest, given that it is currently interpreted).

However, the standard use of Java at the time of writing (August 1998) is for embedding programs in web pages. When a user views that page in a web browser, the compiled `.class` files are downloaded to the user's machine and run locally over an interpreter. Java is ideal for this use because of its extremely high level of portability – the user may have many kinds of hardware or operating system, but Java interpreters now exist in all major web browsers. In addition, the language is inherently secure. For example, since pointers do not exist, the programmer cannot access memory belonging to other programs.

These embedded programs are called **applets**. A class `java.applet.Applet` defines a standard set of methods which all applets must provide. They use the concept of **inheritance**, discussed in the next chapter, to do this. Writing an applet is no different technically from writing normal programs (called **applications**), except that the applet is not allowed to read or write to files (it will be running on somebody else's computer!).

There are two further issues about applets. Firstly, standard text input and output is effectively non-existent. Some web browsers provide a simple text console, but some (such as Microsoft Internet Explorer) do nothing more than logging `println` output to an obscure file.

Secondly, at the time of writing, some major web browsers are not fully JDK 1.1 compliant. This will change, but, until JDK 1.1 support is widespread, you would probably be wise to restrict your code to the JDK 1.0 libraries. The major effect that this has for scientific programming is that `BigInteger` and `BigDecimal` do not exist.

However, leaving these points aside, an applet provides us with a `paint` method very similar to that which we used in the previous section. In fact, we can convert exactly the same program into an applet, leaving all code in the `paint` method unchanged. This program is available at `http://www.jscieng.co.uk/Code/StdLib/WebGraph/`. Note, once again, that Chapter 7 discusses a better way of embedding Java graphics in web pages.

```java
import java.applet.Applet;
import java.awt.*;

// Declare a class capable of being an applet
public class WebGraph extends Applet
{

// ********** COPY EVERYTHING BEFORE HERE **********


  // Steps is the number of points plotted on the graph
  public static final int STEPS = 100;
  // Graphsize is the size of the window for the graph
  public static final int GRAPHSIZE = 300;


  // f is the function which gets drawn
  public static double f(double x)
  {
    return x*x + 0.2 * Math.sin(8*x);
  }


  // The paint method is where you should write your
  // code to draw the graph.
  public void paint(Graphics g)
  {
    // Add a title and status message on the command line.
    g.drawString("A graph", 40, 40);
    System.out.println("Drawing graph...");

    // Step through the points
    for (int i=1; i<=STEPS; i++)
```

```
    {
        // Compute the previous point
        double oldX = (i-1) / ((double) STEPS);
        double oldY = f(oldX);

        // And the current point
        double newX = i / ((double) STEPS);
        double newY = f(newX);

        // Convert these values into screen coordinates
        int goX = (int) (GRAPHSIZE*oldX);
        int goY = GRAPHSIZE - (int) (GRAPHSIZE*oldY);
        int gnX = (int) (GRAPHSIZE*newX);
        int gnY = GRAPHSIZE - (int) (GRAPHSIZE*newY);

        // And draw the line segment
        g.drawLine(goX, goY, gnX, gnY);
    }
  }


  // ********** COPY EVERYTHING AFTER HERE **********
  }
```

In order to embed this program in a web page, we use the <APPLET> tag in our HTML.
The structure is:

```
<APPLET codebase="?" code="?" width=? height=?>
Text for non-Java browsers.
</APPLET>
```

The `codebase` is the path for the base directory of your packages (the `-d` option to
`javac`), whilst the `code` is the relative path to the `.class` file containing the `extends`
`Applet` and `paint` method.

For example, the file `WebGraph.html` contains:

```
<HTML>
<HEAD>
<TITLE>This is Graphing on the Web</TITLE>
</HEAD>
<BODY>
The Java applet's just below this text
and already it's starting to run...
<P>
<APPLET codebase="." code="WebGraph.class" width=300 height=300>
Your browser does not support Java, sorry.
</APPLET>
<P>
This Java applet was written for the book
<EM>Introductory Java for Scientists and Engineers</EM>
by Richard J. Davies.
```

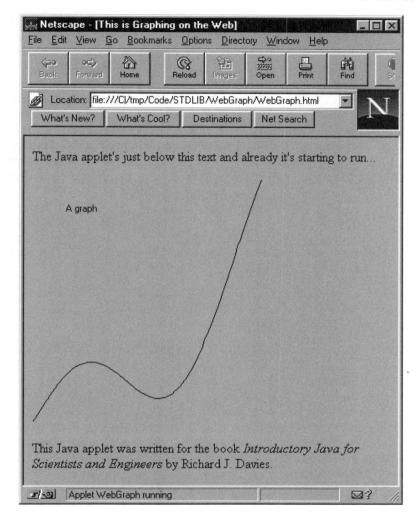

Figure 5.5 The WebGraph applet.

```
    </BODY>
    </HTML>
```

Running `appletviewer WebGraph.html` from the command line (this is part of the JDK), or pointing a web browser at this file, will run the program. Figure 5.5 shows it running in Netscape Navigator under Windows 95.

Once you have reached this stage, making your applet available on the web is simply a matter of copying the `.class` and `.html` files onto your website. You must make sure that you maintain any hierarchical directory structure in which the `.class` files are stored to represent their packaging.

WHERE TO GO FROM HERE

This chapter has covered only those parts of the standard libraries of direct relevance to the scientific programmer. The libraries themselves are huge, and range far beyond the scope of this book. As well as large amounts of support for graphics and user interfaces, they include networking, multi-threading and advanced file handling, to name but a few topics.

Chapters 7 and 8 describe two further libraries, the JSGL and the JNL respectively, which may interest you. The JSGL provides a simple but useful environment for drawing graphs and performing text input and output. It may be used locally or in applets. The JNL provides additional mathematical functionality.

If your requirements go beyond these, then you will need to investigate the standard libraries yourself. A large amount of online documentation is provided with the JDK, and you may find this helpful. Alternatively, you can turn to less specialized books on Java; I would particularly recommend the two volumes of *Core Java 1.1* (Cornell and Horstmann, 1997) or *Java in a Nutshell* (Flanagan, 1997).

CHAPTER 6

Object orientation

6.1   Introduction

In Chapter 4, you were introduced to the concept of objects and wrote programs which used them. However, we have not yet discussed the idea of object oriented programming in any depth or fully explained the syntax for writing your own objects. This chapter covers these gaps. It assumes knowledge of everything discussed in Chapter 4. All sample code is available from the website at http://www.jscieng.co.uk/Code/Objects/.

The contents of this chapter are not required by any later section of the book. However, object orientation is an important programming technique and is one of Java's major features. In addition, in previous and subsequent chapters we use objects, and understanding how these work internally will help you to write programs which use them.

6.2   Simple objects

Many traditional programming languages, such as Fortran, C and Pascal, are based on subroutines, also known as functions or procedures. These lead to a style known as **procedural** programming. As you have seen, Java supports this style of programming with few changes (just declare class variables and methods as `public static`). In addition to this, like many modern languages, Java allows for **object oriented** programming.

6.2.1 Non-static variables and methods

As we discussed in Section 4.3.3, the most simple objects are instances of data types with named parts. These objects behave like `struct` in C, `record` in Pascal or simple use of `class` in C++ or `object` in Modula-3. There is no equivalent structure in FORTRAN 77, whose users have to maintain synchronized parallel arrays for each type of data to be stored. Objects are handled by reference.

Recapping, we remember that we can define a new type of object using a class definition in which there are non-static variables:

```
public class Complex
{
   public double realpart;
   public double imagpart;
}
```

Given this definition, we can use `new` to create objects of this type. Each object stores its own values for each non-static variable named in the class definition. This is different from static class variables, which behave like standard global variables, have a single value and are stored centrally in the class, not in objects of the class's type.

We can access the data stored in an object by appending `.<variable name>` to the name of a reference to the object.

For example, we wrote:

```
public static void main(String[] argv)
{
   Complex a;

   a = new Complex();

   a.realpart = 1.0;
   a.imagpart = 3.4;
}
```

As you know by now, object orientation goes much further than this, and also allows us to write non-static methods. These act on the data stored in a object and are called by appending `.<methodname>(<argument list>)` to the name of a reference to the object.

In Section 4.3.3 we discussed a method

```
public void scalarMultiply(double s)
```

which multiplied a complex number by a scalar and updated the value of the complex number in place. This would be called using

```
Complex a = new Complex();

a.scalarMultiply(5.7);
```

We will now discuss writing that method.

When you call a non-static method, you call it using a reference to the object which that method will act on. As a result, the method effectively has one more argument than it appears to. This extra argument is the object with respect to which it is called, and is called `this` inside the method. Thus the above declaration of `scalarMultiply` is equivalent to

```
public static void scalarMultiply(Complex this, double s);
```

except that we can call it using the syntax above and do not have to write

```
Complex a = new Complex();

Complex.scalarMultiply(a, 5.7);
```

If we think in terms of the equivalent declaration including the `this` parameter, we can see how to write the body of the method. Note that the `this` parameter is passed by reference, which means that the data that it stores can be changed.

```
public class Complex
{
  public double realpart;
  public double imagpart;

  public void scalarMultiply(double s)
  {
    this.realpart *= s;
    this.imagpart *= s;
  }
}
```

In fact, since 'this.' would be a very common piece of code under these rules, we are actually allowed to leave it out and write:

```
public class Complex
{
  public double realpart;
  public double imagpart;

  public void scalarMultiply(double s)
  {
    realpart *= s;
    imagpart *= s;
  }
}
```

This piece of code looks remarkably like the same code with `static` after every `public`. However, the behaviour is different. With `static`, there would be two global class variables, accessible as `Complex.realpart` and `Complex.imagpart`. The method would be called as `Complex.scalarMultiply` and would act on these variables.

Without `static`, nothing can be accessed via `Complex.<>`. The two pieces of data exist inside every object of this type that we create. `scalarMultiply` can only be called in conjunction with an object and acts on the data stored in that object.

Note that, as will be discussed in Section 6.4, non-static variables in complicated classes should probably be accessed indirectly via non-static methods of the class (**accessor methods**) rather than directly as `<object>.<variable>`. This second approach is considered bad program design.

6.2.2 Constructors

As we discussed in Section 4.3.3, the round brackets that appear after the class name in a `new` statement have a meaning. These look like a method call because they are. A class may define special methods, called **constructors**, with no return type and the same name as the class. These methods act to set up the object immediately following its creation. We can pass parameters to the constructor in the brackets of a `new` statement. Like any method, we can write several different constructors and distinguish between them by the argument list. If we do not write any constructors, then we automatically get a default constructor, taking no arguments, which does nothing. This default constructor is not written for us if we write any constructors ourselves, even if they do not include one taking no arguments.

An appropriate constructor for our `Complex` class would allow us to set the initial value of an object. This would look like:

```
public Complex(double r, double i)
{
  realpart = r;
  imagpart = i;
}
```

We would use it in statements such as:

```
Complex c = new Complex(4.5, 7.3);
```

There is one additional piece of constructor syntax. A constructor may call another constructor for the same class, and then perform some additional setup. This is done by placing `this(<argument list>)` in the first line of the constructor. For example, in the complex number example, a constructor taking no arguments which initialized an object to contain `1 + 0i` could be written as:

```
public Complex()
{
  this(1, 0);
}
```

If such a `this` statement is to be used, it must be on the very first line of the constructor.

6.2.3 Example – complex numbers

We now know enough to be able to define simple objects. As an extended example, we now write a more complete complex number class. This is still only an example: the JNL, as discussed in Chapter 8, contains a much better, fully functional, class for complex numbers. This example is available at `http://www.jscieng.co.uk/ Code/Objects/Complex/`.

```java
public class Complex
{
  // Declare the data variable for the type
  public double realpart;
  public double imagpart;

  // Default constructor sets value to 0 + 0i
  public Complex()
  {
    realpart = 0;
    imagpart = 0;
  }

  // Constructor with user specified value
  public Complex(double r, double i)
  {
    realpart = r;
    imagpart = i;
  }

  // Method to add 'other' to this object
  public void add(Complex other)
  {
    realpart += other.realpart;
    imagpart += other.imagpart;
  }

  // Method to multiply 'other' into this object
  public void multiply(Complex other)
  {
    // Declare temporary storage for calculation
    Complex ans = new Complex();

    // Calculate
    ans.realpart = realpart * other.realpart
                 - imagpart * other.imagpart;
    ans.imagpart = realpart * other.imagpart
                 + imagpart * other.realpart;

    // Copy value into this object.
    realpart = ans.realpart;
    imagpart = ans.imagpart;
```

```
        }

        // Main method. Static and so independent
        // of the definition of the object type.
        public static void main(String[] argv)
        {
          // Declare and create some objects
          Complex a = new Complex();
          Complex b = new Complex(4.7, 3.2);
          Complex c = new Complex(3.1, 2.4);

          // Perform some arithmetic
          a.add(b);
          c.multiply(a);

          // Extract the answer
          System.out.print(c.realpart + " + ");
          System.out.println(c.imagpart + "i");
        }
      }
```

Looking at this code, the benefits of being able to declare our own data type are obvious: it is much simpler to be able to write .add and .multiply than to write the whole operation longhand every time. Unfortunately, unlike C++, Java does not support **operator overloading**, which would have allowed us to go even further and use '+' to do the addition. It is not yet clear why being able to make the method non-static was useful: we could reasonably have written static methods taking two arguments. This should become clear when we discuss **inheritance**.

Note how the main method is exactly as normal. Classes may have both static and non-static parts, and the two do not interact.

Also, remember that objects are handled by reference and so = and == act to set/compare what the references refer to, not on the objects. This is what prevented us from writing this = ans; at the end of the multiply method.

6.3   Inheritance

The second fundamental part of object orientation is the idea of **inheritance**. This allows you define new object types as extensions of old ones. The new type inherits all variables and methods defined in the original. It can be treated exactly like the old type for many purposes, but can also provide some additional functionality of its own, or change the original behaviour in some cases.

The language used to describe inheritance is the same as that for family trees. A class is said to be a **descendant** or **subclass** of an **ancestral superclass** from which it **inherits** behaviour. We can then proceed to produce subclasses of the subclass and continue like this as far as we wish. We refer to the immediate ancestor of a class as its **parent**.

The benefits of object orientation are twofold. Firstly, if two objects have identical behaviour in some respect then we can define this in the superclass. This prevents us from

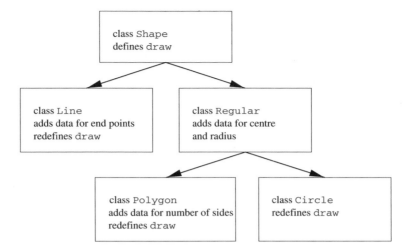

Figure 6.1 Geometrical shapes and inheritance.

having to copy the code out several times and then maintain synchronization between the copies. Secondly, even if the behaviour of the two objects is not identical in some respect, then if the definition of the action to be performed is, for example, that both objects act to display themselves (details of doing this depend on the object's internal structure), we can define the action in the superclass and override it in both subclasses. Other parts of the program can then use the superclass's method on objects of either type without even knowing which they are and the correct version of the action will be performed.

6.3.1 Example – geometrical shapes

As an example, consider the set of geometrical shapes in two dimensions. Imagine that we are defining classes to store data defining lines, circles and regular polygons. We want to be able to draw these shapes and choose to implement drawing through class methods so that the code is kept together with the object definition. To allow all of our objects to be handled uniformly, we define a superclass `Shape` with a method `draw`.

We define the class `Line` as a subclass of `Shape` and add data storage to record the ends of the line. We override the `draw` method to draw the line.

At this point we realize that both regular polygons and circles share some behaviour: they have a centre and a radius. As a result, they should not be written as direct descendants of `Shape`. We define a class `Regular` as a subclass of `Shape`, and add data storage to record the centre and radius.

We can now declare `Polygon` as a subclass of `Regular` which adds support for a number of sides and overrides the `draw` method to draw the polygon. Similarly, `Circle` should be a subclass of `Regular` which merely overrides the `draw` method to draw the circle.

The resulting inheritance tree is shown in Figure 6.1. The extra pieces of syntax that we need to implement this are simple. At the top of our class definition we add an `extends` clause:

public class <class name> **extends** <parent name>

This specifies which superclass a subclass inherits from. The subclass inherits all variables and methods defined by its superclass. To override a superclass method, we just redefine it in the subclass using a standard method definition (C++ programmers should note that all methods are `virtual` in Java). The code for our shapes would look something like:

```
public class Shape
{
  public void draw()
  {
    <generic drawing code. Poss. throw exception>
    <since there is not a sensible default>
  }
}


public class Line extends Shape
{
  int startx, starty, endx, endy;

  public void draw()
  {
    <actually draw the line>
  }
}


public class Regular extends Shape
{
  int centrex, centrey, radius;
}


public class Polygon extends Regular
{
  int sides;

  public void draw()
  {
    <actually draw the polygon>
  }
}


public class Circle extends Regular
```

```
  {
    public void draw()
    {
      <actually draw the circle>
    }
  }
```

Note that when we override a method, the new definition must have exactly the same arguments and return type.

What benefits have we obtained from inheritance, as opposed to just writing Line, Polygon and Circle alone?

Firstly, we have saved some coding. This is not very apparent here, since the extra classes Shape and Regular made up for it. However, we only had to write centrex, centrey and radius in one place: Polygon and Circle both inherited this behaviour unchanged. This could be quite significant if we had written a larger body of code or if the classes shared methods.

Secondly, and perhaps more importantly, a reference to a class is also capable of referring to any subclass of that class. Hence, if we wanted to store a list of shapes we could just create an array of Shape references. Line, Polygon and Circle all descend from Shape and so could all be stored in this array. In addition, since Shape defined draw, a method could move through the array, calling draw for every item. When the function is called, the objects use the subclass's definition, so the different shapes would draw themselves correctly. Note that the code calling draw need only know that Shape defines a draw method – it need not contain explicit code to draw each type of object and need not even know what subclasses of Shape exist.

The code that we have just discussed would look like:

```
Shape[] list = new Shape[100];

Circle c = new Circle;
c.centrex = 15;
c.centrey = 7;
c.radius = 9;
list[0] = c;

<some more code to get the shapes into the array>

for (int i=0; i<100; i++)
{
  list[i].draw();
}
```

Similarly, if we had an array of Regular references, we could move through the array, using radius to double the size of all the shapes without actually considering what kind of shapes they really were.

This ability to handle many cases in a generic way without writing a large switch statement is the major benefit from object orientation.

Thirdly, and much more trivially, the object structure neatly keeps all of the data and methods together in one place. Compare this situation with a similar program in C or

Pascal in which you would have to define several new data types to hold the possible combinations of data and then define several versions of `draw`, with different, memorable names.

6.3.2 Further issues

Note that, although the structures of packages and inheritance are both tree-like, there is no relation at all between them. For example, in the standard library, `java.io.IOException` extends `java.lang.Exception`.

A subclass inherits both the static and non-static members of its superclass. However, by far the most benefit is obtained from inheritance of non-static members. Only these methods can be called without specifying a class, and therefore only with these can we call subclass versions transparently.

If you think back, you have already seen several examples of inheritance. In the discussion of the `java.lang` package, we said that `Byte`, `Short` and the other classes are all descended from `Number`, which is descended from `Object`.

In fact, all object classes in Java are implicitly descended from `java.lang.Object`, which is added by the compiler to any **base class** which does not define a parent. This explains how `Stack` and the other classes from `java.util` are able to work for all classes simply by working for `Object` and also explains how writing a `toString` method will always make your class printable in `println` and how writing `equals` can be a standard interface for equality testing.

You should think of inheritance as an 'is a' relationship. The subclass 'is a' version of the superclass with some additions or changes. For example, in our shapes example, a line is a shape, and a circle is a regular shape. The easy trap to fall into is to use inheritance in 'has a' situations: where a new class needs to be able to perform some actions that another class already does, but the two ideas are not related. This case is better handled by giving the new class a member variable in which it creates an object of the other class. The new class can then call that object's methods.

Finally, note that, although inheritance provides the subclass with all of the methods and variables defined by the superclass, the subclass may override only methods. Variables cannot be overridden. If a subclass defines a new member variable with a name which is already present in the superclass, then **shadowing** occurs. Both variables exist independently. Methods declared in the superclass will still use the superclass variable, whilst methods declared in the subclass will use the subclass variable, unless they explicitly specify the superclass version by casting the `this` reference to the superclass type or using the `super` keyword as discussed later in Section 6.3.4. If the class is stored in an array of superclass references, then these will access the superclass version of the variable. Essentially, shadowing is provided as a bug-prevention tool. You should never want to use it deliberately – why must the subclass use the same name for its variable? However, it ensures that if you do accidentally use the same name twice then both sets of code work and do not interact. For any object orientation gurus amongst you, this, together with dynamic linking, are parts of Java's solution to the problem of the **fragile base class**.

6.3.3 Example – subclassing `java.util.Random`

As another example, consider the random number generating class `java.util.Random` in the standard library. This was discussed in Section 5.11. As we saw in Section 5.4, we can construct a random `BigInteger` by passing an object of the class `Random` to the constructor.

However, imagine that we did not believe the standard class `Random` to be sufficiently well implemented for our purposes. What can we do? Well, we can write a new class, descended from `Random`, and pass an object of this subclass to the constructor. In our subclass we can override the methods that we are concerned about and replace them with versions that work to our specifications.

In the example that follows, which is available at `http://www.jscieng.co.uk/Code/Objects/NewRand/`, we define a new class `NewRandomGenerator` which generates very bad random numbers (in fact they're the same every time). We then pass an object of this class to `BigInteger`'s constructor to create a 'random' `BigInteger` using our algorithm for 'randomness'.

```java
import java.math.BigInteger;
import java.util.Random;

// Declare NewRandomGenerator to descend from Random
class NewRandomGenerator extends Random
{
  // Override nextBytes to return the
  // same byte over and over again.
  public void nextBytes(byte[] bytes)
  {
    for (int i=0; i<bytes.length; i++)
    {
      bytes[i] = 0x52;
    }
  }

  // Override nextInt to return the
  // same integer every time.
  public int nextInt()
  {
    return 52;
  }

  // Override nextLong to return the
  // same value every time.
  public long nextLong()
  {
    return 52;
  }

  // Override nextFloat to return the
  // same value every time.
  public float nextFloat()
```

```
  {
    return 0.634F;
  }

  // Override nextDouble to return the
  // same value every time.
  public double nextDouble()
  {
    return 0.634;
  }

  // Override nextGaussian to return the
  // same value every time.
  public double nextGaussian()
  {
    return 0.634;
  }
}


// Declare a class NewRand which demonstrates the use
// of NewRandomGenerator.
public class NewRand
{
  public static void main(String[] argv)
  {
    // Create new BigInteger using an object of
    // the class NewRandomGenerator
    // as the source of randomness.
    BigInteger b = new BigInteger(128,
                              new NewRandomGenerator());

    // Print the integer. The lack of randomness is
    // obvious in base 16.
    System.out.println("Is this a random integer: " + b);
    System.out.print("In base 16, it clearly is not: ");
    System.out.println(b.toString(16));
  }
}
```

6.3.4 Constructors

When we start writing classes which inherit code from each other, we immediately run into an issue about constructors. In some sense, creating an object of the subclass involves creating an object of the superclass and then performing some additional actions to set up the additional behaviour of the subclass.

Like C++, Java handles this by **chaining** of constructors. After the memory has been allocated for the object, the constructors of all of its superclasses are executed in order, starting from the base class. Finally, the object's own constructor is executed.

The syntax for doing this is very similar to the usage of `this` in a constructor to call a different constructor for the same class. We simply write `super(<argument list>)` on the first line of the subclass constructor, listing the arguments to be passed to the superclass constructor. For example:

```
public class A
{
  public A(int i)
  {
    <code>
  }

  <other methods>
}


public class B extends A
{
  public B(int i, int j)
  {
    super(i);

    <further code>
  }

  <other methods>
}
```

Once again, `super` must be the very first line of the subclass constructor.

There are also two shortcuts. Firstly, if we omit the `super` statement, then `super();` – a call to the default constructor of the superclass – is automatically inserted. Of course, this will fail to compile if the superclass does not have a default constructor, which would occur only if we had specified some constructors ourselves but had not written this one.

Secondly, we have already mentioned that if we do not write any constructors, then a default constructor is written for us, which does nothing. In fact, it does perform one action: it calls the superclass's default constructor. Thus the default constructor that the compiler writes looks like:

```
public <subclass name>()
{
  super();
}
```

Taken together, these two actions mean that constructor chaining will always occur. We cannot forget to implement it.

As a technical point, note that method calls use the subclass versions at all times, even in the superclass constructor, which is run before the subclass constructor. This can mean that the superclass constructor ends up calling a method overridden in the subclass and that the method may fail because it relies on some setup information created in the subclass constructor, which has not yet been executed. This behaviour is different from C++.

In addition to the above role, `super` behaves much like `this` – as a reference to the current object. However, `super` has the type of the superclass. Because of this, you can use `super` to access shadowed variables (see Section 6.3.2).

`super` also has a special role in accessing methods from the superclass that have been overridden. Unlike shadowed variables, a reference to a subclass with the type of its superclass will still use the overridden methods defined in the subclass. However, `super` behaves differently: calling superclass methods using `super` will work. This enables you to override a method from the superclass, but still to be able to call the superclass's version of the method during the implementation of the overridden version. Note that in this form `super` can occur anywhere inside the method, not just on the first line.

6.4   Access control

A pillar of object orientation is the principle that a class should be able to restrict outside access to its data and methods.

Why is this useful? Consider the complex number class that we have already discussed. Complex numbers can be implemented using real and imaginary parts or using modulus and argument. The former is faster for addition/subtraction, while the latter is faster for multiplication/division. We could even write a very sophisticated complex number class which was capable of both representations, and try to use whichever was faster for the type of operations that were performed more frequently.

The issue this raises is that, while the user should be able to get and set both real and imaginary parts and moduli and arguments, the internal storage of the data should be hidden from the user of the class.

Object oriented languages allow this by providing different levels of access to variables and methods. So far, every class, variable or method that you have written has been preceded by `public`, which made it accessible to everything, or has had no qualifier, so was restricted to its package. Several other levels of access control, such as `private`, exist.

The solution to our problems is to restrict access to the object's data by specifying it as `private` and then to provide **accessor methods** which are public and control access to the data. We should write the complex number class as follows (the actual code in methods is omitted):

```
public class Complex
{
  // Constructors are visible to all
  public Complex();
  public Complex(double a, double b);

  // Data is hidden
  private double realpart;
  private double imagpart;
```

```
    // Accessor methods are visible
    public double realpart();
    public double imagpart();
    public double modulus();
    public double argument();

    public void setRealImag(double r, double i);
    public void setModArg(double m, double a);
}
```

Under this definition, code such as `c.realpart` is illegal and will be trapped by the compiler.

Why do we actually prevent access? Surely we could simply remember not to use the variables directly? Well, object oriented techniques are designed for use on very large projects with many programmers. The aim is to separate the design and implementation of the class. With the code as above, a programmer is guaranteed that no other code is using the variables directly. In a large project, this guarantees that changing the internal structure of the class will not break existing code which the programmer may know nothing about. One school of thought goes as far as to say that we should always use accessor methods and should have no public data. This means that we will be able to put logging output into the accessor methods, following which we will be able to see every time anything changes the value of the data. It will also be totally safe to rewrite a class entirely as long as we provide the same methods.

We now move on to the actual syntax. Java defines four levels of access control: `public`, `protected`, the default (no modifiers) and `private`. As you saw above, these modifiers are prefixed to the definitions of classes, methods, constants and variables. Classes may only be `public` or default, whilst methods, constants and variables can be at any level. An additional level, `private protected`, existed in JDK 1.0 but is no longer supported. The meanings are as follows:

- `public`: visible everywhere. There is one exception – if a class uses the default level of access, then even public methods, constants and variables will not be visible in those circumstances where the class itself is not.
- `protected`: visible in its package and to subclasses from different packages.
- The default: visible everywhere inside its package. No access from outside the package.
- `private`: not visible outside the class.

The description of `protected` requires a little further discussion. `protected` methods/data of a superclass are visible to subclasses but only in objects of the subclass's type or subtypes. In other words, if a class C is descended from a class B, which is descended from a class A, and A defines a protected part, then B can access this part within itself or other objects of types B or C, but B cannot access this part within A (unless the packaging overrides this).

There is one area of overlap in some of these definitions. This is the issue of visibility to a subclass which is in the same package as the superclass. In this case the appropriate part is visible if either condition is satisfied. Hence the default is for parts to be visible to subclasses only if the subclass is in the same package.

Table 6.1 Levels of access control.

Access level	public	protected	Default	private
Visible in same package	Y	Y	Y	N
Visible in other package	Y	N	N	N
Visible in subclass in same package	Y	Y	Y	N
Visible in subclass in other package	Y	Y	N	N

These levels of access control are summarized in Table 6.1. Note that `protected` parts are actually less 'protected' than the default!

Subclasses can redefine parts of a superclass to have a greater degree of visibility, but not a lower degree. The `main` method and its class must be `public`. Recall that a `.java` file can contain only one `public` class, but can also contain others of lower visibility.

C++ programmers should note the following:

- Java provides no `friend` statement – the use of packages to group classes for a higher level of access is the closest equivalent.
- `public` and `private` correspond to the C++ levels of access. `protected` is like C++ `protected` with `friend` in use for everything in the package, while the default level is like C++ `private` with `friend` in use.
- Unlike C++, subclass access to parts defined as `protected` in the superclass occurs only in objects of the subclass's type or its subtypes (unless packaging overrides this).
- Unlike C++, every method, constant or variable must have an access specifier. We cannot use the `:` syntax to set the access control for whole groups of parts.

6.5 Special methods

Constructors form a special subset of methods with a specific role in creating objects. As we saw in Section 5.10, all objects are descended from `java.lang.Object` which means that this class defines a further set of special methods which every class should have. It also provides primitive implementations of the methods, which you should override in many cases. A simplified declaration of `java.lang.Object` is as follows:

```
package java.lang;

public class Object
{
  //// Comparison of objects
  // since == compares references
  public boolean equals(Object obj);

  // Duplication of current object
  protected Object clone()
          throws CloneNotSupportedException,
                 OutOfMemoryError;
```

```
//// Conversion to String for '+' and printing
public String toString();

//// Generation of hash code for hash tables
public int hashCode();

//// Finalizer
protected void finalize()
        throws Throwable;
}
```

We can now discuss these methods in more detail.

equals

This defines an equivalence relation on objects. In other words, it must be:

- Reflexive: `a.equals(a)` is true.
- Symmetric: `a.equals(b)` if and only if `b.equals(a)`.
- Transitive: if `a.equals(b)` and `b.equals(c)` then `a.equals(c)`.
- Consistent: it will return the same value every time for the same objects.

Everything should return false when compared with `null`.

Note that the default implementation is to test if the two references refer to the same actual object. This is also the behaviour of `==` and the whole point of this standard method is to provide a more sensible test for equality. You should override this behaviour to test if the actual data in the objects is equal. For example, `Complex` should override this to test if two objects' real and imaginary parts are equal.

clone

This creates a copy of an object. The default behaviour is to copy the object's data exactly, field by field. No constructors get called, a new area of memory is allocated and all of the data copied. To enable this default behaviour, you must define your class to implement the `Cloneable` interface (see next section), otherwise a `CloneNotSupportedException` will be thrown if cloning is attempted. You can also decide not to implement the interface and rewrite `clone` to perform some form of duplication that is more appropriate than simple copying.

Unfortunately, `clone` is `protected`, and so cannot be used to copy arbitrary objects. This would be very useful, since `=` assigns references, so there is no standard copying operation. Certain classes, such as `Hashtable`, and `Vector` redeclare it as `public` so that we can do so. Otherwise, many classes define a constructor from an object of the same sort, which simply duplicates that object.

toString

This generates the string that this object produces when used in `println` statements or with the textual '+' operator. The default implementation is to print the object's class, followed by '@' and then the hashcode. Rewrite this for classes (such as complex numbers) that should be printable.

hashCode

This generates an integer for use in storing the object in a hash table (see Section 5.11). Hashcodes should be constant for any given object over time. They should also be the same for any pair of objects that test as the same using `equals`. However, they should be as widely spread as possible for objects that are not equal. As an example, for complex numbers, bitwise conversion of the real part to an integer would be reasonable, although by no means perfect.

finalize

Unlike languages such as C++, Java does not have **destructors** which are called when an object is deleted to correspond to **constructors** at its creation. The typical use for destructors is to delete memory that a class allocated during creation. This is not necessary in Java, because the language will automatically be garbage collected together with the object itself. There is also a problem in that, due to garbage collection, an object may be deleted some time after it has finished being used.

However, Java does provide a mechanism of **finalizers** (which is vastly inferior to proper destructors). It is guaranteed that, after an object is no longer in use, but before it is garbage collected, the `finalize` method will be called. The default `finalize` method declared by `java.lang.Object` does nothing, and you will probably have no need to write a replacement. However, if you do write a replacement, then it is important to note that finalizers do not automatically chain (unlike constructors or destructors). Therefore any finalizer that you write must end `super.finalize();` in order to let the superclass finalizer do whatever it needs to.

initialize

Finally, there is one special sort of method that has not been mentioned yet. These are **initializers**. An initializer is static, but has no other properties (name, access control, arguments, return type, . . .). As a result, it is written as follows:

```
public class <class name>
{
  // The initializer.
  static
  {
    <some code>
  }
```

```
     <other methods, variables and constants>
}
```

The initializer is called once, at the start of the program. As such, initializers are used to perform any complicated setup for static variables which was too complicated to be written out as an initial value for the variable. For instance, an initializer could be used to set up the starting values for a large array.

6.6   Further inheritance

To finish this chapter and this book's discussion of the Java language, there are a number of special pieces of syntax which add extra features to inheritance of objects.

6.6.1   `abstract`

When we wrote the geometrical shapes example in Section 6.3.1, we had to write a method `Shape.draw`. It was necessary that `Shape` defined a `draw` method, since this is an operation that all shapes can perform, and we want to be able to call `draw` using a reference to a generic `Shape` object (from an array, for instance). However, it was not possible to write any sensible code for `Shape.draw`.

This problem is solved using the `abstract` modifier. An `abstract` method is defined as normal, but has no body of code. The declaration line is followed by a semicolon, and looks rather like the simplified class declarations that we have written for parts of the standard library:

```
public class Shape
{
   public abstract void draw();
}
```

Note that, once again, the arguments and return type must be exactly the same in the superclass and subclasses. `abstract` methods may not be `private` or `final` since these would prevent them from being overridden.

`abstract` can also be used as a class modifier, and must be present if and only if a class has `abstract` methods. Note that a class may have both `abstract` and non-`abstract` methods, and that a subclass may choose to override only some of the `abstract` methods and replace them with actual code. However, all classes with any `abstract` methods, inherited and not overridden or defined in that class, must be declared `abstract`. Objects cannot be created from an `abstract` class.

6.6.2   `final`

When we call an object's method in Java, a fairly large amount of processing must take place. This is necessary because the object may be of the same class as the reference being used to handle it, or it may be of some subclass. In the second case, the subclass may have overridden the method. As a result, the interpreter must test the type of the object and then look up which version of the method to use.

This is, of course, slower than a straightforward function or procedure call in languages such as C or Pascal. C++ provides a solution by defining `virtual` and non-`virtual` functions. The lookup is performed only with `virtual` functions. Non-`virtual` functions perform according to the type of the reference.

This is quite a bad solution: it loses the benefits of object inheritance and method overriding. Therefore, the solution in Java is different. In Java, a method may be declared as `final`. If this is done, then no subclass is allowed to override that method. This means that no lookup need be performed for calls to that method using references to the class or its subclasses. The `final` keyword applies only to the class that uses it and its subclasses: the method may be non-`final` in the superclasses. A whole class may be defined `final`, meaning that no subclasses can be created.

Note that `private` and `static` methods are treated as though they are automatically `final`; they cannot be overridden.

6.6.3 Interfaces

When writing object oriented code, we may want to define a class that is descended from multiple superclasses. For instance, the class may need to be stored in arrays of two different kinds of references, or simply to provide two types of behaviour each of which is defined in a different base class.

C++ allows **multiple inheritance** in which a class can be declared to have multiple parents and to inherit structure and code from all of these. Unfortunately, this leads to a number of complications. Other modern languages such as Java and Modula-3 have chosen to avoid these by allowing inheritance of code from only one parent.

Nevertheless, Java classes may have multiple parents, as long as the others are effectively `abstract` and provide only method declarations and constants, not method definitions or variables. To do this we use some slightly new syntax. An **interface** is much like an `abstract` class, and is defined as follows:

```
interface <interface name>
{
  <method and constant declarations>
}
```

All of these methods are automatically `abstract`, and so have no body of code, just semicolons after the first line. They are also all automatically `public`.

A class `implements` interfaces, just as it `extends` a base class:

```
class <class name> extends <base class>
                   implements <list of interfaces>
{
  ...
}
```

The class must then be declared `abstract` itself or otherwise must override all of the `abstract` methods which it inherits from the interface.

You should note that interfaces may be derived from each other, using `extends`, and that you may create references to interfaces and assign an object that implements the interface to the reference, just as you can assign subclasses to a reference to a superclass.

6.6.4 Example – methods as arguments

As we have mentioned earlier, unlike Fortran, C/C++, Pascal or Modula-3, Java does not provide method pointers. We may want to pass a method as an argument to another method. For example, we could pass a function to be integrated to a method that performs integration. This is possible but a little harder than in these other languages.

We define an interface that declares the method's type, then write classes descended from this which implement the method. To pass the method as an argument, declare the receiving function as taking a reference to the interface, and then pass it an object implementing the method.

As an example, we now write a program to sum a general series. The series is defined in a method which takes an index and returns that element of the series, but the code to sum the series is written to be able to take any such method as one of its arguments. This example is available at `http://www.jscieng.co.uk/Code/Objects/Series/`.

```java
// An interface for objects capable of generating
// the elements of a series from their indices.
interface Generator
{
  double element(int n);
}



// An example of a class that implements this
// interface to generate a series of squares.
class SquareGenerator implements Generator
{
   public double element(int n)
  {
    return n*n;
  }
}



// The public class in the file.
public class Series
{
  // This function takes any object capable of
  // generating a series and sums the terms from
  // zero up to 'number'.
  public static double sum(Generator g, int number)
  {
    double ans = 0;

    for (int i=0; i<=number; i++)
      ans += g.element(i);

    return ans;
  }
```

```
// The main method creates one of our square
// series generators and uses the generic series
// summing method to add the first 10 elements.
public static void main(String[] argv)
{
  SquareGenerator s = new SquareGenerator();

  double x = sum(s, 10);

  System.out.println("Sum of elements 0 to 10 is: " + x);
}
}
```

Note that the interface's method `element` is automatically public and so must be overridden as such in `SquareGenerator`.

6.6.5 Runtime type identification

Inheritance allows us to refer to objects using references of the type of one of their superclasses. We can also cast an object to the type of one of its superclasses. Hence, if a class A is the superclass of a class B, we can write code such as:

```
A aref = new B();

B bref = new B();

aref = (A) bref;  // This cast is actually automatic
```

However, just as for numerical data types, although conversion in one direction is easy, conversion in the other is more difficult. The problem is that an object which appears to be of class A may actually be of class B but may not. This is especially relevant when retrieving data from hash tables and other such classes (see Section 5.11) in which all data is cast to the base class `java.lang.Object`.

Such conversions can be performed using an explicit cast:

```
A aref = new B();

B bref = (B) aref;  // explicit cast
```

Unlike C/C++, these casts are checked. The Java interpreter knows the real type of an object and will throw a `ClassCastException` if the cast is illegal. For instance, in our example the cast would be illegal if the `aref` really did store an object of class A.

In order to access this information about the real type of an object, either before performing such casts or for some other reason, Java provides an operator, `instanceof`, used as follows:

```
<variable name> instanceof <class>
```

It returns a `boolean` stating if it is safe to cast the variable's contents to the given class.

Consider the geometrical shapes example in Section 6.3.1, in which `Polygon` is derived from `Shape`. If we wanted to double the number of sides of all polygons in an array, `shapes`, we could write:

```
Shape[] array = <some setup>;

for (int i=0; i<array.length; i++)
  if (array[i] instanceof Polygon)
    ((Polygon) array[i]).sides *= 2;
```

Although such usage is sometimes necessary, in general it is better design to add a method to the base class and override it appropriately than to perform different actions explicitly based on the type of an object – this defeats the point of object orientation.

6.7 Summary – object orientation

- **Objects** are instances of data types with named parts and associated methods. They are created from class definitions with non-static variables and methods.

- **Constructors** are methods concerned with object creation. They are automatically called by new statements.

- **Inheritance** allows one class to be defined in terms of another existing one. The new class **inherits** all variables and methods that the old one defined. Inheritance relationships are defined using extends. A class may inherit only from one parent class.

- this can be used in non-static methods to refer to the object through which the method was called. 'this.' may be omitted when using that object's variables and methods. this is also used on the first line of a constructor to call another constructor for the same class.

- super allows a subclass to call its superclass's constructors. super is also used to access shadowed variables or overridden methods.

- public, protected, default and private provide varying levels of access control for classes, their methods and variables.

- abstract methods contain no code and merely define the method so that subclasses can override it. A class with abstract methods must itself be defined as abstract.

- **Interfaces** are base classes containing no code, merely defining a set of abstract methods for subclasses to override. Inheritance relationships are defined using implements. A class may implement more than one interface.

EXERCISES

6.1 Complex number division is carried out as follows: if $u = a + ib$ and $v = c + id$ then

$$w = \frac{u}{v} = \frac{ac + bd}{c^2 + d^2} + i\frac{bc - ad}{c^2 + d^2}$$

Write a divide method for Complex such that the call a.divide(b); divides the value of a by that of b and stores the result in a.

6.2 Design a hierarchy of objects for a zoological database. We wish to store turkeys, salmon, trout and penguins. For each we would like a method `hasBeak` returning a `boolean`, a method `canFly` returning a `boolean`, a method `size` returning the animal's size, and a method `cubeSize` returning the cube of this value.

6.3 Write the bodies of the constructors for the following classes. Use `this` and `super` to avoid code duplication.

```
class A
{
  int value1;

  A()
  // default to value1 = 1

  A{int i}
  // sets value1
}

class B extends A
{
  double value2;

  B()
  // default to value1 = 1, value2 = 3.0

  B(int i)
  // sets value1, default to value2 = 3.0

  B(double d)
  // sets value2, default to value1 = 1

  B(int i, double d)
  //sets both value1 and value2
}
```

6.4 Complex number division can also be carried out by subtracting the arguments and dividing the moduli. Write a `divide` method for the version of `Complex` using access controls and accessor methods. Note how much easier it is!

6.5 Consider the zoological database in Exercise 6.2. Which methods and classes should be `abstract`? Which methods should be `final`? Consider an interface `Edible` defined by:

```
interface Edible
{
  String taste();
}
```

We rewrite `Trout`, `Salmon` and `Turkey` to implement this interface. Write code to scan through an array of `Creature` objects outputting the tastes of those which are edible.

6.6 We wish to pass a method taking a single double variable and returning the same to a method that will integrate it over a range. Write code to handle passing this method as an argument.

WHERE TO GO FROM HERE

You now understand all of the syntax of the Java language that will be taught in this book. This is the vast majority of the syntax actually available – the few exceptions are mainly used in areas such as multi-threading (for example, the `synchronized` keyword) and user interface code (for example, inner classes). The remainder of the book is concerned with various libraries of use to the scientific programmer and discussion of algorithms and programming techniques.

Object orientation is a difficult topic. This chapter has taught you everything that you need to know, but you will probably not get a feel for an object oriented design style immediately. One classic area which object orientation handles very well is user interface code. This is beyond the scope of this book, but if you decide to learn this aspect of the standard libraries then your understanding of object orientation will increase at the same time. To move into this area you can turn to less specialized books on Java; I would particularly recommend *Core Java 1.1* (Cornell and Horstmann, 1997) or *Java in a Nutshell* (Flanagan, 1997). Alternatively, I can recommend *Object Solutions: Managing the Object-Oriented Project* (Booch, 1996) as a general book on object orientation, or *Understanding Object-Oriented Programming with Java* (Budd, 1998) as one more closely linked to this language.

PART II

Scientific applications

CHAPTER 7

JSGL, a scientific graphics library for Java

7.1 Introduction

This chapter teaches you how to use the simple graphics library which is associated with this book. This library is called the 'Java Scientific Graphics Library' or JSGL and this book describes version 1.0. The library is not a standard – it was written specifically for this book. However, because it is written entirely in Java using the standard libraries, it will work unchanged on all computer platforms and all compilers. You can use it with confidence that it will be available on any system for which you decide to write programs.

The JSGL provides simple support for text input and output and line-based graphics. Programs are provided with two windows. You can write to the text window using `println` (just like `System.out`) and can also read single lines of user input. The graph window sets up a **virtual coordinate system** so that you do not have to work in pixels, but can use the natural coordinates of your problem instead. This window can display lines and points. We also provide simple methods for drawing graphs of functions, bar charts and line charts so that you need not write this code yourself. Both windows remember their contents and so are scrollable, resizable and movable. The library is available in versions for both JDK 1.0 and JDK 1.1 or later and can be used in both applications (standard programs) and applets (programs embedded in web pages). When used in an application it allows you to save the contents of the text or graph windows. In addition, when used in an application under JDK 1.1 or later it also allows you to print the contents of the graph window.

The JSGL is automatically multi-threaded. Your program runs in one thread, and the user interface code runs in another. This means that you can move, resize and scroll windows or quit the program while computations are in progress. This is useful when a computation takes a significant amount of time, such as the Mandelbrot set example in Section 7.7.

The programming interface to the library consists almost entirely of `public static` methods. This means that you do not need to understand object orientation in order to be able to use it. However, use of the library does require an understanding of Chapter 4 and of Section 5.2.

All example code in this section is on the website at `http://www.jscieng.co.uk/Code/JSGL/`. The JSGL is available as an archive at `http://www.jscieng.co.uk/JSGL.zip` or `http://www.jscieng.co.uk/JSGL.tar.gz`. Appendix B contains installation instructions for the JSGL under Windows 98/NT and Solaris. If you are on a different platform or using non-JDK software then consult your own documentation. I suggest that you install the JSGL before proceeding.

7.2   Overview

The JSGL is implemented using 11 classes. However, it is designed so that the entire programming interface is provided by `public static` methods of a single class `uk.co.jscieng.SciGraph` and of an interface `uk.co.jscieng.Plottable`. This implementation means that, if you add the `import` statement:

```
import uk.co.jscieng.*;
```

to the start of your `.java` files, then you can call all of the methods in the library using the syntax:

```
SciGraph.<method name>(<arguments>);
```

Apart from this `import` statement, application program structure is unchanged. Simply write code as usual and call JSGL methods when you have output to display.

7.3   The text window

The JSGL provides two windows: a text window and a graph window. The text window provides little new functionality: it behaves like `System.out` for output, and offers an improvement over `System.in` for input. The main benefit is that your text appears in a window, where it can be saved or scrolled through, as opposed to appearing at a command line. The exact appearance of the text window will vary between systems. Figure 7.1 shows it on my system (JDK 1.1 under Windows 95) during execution of a typical program.

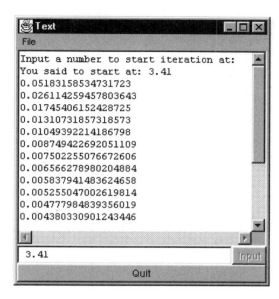

Figure 7.1 The text window.

7.3.1 `showText`

The `showText` method is used to create the text window. You should call it at the start of your program, before you make any calls to `print`, `println` or `readln`, and need not call it again after this. Method overloading is used to give two versions of the method so that you have the option of specifying the height and width of the window.

The declarations of the methods are as follows:

```
//// showText creates and shows the Text window.
// The width and height of the window are
// specified in characters.
public static void showText(int width, int height);
// Default of 80 characters wide, 24 characters high.
public static void showText();
```

As `public static` methods, the syntax for calling them is:

```
SciGraph.showText();
SciGraph.showText(60, 20);
```

7.3.2 `print` and `println`

`SciGraph` implements `print` and `println` methods that behave exactly like `System.out.print` and `System.out.println`. The output is directed to the text window.

Once again, method overloading is used. This time, each method is overloaded with all possible input types to allow the same flexibility as the System.out methods. The declarations are:

```
//// print outputs some text
// without moving to a new line.
public static void print(String s);
public static void print(Object obj);
public static void print(char[] s);
public static void print(char c);
public static void print(int i);
public static void print(long l);
public static void print(float f);
public static void print(double d);
public static void print(boolean b);

//// println outputs some text
// and moves to the start of a new line.
public static void println(String s);
public static void println();
public static void println(Object obj);
public static void println(char[] s);
public static void println(char c);
public static void println(int i);
public static void println(long l);
public static void println(float f);
public static void println(double d);
public static void println(boolean b);
```

You may use the '+' operator to perform string concatenations just as you would with System.out.println.

7.3.3 `readln`

The method `readln` is designed to be simpler to use than the text input commands that you saw in Section 5.8. Calling `readln` causes execution of your program to pause. The user interface code maintaining the windows keeps running and the user can move between the windows and scroll through them whilst deciding what they wish to type. Once they have decided, they type their input into the editable area at the bottom of the text window and then press the 'Input' button. At this point, execution of the program restarts and the `readln` method returns the exact characters that the user typed, stored in a string. This string is also written into the output window.

The declaration of the method is:

```
//// readln waits for the user to type
// some text and press the input button.
// It then returns the text typed.
public static String readln();
```

If you want to use `readln` to input numbers, then the string returned by `readln` can be converted into a number using:

```
String s = SciGraph.readln();
int i = Integer.parseInt(s);
```

under any JDK version or

JDK 1.1

```
String s = SciGraph.readln();
double d = Double.parseDouble(s);
```

under JDK 1.2 or later but

```
String s = SciGraph.readln();
double d = Double.valueOf(s).doubleValue();
```

under earlier versions of the JDK. These methods were discussed in Section 5.10. If the string is not a valid number, then a `NumberFormatException` is thrown.

7.3.4   Example – Euclid's algorithm

We now know all of the text handling methods and so we can write a short example program using them. The program that follows uses Euclid's algorithm to compute the Greatest Common Divisor (GCD) and Least Common Multiple (LCM) of a pair of numbers. It involves text input and output on several occasions. This example is available at `http://www.jscieng.co.uk/Code/JSGL/Euclid/`.

Euclid's algorithm uses the fact that:

$$\mathrm{GCD}(a, b) = \begin{cases} \mathrm{GCD}(b, a \bmod b) & \text{if } a \text{ does not divide by } b \\ b & \text{otherwise} \end{cases}$$

Since $a \bmod b$ is less than b, repeatedly carrying out this procedure produces the answer because the second argument to GCD will be strictly decreasing, integer-valued and bounded below by zero so the program must eventually halt.

```
import uk.co.jscieng.*;

class Euclid
{
  // The gcd method implements Euclid's algorithm.
  // If b does not divide exactly into a, then it is
  // mathematically true that GCD(a, b) = GCD(b, a % b).
  // If b does divide exactly, then GCD(a, b) = b. We
  // catch this case in the recursive call to gcd, as
  // opposed to doing so immediately.
  public static int gcd(int a, int b)
  {
    if (b != 0)
    {
```

```
      return gcd(b, a % b);
    }
    else
    {
      return a;
    }
  }


    // The main method performs a simple loop.
    public static void main(String[] argv)
    {
      String s;
      int a, b, g;

      // Start the program
      SciGraph.showText();
      SciGraph.println("This program computes GCDs/LCMs");

      do
      {
        SciGraph.println();

        // Get the first argument and convert it into an integer.
        SciGraph.print("Enter the first argument: ");
        s = SciGraph.readln();
        a = Integer.parseInt(s);

        // Get the second argument and convert it into an integer.
        SciGraph.print("Enter the second argument: ");
        s = SciGraph.readln();
        b = Integer.parseInt(s);

        // Compute and display their GCD and LCM.
        SciGraph.println("Their GCD is " + gcd(a,b));
        SciGraph.println("Their LCM is " + a*b/gcd(a,b));

        // Loop around again if the user wants to continue.
        SciGraph.print("Do you want to compute another "
                      +"GCD/LCM (y/n)? ");
        s = SciGraph.readln();
      }
      while (s.equals("y"));
    }
  }
```

Note how showText, print, println and readln are all public static members
of the class SciGraph and so can be called using the syntax SciGraph.<method
name>.

7.4 The graph window

The second window that the JSGL provides is the graph window. By contrast to the text window, this provides quite a lot of functionality.

In Section 5.12, we discussed how to use the Java graphics libraries directly in order to draw a simple graph of a function. This was somewhat difficult – there was quite a large amount of code that was not explained, and the program had to work in rather a strange coordinate system with units of pixels and the y-axis pointing downwards.

The JSGL provides a layer between you and the Java graphics libraries which removes these problems. There are a number of `public static` methods defined for `SciGraph`. We will cover these gradually over a number of subsections, but include a brief overview in the remainder of this paragraph. `showGraph` creates a graphics window for your use. At the time of creation, you define a **virtual coordinate system** for the window. From this point onwards, you can refer to points in the window using your chosen coordinates and the JSGL will convert these into pixel values. Simple methods – `clear`, `point` and `line` – are provided for your own graphics, whilst more complicated methods – `functionPlot`, `parametricPlot`, `stepPlot` and `linePlot` – automate drawing of standard types of graph. All graphics can be performed in any colour, and the graph window is both scrollable and printable (JDK 1.1 or later only). The exact appearance of the graph window will vary between systems. Figure 7.2 shows it on my system (JDK 1.1 under Windows 95) during execution of a typical program. Note the scrollbars to allow the user to move around the graph and the text at the top of the window indicating the position of the mouse pointer (not shown) in the virtual coordinate system.

7.4.1 `showGraph`

The `showGraph` method is used to create the graph window. You should call it at the start of your program, before you make any calls to `clear`, `point`, `line`, `functionPlot`, `parametricPlot`, `stepPlot` or `linePlot`.

`showGraph` has two distinct types of arguments. As we mentioned earlier, all subsequent graphics commands use a **virtual coordinate system** to draw to the window. The arguments `left` and `right` define the values of these coordinates at the vertical edges of the window, whilst the arguments `bottom` and `top` define these coordinates of the horizontal edges of the window. The arguments `width` and `height` are distinct from this. These specify the size of the graph window in pixels. It can be larger than the screen: scrollbars will be used to display it.

Method overloading is used to give two versions of `showGraph` so that specification of the height and width of the window is optional. The two declarations are as follows:

```
//// showGraph creates and shows the graphics window.
// Specify coordinate system (left, right, bottom, top)
// to be used in the window and the width and height of
// the window in pixels.
public static void showGraph(double left, double right,
                             double bottom, double top,
                             int width, int height);
// Default to a window 300x300 pixels
```

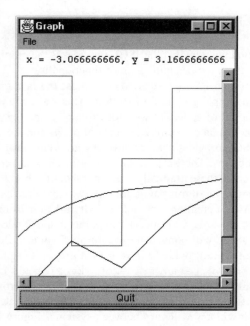

Figure 7.2 The graph window.

```
public static void showGraph(double left, double right,
                             double bottom, double top);
```

As an example, to show a graphics window 600 by 300 pixels in size with a coordinate system in which x takes values between -0.4 and 3.5 and y takes values between 0.001 and 0.03, we would write:

```
SciGraph.showGraph(-0.4, 3.5, 0.001, 0.03, 600, 300);
```

7.4.2 `java.awt.Color`

All of the graphics commands that follow give you the option of specifying a colour for the output to be drawn in. To represent colours, we use the standard library class `java.awt.Color`. This is presented in this chapter, not in Chapter 5, because we do not explain a sufficient amount of the standard libraries to allow you to use it in any context other than with the JSGL. A simplified declaration of `java.awt.Color` is as follows. Note that `NumberFormatException` is a subclass of `RuntimeException` and so need not be handled explicitly.

```
package java.awt;

public class Color
{
    //// Constructors for the class.
```

```
// Firstly from red, green and blue
// values in the range 0 to 255.
public Color(int r, int g, int b);
// Secondly from a single number, with
// binary bits 16-23 storing the red value,
// 8-15 storing green and 0-7 storing blue.
public Color(int rgb);
// Thirdly from red, green and blue values
// in the range 0.0 to 1.0
public Color(float r, float g, float b);

//// Method to create a colour from a string
// containing a single integer as above.
public static Color decode(String nm)
               throws NumberFormatException;

//// Standard colours provided as constants.
public final static Color white     = new Color(255, 255, 255);
public final static Color lightGray = new Color(192, 192, 192);
public final static Color gray      = new Color(128, 128, 128);
public final static Color darkGray  = new Color(64, 64, 64);
public final static Color black     = new Color(0, 0, 0);
public final static Color red       = new Color(255, 0, 0);
public final static Color pink      = new Color(255, 175, 175);
public final static Color orange    = new Color(255, 200, 0);
public final static Color yellow    = new Color(255, 255, 0);
public final static Color green     = new Color(0, 255, 0);
public final static Color magenta   = new Color(255, 0, 255);
public final static Color cyan      = new Color(0, 255, 255);
public final static Color blue      = new Color(0, 0, 255);

//// Getting at the data stored in a Color object
public int getRed();
public int getGreen();
public int getBlue();
// Returns an integer containing the red value in bits
// 16-23, the green value in 8-15 and the blue in 0-7.
public int getRGB();

//// Returns a colour that is related to the existing one.
public Color brighter();
public Color darker();

//// Comparison operators
public boolean equals(Object obj);

//// Conversion to other data types.
public String toString();

//// Generation of a hash code. This is a number used to
```

```
    // reference the object when it is stored in a hash table.
    public int hashCode();
}
```

This declaration is deliberately simplified: the class is also capable of reading the system's standard colour scheme and performing HSB to RGB conversions. You should read the online documentation if you are interested in these features.

From our point of view as scientific programmers, we are probably interested only in distinguishing between several graphs drawn in the same window. As such, we can use the constants that the `Color` class defines.

To do this, we add the line

```
import java.awt.Color;
```

at the top of our `.java` files to enable easy reference to the class. Once this has been done, we can simply use `Color.red`, `Color.green` and so forth whenever a colour is required.

7.4.3   `clear`, `point` and `line`

The JSGL provides three basic drawing operations: `clear`, `point` and `line`. These are more or less self-explanatory. `clear` removes all drawing from the window, `point` plots a point, and `line` joins two points. There are two versions of `line`: one in which you specify both ends and one in which the line continues on from the last position at which drawing occurred.

The declarations are as follows:

```
//// clear removes all previous drawing from the graph window.
public static void clear();

//// point plots a single point.
// Specifying position and colour.
public static void point(double x, double y, Color c);
// Defaulting to black.
public static void point(double x, double y);

//// line joins two points.
// Specifying both ends and a colour.
public static void line(double xstart, double ystart,
                        double xend, double yend, Color c);
// Defaulting to black.
public static void line(double xstart, double ystart,
                        double xend, double yend)
// Continuing on from the end of
// the previous drawing operation
public static void line(double xend, double yend, Color c);
// Continuing from the previous
// operation in that operation's colour.
public static void line(double xend, double yend);
```

Note that all of these methods use the coordinate system that you created with showGraph, and all of them can optionally take a Color object as an argument.

7.4.4 functionPlot

The functionPlot command is the first of four less basic drawing operations. These are designed to automate the process of drawing standard types of graphs. functionPlot handles simple graphs in which the *y*-value is a function of the *x*-value and the function can be expressed as a method.

Unfortunately, Java does not yet provide a mechanism of **function pointers**, unlike Fortran, C/C++, Pascal or Modula-3. As a result, passing methods as arguments to other methods is fairly difficult. This topic is discussed in detail in Section 6.6.4. However, the JSGL is not intended to require that much knowledge, so we provide a simple explanation of the topic here.

As well as the class SciGraph, the package uk.co.jscieng contains an **interface** Plottable. The definition of this is as follows:

```
package uk.co.jscieng;

public interface Plottable
{
  // The method f, to be graphed, that you should override.
  public double f(double x);
}
```

An interface is like a template for a class. We can define classes that **implement** the interface. This means that they define all of the methods that it specifies.

To write a class that implements the Plottable interface, we write the following:

```
public class MyClass implements Plottable
{
  public double f(double x)
  {
    <computation of the return value>;
  }
}
```

Those of you who have not read Section 6.6.4 may be confused by this. Essentially, you can treat the class around the method f as a standard wrapper that enables you to use the method as an argument. You should note that the method f is non-static.

To pass the method as an argument, we create an object of the class and pass that. For example:

```
SciGraph.functionPlot(new MyClass());
```

In addition to the method to be plotted, functionPlot can take several other arguments:

- left and right define a range of x-values for which the function should be plotted. If these are omitted, then it is plotted over the entire width of the graphics window.

- c is the colour in which to plot the graph. The default is black.
- pixelgap is the number of screen pixels horizontally between each point that is computed on the function. The default is 10, which should always be fairly fast. However, if you want to increase the accuracy of the graph then you should decrease the gap between pixels (which will take longer to plot). This argument is a double so that you can specify values such as 0.1 to enable rapidly oscillating functions to be drawn with precision.

functionPlot is overloaded with versions to take all possible combinations of these arguments. The definitions of the versions are as follows:

```
//// functionPlot graphs a function (provided via
//   the Plottable interface). Specifying the range
// to plot, the colour and the number of pixels
// horizontally across the screen between points.
public static void functionPlot(Plottable p, double left,
                                double right, Color c,
                                double pixelgap);
// Defaulting to black.
public static void functionPlot(Plottable p, double left,
                                double right, double pixelgap);
// Defaulting to the whole Graph window.
public static void functionPlot(Plottable p, Color c,
                                double pixelgap);
// Defaulting to the whole Graph window and black.
public static void functionPlot(Plottable p, double pixelgap);
// Defaulting to one point per 10 pixels horizontally.
public static void functionPlot(Plottable p, double left,
                                double right, Color c);
// Defaulting to one point per 10 pixels and black.
public static void functionPlot(Plottable p, double left,
                                double right);
// Defaulting to one point per 10 pixels
// and the whole Graph window.
public static void functionPlot(Plottable p, Color c);
// Defaulting to one point per 10 pixels,
// the whole Graph window and black.
public static void functionPlot(Plottable p);
```

7.4.5 Example – plotting a function

The previous section was fairly complicated, so we now provide an example of plotting a simple function using functionPlot. The function that we use is

$$y = \begin{cases} \sin(1/x) & \text{if } x \le 0 \\ \sqrt{x}\,\sin(1/x) & \text{otherwise} \end{cases}$$

This is only an example; this particular function is of no importance to the program. You can alter the code to plot any function that you are interested in.

We have chosen this particular function for two reasons. Firstly, it is a reminder that when using a programming language functions need not have a simple definition. They can include all aspects of Java syntax: method calls, `if` statements, `for` loops and so forth. Secondly, this function oscillates more and more rapidly as we approach the origin. This means that the default `pixelgap` of `10` will not produce a satisfactory graph – the oscillations occur on a smaller scale than this. Note how we use a smaller `pixelgap` to make the graph more accurate. It is important to realize that the `pixelgap` can be set to values less than 1 in order to obtain very high accuracy pictures.

The actual program is stored in a file `Oscillations.java`. It is printed below. It is also available at `http://www.jscieng.co.uk/Code/JSGL/Oscillations/`. We use two classes: `OscFun` implements the `Plottable` interface and defines the function to be graphed. `Oscillations` contains the `main` method and calls the JSGL methods.

```java
import uk.co.jscieng.*;


// The 'OscFun' class is a wrapper for the method
// 'f' to allow it to be passed as an argument.
class OscFun implements Plottable
{
  // The function to be plotted.
  public double f(double x)
  {
    if (x>0)
      return Math.sqrt(x) * Math.sin(1/x);
    else
      return Math.sin(1/x);
  }
}


// The class containing the main method
public class Oscillations
{
  public static void main(String[] argv)
  {
    // Set up the graph window.
    SciGraph.showGraph(-0.5, 0.5, -1.1, 1.1);

    // And plot the function
    SciGraph.functionPlot(new OscFun(), 0.1);
  }
}
```

7.4.6 `parametricPlot`

`parametricPlot` draws a more general graph in which both the x and y coordinates are functions of a third variable. Several important classes of graph, such as those in polar coordinates or those representing motion over time, can be written in this form.

parametricPlot takes similar arguments to functionPlot, except that it takes two methods – one mapping the third variable to each coordinate. The arguments are:

- x and y are Plottable objects containing methods mapping the third variable to *x* and *y* coordinates, respectively.
- start and finish define a range of values for the third variable over which the graph should be plotted. If these are omitted, then it is plotted between 0 and 1.
- c is the colour in which to plot the graph. The default is black.
- points is the number of points that are computed on the graph. These are equally spaced in the third variable across the range. The default is to use 50 points. However, if you want to increase the accuracy of the graph then you should increase the number of points drawn.

parametricPlot is overloaded with versions to take all possible combinations of these arguments. The definitions of the versions are as follows:

```
//// parametricPlot draws a graph in which both x
// and y coordinates are functions of a third
// variable (the functions are provided via
// the Plottable interface). Specifying the range
// to plot, the colour and the number of points.
public static void parametricPlot(Plottable x, Plottable y,
                                  double start, double finish,
                                  Color c, int points);
// Defaulting to black.
public static void parametricPlot(Plottable x, Plottable y,
                                  double start, double finish,
                                  int points);
// Defaulting to a range from 0 to 1.
public static void parametricPlot(Plottable x, Plottable y,
                                  Color c, int points);
// Defaulting to a range from 0 to 1 and black.
public static void parametricPlot(Plottable x, Plottable y,
                                  int points);
// Defaulting to 50 points.
public static void parametricPlot(Plottable x, Plottable y,
                                  double start, double finish,
                                  Color c);
// Defaulting to 50 points and black.
public static void parametricPlot(Plottable x, Plottable y,
                                  double start, double finish);
// Defaulting to 50 points and a range from 0 to 1.
public static void parametricPlot(Plottable x, Plottable y,
                                  Color c);
// Defaulting to 50 points, a range from 0 to 1 and black.
public static void parametricPlot(Plottable x, Plottable y);
```

7.4.7 `stepPlot`

`stepPlot` draws a bar chart given an array of values for the bars. All bars are drawn with equal width.

The method takes several arguments. There are also overloaded versions which use default values for the arguments that they omit. The arguments are:

- `array`. This is the array whose values are to be used for the bar heights. `stepPlot` uses `array.length` to determine the size of the array and draws one bar for every entry, starting at `array[0]` and working up to `array[array.length-1]` (note that arrays do not contain the element `array[array.length]` since they start at 0).

- `left` and `right`. These define the left- and right-hand edges of the area in which the bar chart will be drawn. `left` is the left-hand edge of the leftmost bar, whilst `right` is the right-hand edge of the rightmost bar. If they are omitted, it is drawn across the entire width of the graph window.

- `c`. This is the colour in which the bar chart will be drawn. It is black by default.

The declarations of `stepPlot` are as follows:

```
//// stepPlot draws a chart of equal width
// bars based on an array of values.
// Specifying the range to plot and the colour.
public static void stepPlot(double[] array, double left,
                            double right, Color c);
// Defaulting to black.
public static void stepPlot(double[] array, double left,
                            double right);
// Defaulting to the whole Graph window.
public static void stepPlot(double[] array, Color c);
// Defaulting to the whole Graph window and black.
public static void stepPlot(double[] array);
```

and an example call to this method would look like:

```
double[] values = {-3.4, 2.3, 1.2, 0.9};
SciGraph.stepPlot(values, 0, 4, Color.red);
```

7.4.8 `linePlot`

`linePlot` draws a line chart linking a series of points. The points are equally spaced horizontally, and their vertical coordinates are passed to the method in an array.

`linePlot` takes exactly the same arguments as `stepPlot` and provides similar overloading to give them default values. The arguments are:

- `array`. This is the array whose values are to be used for the points. `linePlot` uses `array.length` to determine the size of the array and puts one point in the graph for every entry, starting at `array[0]` and working up to `array[array.length-1]` (note that arrays do not contain the element `array[array.length]` since they start at 0).

- left and right. These define the left- and right-hand edges of the area in which the line chart will be drawn. left is where the leftmost point will be and right is the position of the rightmost point. If they are omitted then the chart is drawn across the entire width of the graph window.

- c. This is the colour in which the bar chart will be drawn. It is black by default.

The declarations of linePlot are as follows:

```
//// linePlot draws a line chart based on an array of values.
// Specifying the range to plot and the colour.
public static void linePlot(double[] array, double left,
                            double right, Color c);
// Defaulting to black.
public static void linePlot(double[] array, double left,
                            double right);
// Defaulting to the whole Graph window.
public static void linePlot(double[] array, Color c);
// Defaulting to the whole Graph window and black.
public static void linePlot(double[] array);
```

and an example call to this method would look like:

```
double[] values = {-1.7, 4.5, 2, 1.97};
SciGraph.linePlot(values);
```

7.5 Applets

We have now provided a complete replacement for the graphics commands that we discussed in Section 5.12. Following on from that section, Section 5.13 discussed writing **applets**, Java programs that can be embedded in web pages and run over the Internet.

The JSGL can be used in applets as well as in **applications** (standard programs). Unlike applications, for which we wrote code as normal and simply called the JSGL methods, writing a JSGL applet is radically different from writing a normal applet. In fact, writing a JSGL applet is very similar to writing a JSGL application. It is possible to write programs that work as both.

To recap, a simple JSGL application has the following structure:

```
import uk.co.jscieng.*;

public class MyApplication
{
  <other methods>

  public static void main(String[] argv)
  {
    <write program as normal here, calling JSGL methods>
  }
}
```

A JSGL applet has the following, similar structure:

```
import uk.co.jscieng.*;

public class MyApplet extends SciGraph
{
  <other methods>

  public void main()
  {
    <write program as normal here, calling JSGL methods>
  }
}
```

Note the extra `extends` clause in the class definition and that the `main` method is no longer static and takes no arguments.

Apart from this change in program structure (which you will understand only if you have read Chapter 6), you can program in exactly the same way that you would for an application. In fact, the two are so similar that, using method overloading, we can write both types of `main` method in the same class, set the second to call the first and produce a program that will work as either an application or an applet. The structure of this would be:

```
import uk.co.jscieng.*;

public class MyBoth extends SciGraph
{
  <other methods>

  public static void main(String[] argv)
  {
    <write program as normal here, calling JSGL methods>
  }

  public void main()
  {
    // Simply call the first 'main' method.
    main(new String[1]);
  }
}
```

As we noted in Section 5.13, to embed the applet in a web page we use the `<APPLET>` tag in our HTML. The structure is:

```
<APPLET codebase="?" code="?" width=? height=?>
Text for non-Java browsers.
</APPLET>
```

The `codebase` is the path for the base directory of your packages (the `-d` option to `javac`), whilst the `code` is the relative path to the `.class` file containing the `main` method. The width and height parameters are irrelevant – the JSGL creates text and drawing windows as normal, and simply places a message on the actual web page.

An example, an HTML file, `MyBoth.html`, for the above class might look like:

```
<HTML>
<HEAD>
<TITLE>This is the JSGL on the Web</TITLE>
</HEAD>
<BODY>
The JSGL applet's just below this text
and already it's starting to run...
<P>
<APPLET codebase="." code="MyBoth.class" width=100 height=50>
Your browser does not support Java, sorry.
</APPLET>
<P>
This Java applet was written using the JSGL, a Scientific
Graphics Library for Java. This library was written for the
book <EM>Introductory Java for Scientists and Engineers</EM>
by Richard J. Davies and is bundled with it.
</BODY>
</HTML>
```

Running '`appletviewer MyBoth.html`' from the command line (this is part of the JDK) or pointing a web browser at this file will run the program.

Once you have reached this stage, making your applet available on the web is simply a matter of copying the `.class` and `.html` files onto your website. You must make sure that you maintain any hierarchical directory structure in which the `.class` files are stored to represent their packaging. You must also copy the `.class` files for the JSGL to the website, since they must be accessible to the users' web browsers. You should copy the entire directory `uk` (in the directory `classes` in the directory `JDK1.0` in the JSGL directory) to the directory on your website that you specified as the `codebase`.

Note that, at the time of writing (August 1998), some major web browsers are not fully JDK 1.1 compliant. This will change, but, until JDK 1.1 support is widespread, you would probably be wise to restrict your code to the JDK 1.0 standard libraries and to copy the JDK 1.0 version of the JSGL to your website. The major effect that this has for scientific programming is that `BigInteger` and `BigDecimal` do not exist.

Applets are not allowed to read or write to files (since they will be running on somebody else's computer!). As a result, the 'save' and 'print' options are disabled in JSGL when it is used by an applet.

7.6　Example – the binomial distribution

The next example uses the graphical features that we have discussed and is implemented as both an application and an applet.

This program considers a simple statistical problem. A series of experiments are conducted, in each of which a fair coin is thrown a set number of times and the number of heads that occur are counted. We then use the observed frequencies of each number of heads to estimate their probabilities.

Theory states that the probability that each number of heads will occur follows a binomial distribution:

$$H \sim \text{Bin(throws, } 1/2)$$

giving

$$\text{P}(H = h) = \frac{\text{throws!}}{(\text{throws} - h)!h!}$$

In addition, as the number of throws increases, we would expect this binomial distribution to tend to a normal distribution:

$$\frac{H - \text{throws}/2}{\sqrt{\text{throws}/4}} \simeq \text{N}(0, 1)$$

where $\text{N}(0, 1)$ is a normal distribution of mean 0 and variance 1.

The following program is called `Binomial.java` and is available at `http://www.jscieng.co.uk/Code/JSGL/Binomial/`. It performs the experiment, using the random number generator, and plots the estimated probabilities for each number of heads in red. Next, it plots the theoretical, binomial distribution of these probabilities in blue and finally it plots the normal distribution, to which the results should tend, in green.

```java
import uk.co.jscieng.*;
import java.awt.Color;


// The 'Normal' class is a wrapper to contain the function f,
// the density of the normal distribution, which must be passed
// as an argument to functionPlot.
class Normal implements Plottable
{
  // f is the density of the normal distribution to which the
  // binomial distribution should tend.
  public double f(double x)
  {
    // Convert the point on the real normal distribution
    // into a point on a N(0,1) normal distribution
    double normPt = (x - Binomial.getThrowNo()/2.0)
                    / Math.sqrt(Binomial.getThrowNo()/4.0);

    // Calculate the density at that point
    // on the N(0,1) distribution
    double normDensity = Math.exp(-normPt*normPt/2)
                         / Math.sqrt(2 * Math.PI);

    // Convert back to the density
    // of the real normal distribution
    return normDensity / Math.sqrt(Binomial.getThrowNo()/4.0);
  }
```

```java
    }


    // This class implements the main body of the program.
    // It extends SciGraph so that the program can be an applet.
    public class Binomial extends SciGraph
    {
      // The number of throws per experiment
      private static int throwNo;

      // An accessor method for throwNo
      public static int getThrowNo()
      {
        return throwNo;
      }

      // The number of experiments
      private static int experimentNo;


      // A utility function to compute factorials.
      public static double fact(int x)
      {
        double ans = 1;

        for (int i=2; i<=x; i++)
          ans *= i;

        return ans;
      }


      // The 'main' method for use as an application
      public static void main(String[] argv)
      {
        // A few useful variables
        String answer;
        int i, j;

        // Create the text window
        SciGraph.showText();

        // Prompt the user for a number of throws per experiment
        SciGraph.println("This program simulates "
                        +"repeated tossing of a coin.");
        SciGraph.println();
        SciGraph.print("Enter a number of throws per experiment: ");

        // And read their answer
        answer = SciGraph.readln();
```

```java
throwNo = Integer.parseInt(answer);

// Create a graph window with the right scale for that
// kind of experiment
SciGraph.showGraph(0, throwNo, 0, 1.5 * fact(throwNo)
        / (fact(throwNo/2) * fact(throwNo - throwNo/2)
            * Math.pow(2, throwNo)));

do
{
  // Clear the graph and prompt for a number of experiments
  SciGraph.clear();
  SciGraph.print("Enter a number of experiments "
               +"to perform: ");

  // And read the answer
  answer = SciGraph.readln();
  experimentNo = Integer.parseInt(answer);

  // EXPERIMENTAL CALCULATION

  // Create an array to store the experimental results
  double[] experimentValues = new double[throwNo+1];

  // Perform the appropriate number of experiments
  for (i=0; i<experimentNo; i++)
  {
    int count = 0;

    // In each of which we count heads over the throws
    for (j=0; j<throwNo; j++)
      if (Math.random() > 0.5)
        count++;

    // And record our result
    experimentValues[count] += 1;
  }

  // Divide all frequencies by the number of experiments
  // to get estimated probabilities for each number of heads.
  for (i=0; i<=throwNo; i++)
    experimentValues[i] /= experimentNo;

  // Plot a graph of the estimated probabilities
  SciGraph.stepPlot(experimentValues, Color.red);

  // BINOMIAL DISTRIBUTION

  // Create an array to store the binomial distribution
  double[] binomValues = new double[throwNo+1];
```

```
        // Step through it, filling in the probabilities
        for (i=0; i<=throwNo; i++)
          binomValues[i] = fact(throwNo)
                        / (fact(throwNo-i) * fact(i)
                        * Math.pow(2, throwNo));

        // Plot a graph of the binomial distribution
        SciGraph.stepPlot(binomValues, Color.blue);

        // NORMAL DISTRIBUTION

        // Plot the normal distribution's density
        SciGraph.functionPlot(new Normal(), Color.green);

        // Ask if the user wants to repeat the experiment
        SciGraph.println();
        SciGraph.print("Do you want to have another go (y/n) ? ");
        answer = SciGraph.readln();
      }
      while (answer.equals("y"));
    }


    // The 'main' method for use as an applet
    public void main()
    {
      // Simply call the other 'main' method.
      main(new String[1]);
    }
  }
```

Because this program defines both types of `main` methods and the class `Binomial` extends `SciGraph`, it can be used as an applet, as well as an application. The file `Binomial.html` is a suitable web page, including an appropriate `<APPLET>` tag. This file is reproduced below. Figure 7.3 shows the applet running in Netscape Navigator under Windows 95.

```
<HTML>
<HEAD>
<TITLE>This is Statistics on the Web</TITLE>
</HEAD>
<BODY>
The Java applet's just below this text
and already it's starting to run...
<P>
<APPLET codebase="." code="Binomial.class" width=100 height=50>
Your browser does not support Java, sorry.
</APPLET>
<P>
This Java applet was written for the book
```

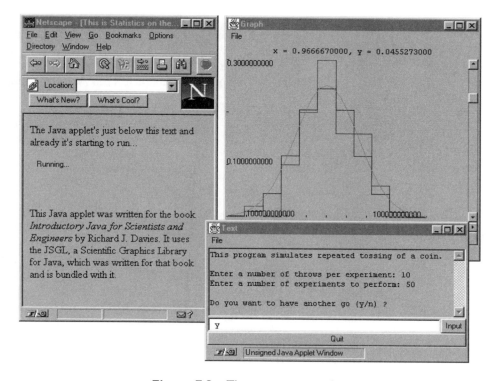

Figure 7.3 The `Binomial` applet.

```
<EM>Introductory Java for Scientists and Engineers</EM>
by Richard J. Davies. It uses the JSGL, a Scientific
Graphics Library for Java, which was written for that
book and is bundled with it.
</BODY>
</HTML>
```

7.7 Example – the Mandelbrot set

The **Mandelbrot set** is the world's most famous fractal. It is generated using complex arithmetic. We consider a point c in the complex plane and set up the iteration

$$
\begin{aligned}
z_0 &= c \\
z_n &= z_{n-1}^2 + c
\end{aligned}
$$

Under this iteration, some values of c cause z_n to diverge to infinity, whilst for other values z_n stays bounded indefinitely.

To draw the Mandelbrot set, we simply perform this iteration, counting how many steps each point takes to leave a circle of radius 2, centred on the origin. Those points which never leave are part of the set, while those which leave are not. We can make the picture look prettier by colouring points outside the set according to how many steps it takes them to leave the circle.

The following program draws the set. It uses the `Complex` class from the JNL (as described in the next chapter). The code is available at `http://www.jscieng.co.uk/Code/JSGL/Mandlebrot/`.

```java
import uk.co.jscieng.*;
import VisualNumerics.math.*;
import java.awt.Color;


public class Mandelbrot
{
  // The size of the window in pixels
  public static final int SIZE = 300;

  // The area of the set to show in the window
  public static final double LEFT = -2.1;
  public static final double RIGHT = 2.1;
  public static final double BOTTOM = -2.1;
  public static final double TOP = 2.1;

  // The maximum number of iterations to perform
  public static final int MAXITER = 100;

  // The colours to cycle to show iteration depth
  public static final Color[] colors =
    { Color.red, Color.pink, Color.yellow,
      Color.cyan, Color.green, Color.magenta };


  // This method returns a color for an iteration depth.
  public static Color indexColor(int i)
  {
    // Return black if we hit our iteration limit.
    // Cycle through the colours array otherwise
    if (i == MAXITER)
      return Color.black;
    else
      return colors[i % colors.length];
  }


  // This method performs the iteration until
  // the complex number leaves a circle of radius
  // 2 about the origin or MAXITER is reached.
  // It returns the number of iterations performed.
  public static int iterate(Complex c)
  {
```

```
    Complex z = c;
    int count = 0;

    while ((Complex.abs(z) < 2) && (count < MAXITER))
    {
      z = Complex.add(Complex.multiply(z, z), c);
      count++;
    }

    return count;
  }


  // The 'main' method controls the drawing.
  public static void main(String[] argv)
  {
    double real, imag;
    int count;

    // Set up a graph window of the right size.
    SciGraph.showGraph(LEFT, RIGHT, BOTTOM, TOP,
                       SIZE, SIZE);

    // Iterate through all of its pixels
    for (int i=0; i<SIZE; i++)
      for (int j=0; j<SIZE; j++)
      {
        // Working out their position in the
        // complex plane
        real = LEFT + i * (RIGHT - LEFT) / SIZE;
        imag = BOTTOM + j * (TOP - BOTTOM) / SIZE;

        // Counting the number of iterations
        // needed at that point
        count = iterate(new Complex(real, imag));

        // And plotting that point in the
        // appropriate colour.
        SciGraph.point(real, imag, indexColor(count));
      }
  }
}
```

7.8   Example – ODE contours

A common problem in scientific computing is the numerical solution of **ordinary differential equations (ODEs)**. Consider a simple pendulum, of length l, hanging from a

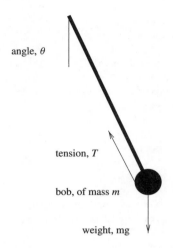

angle, θ

tension, T

bob, of mass m

weight, mg

Figure 7.4 A simple pendulum.

fixed point, as shown in Figure 7.4. If we apply Newton's Second Law, we find that θ varies over time according to the differential equation

$$\ddot{\theta} + \frac{g}{l}\sin\theta = 0$$

Setting $x = \theta$ and $y = \dot{\theta}$, we obtain the system

$$\dot{x} = y$$
$$\dot{y} = -\frac{g}{l}\sin x$$

We can now plot contours solving this differential equation in **phase space** (the space defined by x and y). The simplest method of doing so is to set up a lattice of points across the phase plane. At each point, we compute the derivative and draw a small line from the point in the direction of the derivative whose length is proportional to the magnitude of the derivative. This creates a diagram which looks rather like iron filings in a magnetic field. The direction that a solution would take at any given point is made clear.

The following program is called ODE.java and is available at http://www.jscieng.co.uk/Code/JSGL/ODE/. It draws the diagram as described above for the case $g/l = 1$.

```
import uk.co.jscieng.*;

class ODE
{
  // Constants defining an area of phase plane.
  public static final double LEFT = -1;
  public static final double RIGHT = 7;
  public static final double BOTTOM = -2;
```

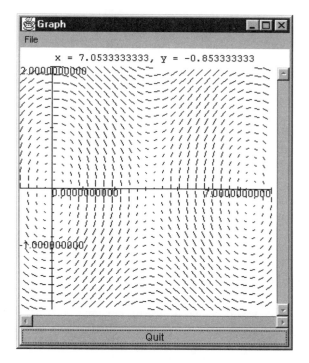

Figure 7.5 ODE contours.

```
public static final double TOP = 2;

// The number of points across either side to
// use for the lattice.
public static final int POINTS = 30;


// The main method
public static void main(String[] argv)
{
  double x, y, dx, dy;

  // Start the JSGL
  SciGraph.showGraph(LEFT, RIGHT, BOTTOM, TOP);

  // Step through all points in the lattice.
  for (int i=0; i<=POINTS; i++)
    for (int j=0; j<=POINTS; j++)
    {
      // Calculating their real coordinates.
      x = LEFT + i * (RIGHT - LEFT) / POINTS;
```

```
            y = BOTTOM + j * (TOP - BOTTOM) / POINTS;

            // Work out the derivative at that point.
            dx = y;
            dy = - Math.sin(x);

            // And draw a small flow line from the
            // lattice point in that direction.
            SciGraph.line(x, y, x + dx/10, y + dy/10);
        }
    }
}
```

Figure 7.5 shows the program running under Windows 95. Note how the small line segments can be joined up to create contours. These contours are equivalent to solutions of the differential equation. The circular contours at the origin correspond to small periodic oscillations of the pendulum about the vertical.

WHERE TO GO FROM HERE

The JSGL was designed to provide a simple interface to a powerful set of graphical operations. The hope is that it will satisfy many readers' needs, and will mean that you do not have to understand the full complexities of the support for graphics and user interface design present in the standard libraries.

For some of you the JSGL will not be sufficient. If this is the case, then you have no choice other than to use the standard libraries directly and write your own graphics methods. This is a substantial topic to cover and is beyond the scope of this book. If you intend to move into this area you can turn to less specialized books on Java; I would particularly recommend *Core Java 1.1* (Cornell and Horstmann, 1997) or *Java in a Nutshell* (Flanagan, 1997).

CHAPTER 8

JNL, a numerical library for Java

8.1   Introduction

This chapter describes the JNL version 1.0, revision F. This is a free library, designed and implemented by Visual Numerics, which they propose as a standard numerical programming interface for Java.

Visual Numerics have produced numerical and statistical libraries for other platforms for over 25 years. Their software has a worldwide installed base of over 30 000 licences and 500 000 users and includes PV-WAVE. Visual Numerics are providing the JNL free as a well-defined common numerical library in order to help Java fulfil its potential in cross-platform numerical computing. They are also campaigning for **operator overloading** to be introduced into the language so that numerical data types such as complex numbers and matrices can be handled using natural mathematical syntax such as 'a + b'.

The JNL provides the following features:

- Elementary functions. The standard library class `java.lang.Math` provides basic functions such as `sin` and `cos`. The JNL extends this to include hyperbolic functions and many others, including statistical functions.

- Complex numbers. The JNL defines a fully functional class for complex numbers.

- Matrices and vectors. The JNL represents these using arrays. For example, a matrix is represented by `double[][]`. It provides a large collection of methods for performing multiplication and other operations on these types.

- Matrix decomposition. The JNL provides methods to perform Cholesky, LU, QR and singular value decompositions of matrices. The algorithms used are based on the LINPACK libraries.

Note that the JNL is a library for manipulation of general matrices and does not provide specialized support for sparse matrices (those with few non-zero entries). These can frequently be handled much more efficiently than the general case if the correct algorithms are used.

This chapter assumes understanding of Chapter 4 and of Section 5.2. All substantial example programs in this chapter are available on the website at `http://www.jscieng.co.uk/Code/JNL/`. The JNL is available from Visual Numerics at `http://www.vni.com/` or by following the links from this book's accompanying website. Appendix B contains installation instructions for the JNL under Windows 98/NT and Solaris. If you are on a different platform or using non-JDK software then consult your own documentation. I suggest that you install the JNL before proceeding.

8.2 Standard functions

In Section 5.2, we discussed the class `java.lang.Math`, which provides elementary functions such as `sin` and `sqrt`. This class is inadequate for serious numerical computing since it fails to define other common methods, such as those from hyperbolic trigonometry. The JNL includes two classes, `VisualNumerics.math.Sfun` and `VisualNumerics.math.Statistics`, which define many of these additional functions. Add the line

```
import VisualNumerics.math.*;
```

to the start of your `.java` files to enable you to use these classes and the rest of the JNL.

8.2.1 More elementary functions

The class `Sfun` is structured exactly like `java.lang.Math` and simply provides extra functions and constants that should be in the standard library:

```
package VisualNumerics.math;


public class Sfun
{
  // Smallest relative spacing for doubles.
  public static final double EPSILON_SMALL
                        = 1.11022302462515e-16;


  // Greatest relative spacing for doubles.
  public static final double EPSILON_LARGE
                        = 2.2204460492503e-16;


  // Euler's constant
  public static final double Euler
                        = 0.57721566490153286;


  // Trigonometric functions
  public static double cot(double x);


  // Hyperbolic functions
```

```
public static double sinh(double x);
public static double cosh(double x);
public static double tanh(double x);

// Inverse hyperbolic functions
public static double asinh(double x);
public static double acosh(double x);
public static double atanh(double x);

// Gamma and logarithm gamma functions
public static double gamma(double x);
public static double logGamma(double x);

// The error function and its complement
public static double erf(double x);
public static double erfc(double x);

// Logarithms taken to base 10
public static double log10(double x);

// Return the value of x with the sign of y
public static double sign(double x, double y);

// Return the nearest integer to x
public static int nearestInteger(double x);
}
```

We can call these as shown in the following example:

```
import VisualNumerics.math.*;

double x = Sfun.cosh(7.6);
```

8.2.2 Statistical functions

The class Statistics is very similar and provides extra statistical functions. These are divided into those which compute properties of a data set and cumulative distribution functions for a few standard distributions. It is defined as follows:

```
package VisualNumerics.math;

public class Statistics
{
  // Properties of a data set
  public static double average(double[] x);
  public static double median(double[] x);
  public static double minimum(double[] x);
  public static double maximum(double[] x);
  // The sample variance (dividing by n-1)
  public static double variance(double[] x);
```

```
// Sample standard deviation (dividing by n-1)
public static double standardDeviation(double[] x);
public static double skew(double[] x);
public static double kurtosis(double[] x);
public static double range(double[] x);

// Least squares linear fit to a data set.
// If coef is the returned array from linearFit
// then the line of fit is: y = coef[0] + x * coef[1]
public static double[] linearFit(double[] x, double[] y);
public static double slope(double[] x, double[] y);

// Cumulative F distribution function and inverse
public static double FCdf(double x,
                double degreesFreedomNumerator,
                double degreesFreedomDenominator);
public static double inverseFCdf(double p,
                double degreesFreedomNumerator,
                double degreesFreedomDenominator);

// Cumulative Student's t distribution function and inverse
public static double tCdf(double t, double degreesFreedom);
public static double inverseTCdf(double p,
                double degreesFreedom);

// Cumulative Normal/Gaussian distribution
// function and inverse.
public static double normalCdf(double x);
public static double inverseNormalCdf(double p);
}
```

Note that `variance` and `standardDeviation` return the sample variance and sample standard deviation. These are the forms obtained by dividing by one less than the number of samples. If x_i are the samples, and there are n of them, then

$$\bar{x} \;=\; \frac{\sum x_i}{n}$$

$$\text{sample variance} \;=\; \frac{\sum (x_i - \bar{x})}{(n-1)}$$

$$\text{sample standard deviation} \;=\; \sqrt{\text{sample variance}}$$

8.3   Complex numbers

In Chapter 6, we wrote a simple class for handling complex numbers. The JNL provides such a class, with much more functionality. The definition is as follows:

```
package VisualNumerics.math;
```

```
public class Complex
{
  // Complex infinity
  public static final Complex INFINITY;

  // Constructors
  public Complex(Complex z);
  public Complex(double re, double im);
  public Complex(double re);
  public Complex();

  // Real and imaginary parts of the object.
  // Variables are directly accessible.
  public double re;
  public double im;

  // Modulus and argument of the object
  public static double abs(Complex z);
  public static double argument(Complex z);

  // Addition
  public static Complex add(Complex z, Complex w);
  public static Complex add(double x, Complex w);
  public static Complex add(Complex z, double y);
  public Complex add(Complex w);
  public Complex add(double x);

  // Subtraction
  public static Complex subtract(Complex z, Complex w);
  public static Complex subtract(double x, Complex w);
  public static Complex subtract(Complex z, double y);
  public Complex subtract(Complex w);
  public Complex subtract(double y);

  // Multiplication
  public static Complex multiply(Complex z, Complex w);
  public static Complex multiply(double x, Complex w);
  public static Complex multiply(Complex z, double y);
  public Complex multiply(Complex w);
  public Complex multiply(double y);

  // Division
  // note only four as opposed to five forms.
  public static Complex divide(Complex z, Complex w);
  public static Complex divide(Complex z, double y);
  public Complex divide(Complex w);
  public Complex divide(double y);

  // Other arithmetic operations
  public static Complex negate(Complex z);
```

```
public static Complex conjugate(Complex z);
public static Complex sqrt(Complex z);
public static Complex pow(Complex z, Complex w);
public static Complex pow(Complex z, double x);

// Elementary functions
public static Complex exp(Complex z);
public static Complex log(Complex z);
public static Complex sin(Complex z);
public static Complex cos(Complex z);
public static Complex tan(Complex z);
public static Complex asin(Complex z);
public static Complex acos(Complex z);

// String used during conversion of a complex
// number into a string. Initially, this is set
// to "i". You can change it to "j" if you want.
// Note that it is static and so set once, not
// once per object.
public static String suffix;

// Conversions to other data types.
public String toString();

// Comparison operators
public boolean equals(Complex z);
// This version of equals is for use in hash tables.
// It treats two NaN doubles as equal, which is not
// the IEEE standard.
public boolean equals(Object obj);

// Checking for special values.
// NaN means Not-A-Number (maths error occurred)
public static boolean isNaN(Complex z);
public static boolean isInfinite(Complex z);
}
```

If you have not read Chapter 6 then you will need a good grasp of Section 4.3.3 to be able to understand how to use this class. It is important to inspect every method in the class to see whether it is static or non-static. This tells you whether it will be called using the syntax `Complex.<method>` or `<object>.<method>`. In the second case, the method will use the object with which it is called as an extra argument.

For example, if we look at the many versions of `add`, we find among them:

```
public static Complex add(Complex z, Complex w);
public Complex add(Complex w);
```

The first of these adds its two arguments and returns their sum. Hence, a simple piece of code such as

```
double a = 5.7;
double b = -3.5;

double c = a + b;
```

has the same logical structure as the following code, which uses `Complex` arithmetic:

```
Complex a = new Complex(5.7, 2.3);
Complex b = new Complex(-3.5);

Complex c = Complex.add(a, b);
```

In contrast, the second version of `add` is non-static so we could also write the last line of the above as:

```
Complex c = a.add(b);
```

If you consider the static or non-static nature of the remaining methods then you should now be able to see how the rest of the class works.

8.4   Vectors and matrices

The JNL does not declare any extra data types to handle vectors or matrices. Instead, both are implemented using arrays of `double` values or `Complex` objects: a vector is declared as `double[]` or `Complex[]` and a matrix is declared as `double[][]` or `Complex[][]`.

Section 4.3.1 discusses the use of arrays in depth. You should remember that you can initialize an array by giving a set of values in curly brackets:

```
double[] a = { 1.4, 3.2, -5.6 };
```

This is also true for matrices of complex numbers. However, in this case the set of values must be `Complex` objects. Hence we must write:

```
Complex[] b = { new Complex(1.4, 2.3), new Complex(-3.4) };
```

which is rather more cumbersome.

One problem arises from this representation of matrices. As we discussed in Section 4.3.1, a multidimensional array need not be rectangular: the rows may be of different lengths. This is clearly impossible for matrices and you must make sure that all of the arrays that you use are indeed rectangular.

8.4.1   Exceptions

The JNL uses exceptions to handle errors during vector and matrix operations. Refer to Section 4.4.1 in order to understand how exceptions are thrown and caught.

Two classes of exceptions are used:

- `java.lang.IllegalArgumentException`, which is defined in the Java standard library. This is a subclass of `RuntimeException` and so need not be handled explicitly.

- `VisualNumerics.math.MathException`, which the JNL defines as follows:

```
package VisualNumerics.math;

public class MathException extends Exception
{
    // Constructors with optional message.
    public MathException();
    public MathException(String s);
}
```

The two exceptions are used to signify two different sorts of errors. `IllegalArgumentException` is used to signify that one of the arguments passed to a method was malformed and the method could not start its computation. For example, this exception will be thrown if a non-rectangular array is used as a matrix or if you try to multiply two matrices in which the row length of the first is different from the column length of the second.

By contrast, `MathException` is used to signify that an error occurred during the actual computation. For instance, this exception will be thrown if you try to invert a singular matrix or try to Cholesky-decompose a matrix that is not symmetric and positive definite. `MathException` is also used when a matrix is supposed to be square and is not.

8.4.2 Vectors

Vectors are implemented as arrays. However, array syntax does not provide many of the operations that we would like to perform on vectors, so the JNL includes two classes, `DoubleVector` and `ComplexVector`, of useful static methods. The declaration of `DoubleVector` is as follows. Note that `IllegalArgumentException` is a subclass of `RuntimeException` and so need not be handled explicitly.

```
package VisualNumerics.math;

public class DoubleVector
{
    //// Arithmetic operations
    // Addition of two vectors
    public static double[] add(double[] v1, double[] v2)
                throws IllegalArgumentException;
    // Subtraction of two vectors
    public static double[] subtract(double[] v1, double[] v2)
                throws IllegalArgumentException;
    // Multiplication of a vector by a scalar
    public static double[] multiply(double da, double[] v);
    // Dot product of two vectors.
```

```
    public static double innerProduct(double[] a, double[] b);


    //// Vector norms
    // Sum of the absolute values of the elements
    public static double oneNorm(double[] a);
    // The Euclidean norm
    public static double twoNorm(double[] a);
    // The maximum of the absolute values of the elements
    public static double infinityNorm(double[] a);


    //// Other operations
    // Addition of a scalar to all elements of a vector
    public static double[] add(double a, double[] v);
    // Multiplication of the elements of the same index
    public static double[] multiply(double[] v1, double[] v2)
                throws IllegalArgumentException;
    // Summation of the elements
    public static double sum(double[] a);
    // Multiplication of the elements.
    public static double product(double[] a);
}
```

Using this class, we can write code such as:

```
double[] a = { 3.7, 4.5, 1.2 };
double[] b = { 1.2, -3.5, 1.2 };
double[] c = DoubleVector.add(a, b);
System.out.println(DoubleVector.twoNorm(c));
```

A similar class called ComplexVector exists for handling vectors that were declared as Complex[]. This class contains methods that correspond to each of the methods of Double, but which take and return Complex or Complex[] arguments (except for the norms, which still return double). In addition, it provides the following extra methods for complex arithmetic:

```
// Complex conjugate components
public static Complex[] conjugate(Complex[] z);
// Real parts of components
public static double[] real(Complex[] z)
// Imaginary parts of components
public static double[] imag(Complex[] z)
```

It also provides some additional versions of arithmetic functions that take a mixture of double and Complex arguments for convenience. The double arguments are taken to be the real part of a complex number with no imaginary part:

```
//// Arithmetic operations
// Addition of two vectors
public static Complex[] add(double[] b, Complex[] z);
// Subtraction of two vectors
public static Complex[] subtract(Complex[] z, double[] b);
```

```
public static Complex[] subtract(double[] b, Complex[] z);
// Multiplication of a vector by a scalar
public static Complex[] multiply(double b, Complex[] z);

//// Other operations
// Addition of a scalar to all elements of a vector
public static Complex[] add(double b, Complex[] z);
// Subtraction of a scalar from all elements of a vector
public static Complex[] subtract(Complex[] z, double b);
public static Complex[] subtract(Complex[] z, Complex b);
// Multiplication of elements of the same index
public static Complex[] multiply(double[] b, Complex[] z);
```

Note that the subtract method for ComplexVector is capable of subtraction of a scalar from all elements of a vector. DoubleVector does not implement such a method.

8.4.3 Matrices

The JNL provides two classes, DoubleMatrix and ComplexMatrix, to manipulate two-dimensional arrays of double or Complex as matrices. The declaration of DoubleMatrix is as follows. Section 8.4.1 explained when each of the two types of exception will be thrown. Note that IllegalArgumentException is a subclass of RuntimeException and so need not be handled explicitly.

```
package VisualNumerics.math;

public class DoubleMatrix
{
    //// Arithmetic operations
    // Addition of two matrices
    public static double[][] add(double[][] a, double[][] b)
                throws IllegalArgumentException;
    // Subtraction of two matrices
    public static double[][] subtract(double[][] a, double[][] b)
                throws IllegalArgumentException;
    // Multiplication of two matrices
    public static double[][] multiply(double[][] a, double[][] b)
                throws IllegalArgumentException;
    // Multiplication of a matrix and a vector
    public static double[] multiply(double[][] a, double[] x)
                throws IllegalArgumentException;
    // Multiplication of a vector and a matrix
    public static double[] multiply(double[] x, double[][] a)
                throws IllegalArgumentException;

    //// Properties of a single matrix
    public static double[][] transpose(double[][] a)
                throws IllegalArgumentException;
    public static double[][] inverse(double[][] a)
                throws IllegalArgumentException, MathException;
```

```
public static double determinant(double[][] a)
               throws IllegalArgumentException, MathException;
public static double trace(double[][] a)
               throws MathException;

//// Matrix norms. Defined as discussed below.
public static double oneNorm(double[][] array);
public static double frobeniusNorm(double[][] array);
public static double infinityNorm(double[][] array);

//// Other operations
// Solve the system Ax = b using the LU factorization.
// MathException is thrown if A is singular.
public static double[] solve(double[][] A, double[] b)
               throws IllegalArgumentException, MathException;
// Solve the system Ax = b using the QR factorization.
// MathException is thrown if R has a zero element.
// Returns the least squares solution if A is not square.
public static double[] QRsolve(double[][] A, double[] b)
               throws IllegalArgumentException, MathException;
}
```

The three matrix norms are defined for a square matrix A of order n as:

$$\|A\|_1 = \max_{\|v\|_1=1} \|Av\|_1$$

$$\|A\|_F = \sqrt{\sum_{i,j=1}^{n} |A_{ij}|^2}$$

$$\|A\|_\infty = \max_{\|v\|_\infty=1} \|Av\|_\infty$$

The class `ComplexMatrix` is identical, except that all methods take and return `Complex[][]` or `Complex[]` (except for the norms, which still return `double`). There is one additional method:

```
public static Complex[][] adjoint(Complex[][] a);
```

8.5 Matrix decompositions

In numerical work, it is often found that computations involving a matrix can be performed more quickly by expressing the matrix as the product of several other matrices, each of which is of a standard form. The process of factorizing the original matrix is called **matrix decomposition**. The JNL provides classes to perform Cholesky, LU, QR and singular value decompositions of real and complex matrices. Each of these algorithms is based on a method from the LINPACK numerical library for linear analysis.

All of the decompositions are implemented via the constructor for a class. To perform a decomposition, you construct a new object, passing the matrix to be decomposed to the constructor. The constructor performs the decomposition, storing the results inside the object. Finally, you can use the object's methods to extract the parts of the decomposed matrix. The object also has methods to perform computations involving the matrix, such as inverting it. These methods use the decomposition that has been computed and so are faster than performing the computation directly.

8.5.1 Cholesky decomposition

The first of the decomposition classes implements Cholesky decomposition. We will discuss this in more detail than for the later classes since their overall structure is shared. There are two versions of the class, DoubleCholesky for real matrices and ComplexCholesky for complex matrices. We will discuss DoubleCholesky first.

The Cholesky decomposition is defined for a real symmetric positive definite matrix, A. Such matrices are diagonalizable, and it turns out that we can write

$$A = LDL^T$$

where D is a diagonal matrix and L is a lower triangular matrix. If we define $D^{1/2}$ to be the diagonal matrix whose diagonal elements are the square roots of those in D, then we can write

$$A = (LD^{1/2})(D^{1/2}L^T)$$
$$U = D^{1/2}L^T$$
$$A = U^TU$$

where U is upper triangular. The Cholesky decomposition consists of finding this matrix, U.

The class DoubleCholesky is defined as follows:

```
package VisualNumerics.math;

public class DoubleCholesky
{
  //// Constructor.
  // This actually computes the decomposition.
  // Algorithm: LINPACK DPOFA
  public DoubleCholesky(double[][] A)
         throws IllegalArgumentException, Math Exception;

  //// Accessor methods for the decomposition.
  // R is a symmetric square matrix with Cholesky
  // factor, U, in both upper and lower triangles.
  public double[][] R();

  //// Operations using the decomposition
  // Computation of inverse for A
  public double[][] inverse()
         throws MathException;

  // Computation of determinant for A
```

```
    public double determinant();


    // Solution of Ax = b.
    // Algorithm: LINPACK DPOSL
    public double[] solve(double[] b)
            throws MathException;


    // Estimation of reciprocal of L1 condition number
    // of the matrix. This is defined as the product of
    // the oneNorms of A and A inverse.
    // Algorithm: LINPACK DPOCO.
    // A small value indicates that the linear
    // system Ax = b is unstable under changes in A.
    public double condition()
            throws MathException;
  }
```

Note that the matrix R that is returned contains U in both its upper and lower triangles.

The class `ComplexCholesky` is very similar and works for complex Hermitian positive definite matrices. The constructor is equivalent to LINPACK's `ZPOFA`, the determinant to `ZPODI`, the solve method to `ZPOSL`, and the condition method to `ZPOCO`.

8.5.2 Example – using `DoubleCholesky`

In order to help you to understand these matrix decomposition classes, we now write an example program using `DoubleCholesky`. This program performs a Cholesky decomposition on a matrix. It also computes the matrix inverse, once directly and once using the decomposition. The code is available at `http://www.jscieng.co.uk/Code/JNL/Cholesky/`.

```
import VisualNumerics.math.*;


public class Cholesky
{
  // A utility method to print a matrix
  public static void printMatrix(double[][] m)
  {
    for (int i=0; i<3; i++)
    {
      // Print each row, elements separated by tabs
      for (int j=0; j<3; j++)
        System.out.print(m[i][j] + "\t");

      // Start a new line at the row's end
      System.out.println();
    }

    // Leave a gap after the entire matrix
```

```java
            System.out.println();
    }


    // The 'main' method contains the body of the program
    public static void main(String[] argv)
    {
        // Define the matrix that we are going to operate on.
        double[][] A = { { 1.3, 1.2, 0.1 },
                         { 1.2, 3.4, 1.1 },
                         { 0.1, 1.1, 3.1} };

        // Print it out
        System.out.println("A is the matrix");
        printMatrix(A);

        try
        {
            // Invert the matrix and print the inverse.
            System.out.println("The inverse of A is");
            printMatrix(DoubleMatrix.inverse(A));;
        }
        catch(MathException e)
        {
            // Error message if inverse fails.
            System.out.println("A is singular");
        }

        try
        {
            // Perform the Cholesky decomposition
            DoubleCholesky decomp = new DoubleCholesky(A);

            // Print the Cholesky factor
            System.out.println("The Cholesky factor of A is");
            printMatrix(decomp.R());

            // Invert the matrix using the decomposition
            System.out.println("The inverse of A via Cholesky is");
            printMatrix(decomp.inverse());
        }
        catch(MathException e)
        {
            // Error message if decomposition fails
            System.out.println("That matrix is not symmetric "
                               + "positive definite");
        }
    }
}
```

You should note the use of the `DoubleCholesky` class: the decomposition is performed by constructing an object. Once it has been performed, we use that object to return the result of the decomposition or to use the decomposition in computations.

Other points worth noting include the use of '\t', a special character for tab, and the exception handling.

Timing this example code, with repetitions added for each inversion operation, it is clear that inversion using the decomposed form is more than twice as fast as direct inversion. This speed is the main benefit of matrix decompositions. It is most important in cases where you will have to perform an action, such as solving a set of equations, repeatedly using the same matrix. One decomposition action will speed up all subsequent stages.

8.5.3 LU decomposition

The LU factorization is defined for any square non-singular matrix, A. We can write

$$A = LU$$

where L is a lower triangular matrix and U is an upper triangular matrix.

The decomposition is performed by a class `DoubleLU`, which behaves just like `DoubleCholesky`:

```
package VisualNumerics.math;

public class DoubleLU
{
    //// Constructor.
    // This actually computes the decomposition.
    // Algorithm: LINPACK DGECO
    // (this uses scaled partial pivoting)
    public DoubleLU(double[][] A)
            throws IllegalArgumentException, MathException;

    //// Accessor methods for the decomposition.
    // Vector of pivoting information from LU.
    // The kth element is the index of the column that
    // has been interchanged into the kth column.
    public int[] ipvt();

    //// Operations using the decomposition
    // Computation of inverse for A.
    public double[][] inverse();

    // Computation of determinant for A.
    // Algorithm: LINPACK DGEDI
    public double determinant();

    // Solution of Ax = b.
    // Algorithm: LINPACK DGESL
```

```
     public double[] solve(double[] b);

     // Estimation of reciprocal of L1 condition
     // number (see Cholesky).
     // Algorithm: LINPACK DGECO.
     public double condition();
}
```

The class `ComplexLU` is very similar and works for complex non-singular matrices. The constructor is equivalent to LINPACK's `ZGECO`, the determinant to `ZGEDI`, the solve method to `ZGESL`, and the condition method to `ZGECO`.

8.5.4 QR decomposition

The class `DoubleQR` computes the QR decomposition of a matrix A using Householder transformations. For a general matrix, A, which need not be square, we can write

$$AP = QR$$

where Q is an orthogonal matrix, R is upper triangular and P is a permutation chosen so that R has non-increasing diagonal elements (in other words, pivoting occurs).

The class definition is:

```
package VisualNumerics.math;

public class DoubleQR
{
  //// Constructor.
  // This actually computes the decomposition.
  // Algorithm: LINPACK DQRDC
  // (uses Householder transformations and pivoting)
  public DoubleQR(double[][] A)
        throws IllegalArgumentException;

  //// Accessor methods for the decomposition.
  // Return Q, an orthogonal matrix
  public double[][] Q();
  // Return R, an upper triangular matrix
  public double[][] R();
  // Vector of pivoting information, defining P.
  // The format is the same as DoubleLU.
  public int[] ipvt();

  //// Operations using the decomposition.
  // Rank of A with tolerance for rounding.
  // Count diagonal elements of R > tol.
  public int rank(double tol);

  // Computation of the rank of A
  // with default tol = 2.22e-16;
```

```
public int rank();

// Solution to the least squares problem
// Ax = b. The rank of A is determined using
// the tolerance tol.
// Algorithm: LINPACK DQRSL
public double[] solve(double[] b, double tol)
        throws MathException;

// Solution to the least squares problem
// Ax = b. tol = 2.22e-16
public double[] solve(double[] b)
        throws MathException;
}
```

The class ComplexQR is very similar and works for complex matrices. The constructor is equivalent to LINPACK's ZQRDC and the solve method to ZQRSL.

8.5.5 Singular Value decomposition

The class DoubleSVD performs a singular value decomposition of a matrix A, which need not be square. If A is an i by j matrix, we can find an i by i orthogonal matrix U and a j by j orthogonal matrix V such that we can write

$$U^{T}AV = \begin{cases} \begin{pmatrix} S \\ 0 \end{pmatrix} & \text{if } i \geq j \\ \begin{pmatrix} S & 0 \end{pmatrix} & \text{otherwise} \end{cases}$$

where S is a diagonal matrix with non-negative entries whose order is the minimum of i and j. The diagonal values of S are called the **singular values** of A, the columns of U are called the **left singular vectors** and the columns of V are called the **right singular vectors**.

The class declaration is:

```
package VisualNumerics.math;

public class DoubleSVD
{
  //// Constructor.
  // This actually computes the decomposition.
  // Algorithm: LINPACK DSVDC
  // The value tol is a tolerance used to test
  // if singular values are negligible. If it is
  // positive, then it is compared directly. If
  // negative, then abs(tol) * infinity norm of A
  // is used.
  public DoubleSVD(double[][] A, double tol)
        throws IllegalArgumentException;
  // A version with default tol = 2.22e-14
```

```
public DoubleSVD(double[][] A);


//// Accessor methods for the decomposition.
// Left singular vectors.
public double[][] U();
// Right singular vectors.
public double [][] V();
// Singular values in order of decreasing magnitude
public double[] S();
// Convergence information. Convergence occurs for all
// singular values and their vectors from the returned
// index onward.
public int info();


//// Operations using the decomposition.
// Rank of A (uses tolerance value).
// MathException is thrown if convergence
// was not obtained for all singular values.
public int rank()
       throws MathException;


// The Moore-Penrose generalized inverse.
// MathException is thrown if the rank could
// not be computed.
public double[][] inverse()
       throws MathException;
}
```

The class `ComplexSVD` is very similar and operates on complex matrices. The constructor is similar to LINPACK's `ZSVDC`.

WHERE TO GO FROM HERE

Unlike more established languages, such as Fortran or C/C++, at the time of writing (August 1998) Java suffers from a scarcity of numerical libraries. I cannot recommend anything remotely comparable to the NAG libraries for Fortran. This book's accompanying website, at `http://www.jscieng.co.uk/`, contains links to many of those resources which are available. These are updated as more software comes into the public arena, and may point you to something relevant to your needs. Alternatively, I can only recommend a good book on numerical algorithms, such as *Numerical Recipes in C* (Press, Flannery, Teukolsky and Vetterling, 1988).

CHAPTER 9

Numerical computation

9.1 Introduction

This chapter is a brief introduction to some important issues in numerical computation. It is divided into two sections. Section 9.2 is a general discussion of possible sources of error in a computation and how these can be minimized. Section 9.3 discusses some of the simpler algorithms in standard use and contains code implementing these. The discussions will probably only be at a suitable level if you have not encountered these subjects before.

The sample code in this chapter assumes knowledge of Chapter 4 and of Section 5.2. All sample code is available from the website at http://www.jscieng.co.uk/Code/ NumComp/.

9.2 Numerical errors

The mathematical concept of a number is, unfortunately, one that cannot be simulated by most programming languages. In mathematics and computer algebra packages, numbers may be unboundedly large and are given with perfect precision. When working with a programming language, we want to represent numbers by storing their binary digits in a fixed, finite amount of memory. However, even a simple fraction such as 1/10 cannot be expressed by a finite number of binary digits, just as 1/3 cannot be expressed by a finite number of decimal digits. As a result, we must compromise.

Computer arithmetic is available for integers, as represented by the types `byte`, `short`, `int` and `long`, and floating point numbers, as represented by `float` and `double`. Both of these types of arithmetic have their limitations.

The limitation of integer arithmetic is simple – any of the data types can only store a fixed range of values. For example, a variable declared as `short` is capable of storing integers from $-32\,768$ to $32\,767$. If the result of a calculation is outside this range, then the values wrap around: arithmetic is treated as if it were modulo $65\,536$. In Java, this happens automatically and there is no mechanism to tell if it has taken place. For example, there is no exception thrown to signal a calculation whose result is too large to be represented. This behaviour can have unexpected consequences. Consider the code

```
short k = 40;
k *= 1000;
System.out.println(k);
```

which will produce a negative result. There is one even stranger consequence, as demonstrated by the method:

```
public static int abs(int a)
{
  if (a < 0)
    return -a;
  else
    return a;
}
```

It would appear that this method always returns the positive value of an integer. However, `abs(-2147483648)` returns `-2147483648`! The reason is that all integer data types have ranges which include one more negative number than they do positive numbers. As a result, when we pass this number and try to negate it, the program is incapable of storing the positive value so this wraps around and produces a negative result.

Programmers learn to deal with these problems fairly easily – they learn to restrict themselves to small integer values, which are handled perfectly. In general, even when wraparound does occur it is easy to spot, since the result is dramatically different from that expected.

Floating point arithmetic is much harder to use properly. Ironically, the first difference is that the problems with integer arithmetic that we have just discussed no longer exist. As we saw in Section 5.10, there are special constants, such as `double.POSITIVE_INFINITY`, which indicate a value which the floating point data type cannot represent. If a calculation's result overflows or underflows then one of these constants is returned. If we perform any subsequent calculations in which that value is used then they too return one of the constants, so the error eventually reaches the programmer's attention.

The second difference is that floating point numbers store only approximations to actual values calculated. To understand the issues raised we must discuss how floating point numbers are represented in a computer. As we mentioned earlier, even a simple fraction such as $1/10$ would require an infinite number of binary digits to store exactly. Floating point data types store binary digits to represent numbers, which means that they are inherently approximate. Numbers are stored in a format very similar to scientific notation: as a **mantissa** (a number between $\frac{1}{2}$ and 1), an **exponent** (an integer) and a sign bit, which together represent the value

$$\text{sign} * \text{mantissa} * 2^{\text{exponent}}$$

Both mantissa and exponent are allocated an exact amount of storage space. For the `double` type, this corresponds to a mantissa capable of storing 16 decimal significant figures of accuracy (see Table 2.1 for ranges of the exponent and the other data types). This means that all floating point computations are subject to **rounding errors** – the value produced will be at best an approximation to the real answer since it may have been rounded up or down at each operation. As a result, we can meet behaviour such as that in Exercise 2.5:

```
double a = 3;

a /= 17;

if (5*a == 15.0/17)
   System.out.println("This line will not be printed!");
```

If you run this program you will see that the line is indeed not printed. The two methods of calculating 15/17 have produced different results, although only in the 16th significant figure! What has happened is that the calculation of 3/17 produced a result, which was rounded to 16 significant figures. When this result is multiplied by 5 the exact details of the rounding do not correspond to that performed during a direct division, so we get two slightly different results.

From a naive viewpoint we might expect no further problems – any computation carried out using `double` would produce a result accurate to 16 significant figures and the 16th place probably should not be trusted. Unfortunately this is not the case: errors accumulate over a series of operations. One of the arts of numerical computation is to understand and control the growth of these errors in algorithms that require very large numbers of arithmetic operations.

9.2.1 Stability and instability

As we just demonstrated, floating point arithmetic is inherently approximate. When we design a numerical method we try to minimize the effect that this has on our results. A method is said to be **stable** if rounding errors in the computation tend to keep a constant size to or to be eliminated over time, or **unstable** if the method magnifies the rounding errors. Stability is one of the key requirements for a good numerical method.

There is one particularly bad case of amplification of rounding errors. This occurs when we add and subtract a number of terms, producing a result which is small compared to the terms themselves. Consider the subtraction $1.628\,325 - 1.627\,856 = 0.000\,569$. It is clear from the way in which this was written that even if both of the original numbers are accurate to seven significant figures then the result will be accurate to only three. We find exactly the same behaviour in many other problems. Consider evaluating e^{-30} using the series expansion

$$e^{-30} = 1 - \frac{30}{1!} + \frac{30^2}{2!} - \frac{30^3}{3!} + \ldots$$

We could perform the evaluation of the series using the code

```
double term = 1;
double sum = term;
```

```
for (int i=1; i<100; i++)
{
  term *= -30.0/i;
  sum += term;
}

System.out.println(sum);
```

which returns $6.1 * 10^{-6}$, not $9.4 * 10^{-14}$ – an error by a factor of 10^8. The problem is that some of the terms in the series are as large as $7.7 * 10^{11}$. For terms of this size, the 16th decimal place is at 10^{-5}, so we would expect the final error to be around this size.

Difficulties with taking differences of terms of approximately equal size are a lot more common than this, somewhat contrived, example might suggest. For example, the standard formula for solving quadratic equations,

$$\frac{-b \pm \sqrt{b^2 - 4ac}}{2a}$$

will cause problems if $b^2 \gg 4ac$ since the square root is almost equal to b. Similarly, imagine computing the cosine of an angle near $\pi/2$. We know that

$$\cos\left(\frac{\pi}{2} + \epsilon\right) = -\sin \epsilon$$

However, computation using the cosine will produce fewer digits of accuracy than computation using the sine because the act of adding $\pi/2$ to x will reduce the accuracy of x from 16 significant figures to 16 decimal places, which is a very different concept indeed. For example, if $\epsilon = 10^{-20}$ then the cosine returns $6.1 * 10^{-17}$ while the sine returns a much more accurate answer, $1.0 * 10^{-20}$.

9.2.2 Example – the leapfrog method

As a good example of an unstable method, we consider solving the first-order ordinary differential equation

$$\dot{y}(t) = -10y(t)$$

subject to $y = 1$ at $t = 0$ by the leapfrog method. This method approximates the continuous function $y(t)$ by values at a series of discrete points, y_n. We choose a step size of 0.001, which means that y_n is an approximation to $y(n/1000)$. We can approximate the derivative by a central difference formula:

$$\dot{y}(n/1000) \approx \frac{y_{n+1} - y_{n-1}}{2 * 0.001}$$

This means that the differential equation is approximated by the difference equation

$$
\begin{aligned}
y_{n+1} &= 2 * 0.001 * \dot{y}(n/1000) + y_{n-1} \\
&= -2 * 0.01 * y_n + y_{n-1}
\end{aligned}
$$

and, given values for y_0 and y_1, we can iterate this expression to estimate $y(t)$ at any t.

The following program implements this iteration. It also computes the exact solution, $y(t) = e^{-10t}$, and compares the values. The program is called `Leapfrog.java` and is available at `http://www.jscieng.co.uk/Code/NumComp/Leapfrog/`.

```java
public class Leapfrog
{
  // Constants for the iteration
  public static final double STEPSIZE = 0.001;
  public static final int STEPS = 2000;


  // The 'main' method actually implements
  // the Leapfrog method.
  public static void main(String[] argv)
  {
    // Set up array for y_n values and
    // insert initial data.
    double[] y = new double[STEPS + 1];
    y[0] = 1;

    // Perform first step by another method
    // as leapfrog needs two points.
    y[1] = y[0] - STEPSIZE * 10 * y[0];

    // Perform iteration
    for (int i=2; i<=STEPS; i++)
    {
      y[i] = -2 * STEPSIZE * 10 * y[i-1] + y[i-2];

      // Print computed value and error.
      System.out.println("At t=" + i * STEPSIZE
                  + " y estimated at " + y[i]
                  + " an error of "
                  + (y[i] - Math.exp(-10*i*STEPSIZE)));
    }
  }
}
```

When we run this program, we discover that the errors produced are large and growing in size. For example, at $t = 2$, the error is more than $12\,000$, whereas $y(t)$ is less than 10^{-8}.

The problem is that we are modelling the first-order differential equation by a second-order difference equation. The algebraic solution of the difference equation is:

$$
\begin{aligned}
y_n &= A*(-0.01 + \sqrt{0.01^2 + 1})^n + B*(-0.01 - \sqrt{0.01^2 + 1})^n \\
&\approx A*0.990^n + B*(-1.010)^n
\end{aligned}
$$

for some constants A and B. The first of these terms approximates the exact solution of the differential equation: y_n approximates $y(n/1000)$ and $0.990^n \approx e^{-10n/1000}$.

The second term was introduced by the fact that we moved to a second-order equation, and has nothing to do with the original problem. This term grows exponentially in size, which means that if B is non-zero then it will eventually dominate. This is our error term. The initial values for y_0 and y_1 give B a very small value and following this its term grows and dominates the problem. Note that this would happen even if $B = 0$ initially, since rounding errors during iteration quickly give B a non-zero value.

This is a good example of the behaviour of an unstable method. If we consider the method from a purely mathematical viewpoint then it appears to be satisfactory: the initial conditions set $B = 0$, so the computation should approximate to the differential equation successfully. However, when we view it as a numerical computation, we have to acknowledge that rounding errors will occur and the suitability of the method depends on its ability to produce accurate results subject to these errors.

9.2.3 Properties of methods

Even when we restrict ourselves to stable methods, they can still show interesting numerical behaviour. Many methods involve splitting the range of a continuous variable into discrete steps. For example, most methods of numerical integration (such as the leapfrog method) involve taking values at a fixed number of distinct points along a function and then computing an integral from these. When we use such methods, we incur **discretization errors**, errors introduced by our discretization of the problem, in addition to rounding errors from the actual computation.

This presents an interesting question. The choice of the number of steps is frequently left to the programmer. How many steps should we choose? Assuming that computer time is not an issue (frequently it will be!), the answer is that the optimal number of steps is chosen to minimize the sum of the discretization and rounding errors.

In general, discretization errors decrease as the number of steps increases and the distinct points approximate to a continuum more and more successfully. By contrast, as we add more points the number of arithmetic operations that we perform during computations increases and so the total rounding error increases.

In Section 2.13, we wrote a simple program to integrate a function by the trapezium rule. We now move on to discuss these types of error using that example. We will not discuss the details of this method or the exact program used; you should refer back for these.

The trapezium rule is a good example of the problem that we have just discussed. It approximates an integral as the sum of the areas of a number of trapezoidal strips under the graph of the integrand. The number of strips to use is set by the programmer, so we must consider the issues in the previous subsection to decide what to do.

Table 9.1 shows what happens as we vary the number of steps for a sample integration, carried out using `float` arithmetic (note that the extreme numbers of steps at either end are not sensible for this method, and that significantly better methods of integration exist; this is just an example). The integration that we chose was

$$\int_{-4}^{4} x^2 \mathrm{d}x = \frac{128}{3}$$

which enables us to calculate the error in the computation for each number of steps.

Table 9.1   Errors using the trapezium rule.

Number of steps	Result	Error
128	42.671 875	0.005 208 0
256	42.667 970	0.001 301 8
512	42.666 992	0.000 325 2
1 024	42.666 473	0.000 193 6
2 048	42.666 588	0.000 079 2
4 096	42.666 840	0.000 172 6
8 192	42.666 798	0.000 130 7
16 384	42.666 832	0.000 165 0
32 768	42.666 595	0.000 071 5
65 536	42.666 430	0.000 235 6
131 072	42.665 990	0.000 678 1
262 144	42.664 870	0.001 795 8
524 288	42.661 820	0.004 847 5
1 048 576	42.650 875	0.015 791 9

It is clear from this table that there is indeed an optimal number of steps: 128 is too few, and produces a result with large discretization error, whilst 1 048 576 is too many, and produces a result with large rounding error. Your programs may not always show such an optimal point – you may find that your method is still improving at the point at which the computation becomes too slow to perform. However, the optimum is a general feature of this type of method and would eventually occur in all cases. You should always choose the number of steps carefully and should experiment with other values to obtain the optimum.

9.3   Numerical algorithms

We now move on to discuss some of the simpler numerical algorithms that are in standard use. In the earlier chapters of this book, most of the examples were concerned with demonstrating language features, rather than implementing numerical algorithms. Nevertheless, we have already met a few algorithms that can be used in more serious work. These were discussed in the following places:

- Section 5.5. RSA is the famous public key encryption algorithm based on large prime numbers which is used by the program PGP and all good intelligence agencies (using primes several hundred digits long). The algorithm as presented in the example is correct, but lacks the ability to spot the special cases that are known to be more easily solvable.

- Section 7.3.4. Euclid's algorithm is a much faster method of finding GCDs than prime factorization, and can also be used for finding inverses of a number modulo some base and many other basic operations in computational number theory.

In addition, the JSGL and JNL libraries are written for serious numerical work. The JNL uses standard algorithms, taken from LINPACK, to perform many of its matrix computations. However, it does not provide specialized support for sparse matrices, which may limit its use in some contexts.

In the following sections, we cover integration (Simpson's rule), finding roots of functions (bisection and Newton's method), finding minima of equations (simplex method), solution of differential equations (Runge–Kutta methods) and data analysis (least squares fits).

9.3.1 Simpson's rule integration

In Section 2.16, we discussed numerical integration using the **trapezium rule**. This states that, if a function $f(x)$ is to be integrated, then

$$\int_a^b f(x)\mathrm{d}x = h\left(\frac{1}{2}f_1 + f_2 + f_3 + \dots + f_{N-1} + \frac{1}{2}f_N\right) + O\left(\frac{1}{N^2}\right)$$

where f_i are the values of f evaluated at equally spaced steps in x, h is the step size and N is the number of steps.

A higher degree of accuracy is given by **Simpson's rule**:

$$\int_a^b f(x)\mathrm{d}x = \frac{h}{3}(f_1 + 4f_2 + 2f_3 + 4f_4 + \dots + 2f_{N-1} + 4f_{N-1} + f_N) + O\left(\frac{1}{N^4}\right)$$

These rules are useful if we are forced to pick sample points on the function at regular intervals. This might be the case if we were integrating a function whose values had been determined experimentally. If we are free to pick the points at which the function is evaluated, then we have more degrees of freedom for the same number of function evaluations, since we can choose to space these non-uniformly across the interval. **Gaussian quadrature** formulae use this technique and are more accurate.

Such formulae have another useful property. The trapezium rule and Simpson's rule work by approximating the shape of the curve by polynomials between each pair of points. For a quadrature formula, we can arrange the points of evaluation and the weightings so that the integral will be computed by approximating the shape of the curve by polynomial multiples of a known function, $F(x)$. This allows for much more accurate integration of functions which do not have a good polynomial approximation.

Unfortunately, the task of computing the points of evaluation and weightings for a quadrature formula is not simple and itself involves a program, so it is not within the scope of this book. However, if you are interested, you might consider reading an algorithms book, such as *Numerical Recipes in C* (Press, Flannery, Teukolsky and Vetterling, 1988).

9.3.2 Finding a root by bisection

Bisection is the simplest method for finding a root of a function, but is also remarkably efficient and applicable to a wide range of problems. The only assumption made is that the function is continuous.

Under this assumption, if the function's value changes sign over an interval, then the function must have a root in that interval. To find the root, we evaluate the function at the midpoint of the interval. Examining the sign here tells us which half-interval the zero is in. We repeat this procedure until our interval has contracted to locate the root to the desired accuracy.

The code for this example is available at `http://www.jscieng.co.uk/ Code/NumComp/Bisect/`.

```
public class Bisect
{
  // The function that we are going to
  // find a root for.
  public static double f(double x)
  {
    return 2 + x*x - (x-1)*x*x;
  }


  // The 'main' method at which program
  // execution starts.
  public static void main(String[] argv)
  {
    double left, right, middle, middley;

    // Start considering the interval from
    // 0 to 3. We assume that the function
    // changes sign over this interval.
    left = 0;
    right = 3;
    if (f(left) * f(right) > 0)
      System.out.println("Function does not change sign");
    else
    {
      // Keep halving the size of the interval
      // until it is as small as our required
      // accuracy.
      while (right - left > 0.0001)
      {
        // Compute the value of the function
        // at the middle of the interval
        middle = (left + right) / 2;
        middley = f(middle);

        // Switch to using whichever half
        // the sign now changes in.
        if (middley * f(right) <= 0)
        {
          left = middle;
        }
        else
        {
          right = middle;
```

```
            }
        }

        // Output our result.
        System.out.println("Root is at");
        System.out.println(left);
    }
  }
}
```

9.3.3 Newton's method

In the previous section we discussed bisection – a simple and fairly fast method of finding roots.

Newton's method (also called the **Newton–Raphson method**) is in general a much faster alternative to bisection. Unfortunately, it is not stable and must be used with some care. To understand the method, we must consider the Taylor series expansion of a function f in the neighbourhood of a point x.

$$f(x + h) \approx f(x) + hf'(x) + \frac{h^2}{2} f''(x) + \ldots$$

If h is small and the function is well behaved then terms of quadratic order or above in h are small, so $f(x + h) = 0$ implies

$$h \approx -\frac{f(x)}{f'(x)}$$

Hence, the iterative formula

$$x_{n+1} = x_n - \frac{f(x_n)}{f'(x_n)}$$

should converge to the root. This is equivalent to taking a linear approximation to the graph at each point and then moving to the root of that linear approximation as the next point.

If this method works, then it can be very fast – for example, in the program below, we obtain the root to 15 decimal places within four iterations! However, the algorithm is not always stable. If the iteration is started too far away from a root then the approximation is invalid and the iteration may not converge – it may display other behaviour such as moving towards a periodic limit cycle between several points on the function. In general, this is a method to be used with more caution than bisection.

There is an additional issue to be discussed. The iteration uses a derivative of the function f. Numerical derivatives can be computed by the approximation

$$f'(x) = \frac{f(x + h) - f(x - h)}{2h}$$

for some small value of h. The exact value of this increment is very important. If this number is too large then the derivative is inaccurate because the curve is not sufficiently close to being linear in the region of the increment. On the other hand, if it is too small then we lose accuracy because the numbers f(x+h) and f(x-h) differ only in their last few decimal places, so subtraction gives a result that is accurate only to this number of places, as opposed to the full 16 significant figures that a double can store. You are strongly advised to differentiate your function algebraically and provide an exact expression for the derivative if this is possible. You may find a computer algebra system useful for doing this.

The program that follows uses Newton's method to find a root of the equation $\sin(x) - 1/2 = 0$, using numerical differentiation. This root should be at $\pi/6$, and we check this. The code for this example is available at http://www.jscieng.co.uk/Code/NumComp/Newton/.

```java
public class Newton
{
  // The starting point for Newton's method
  public static final double START = 0.5;

  // The closeness to f(x) = 0 that we want to obtain
  // before giving x as the root.
  public static final double CLOSENESS = 1e-14;

  // The maximum number of steps to take before
  // giving up.
  public static final double MAXSTEPS = 100;

  // A small number for use in numerical
  // derivatives.
  public static final double BIT = 1e-8;


  // The function that we are going to
  // find a root for.
  public static double f(double x)
  {
    return Math.sin(x) - 0.5;
  }


  // A numerical derivative of that
  // function
  public static double deriv(double x)
  {
    return (f(x+BIT) - f(x-BIT)) / (2*BIT);
  }


  // The 'main' method actually implements
  // Newton's method.
  public static void main(String[] argv)
  {
    // Set up the starting point
```

```
double x = START;
int steps = 0;

// And print it out
System.out.println(x);

// Until we are sufficiently close to a root...
while((Math.abs(f(x)) > CLOSENESS) && (steps < MAXSTEPS))
{
  // Iterate by Newton's method
  x = x - f(x) / deriv(x);

  // Print the new position and update the counter
  System.out.println(x);
  steps++;
}

System.out.println();

// Print out the result
if (steps<MAXSTEPS)
{
  System.out.println("Root at x = " + x);

  // The eqn to solve was sin(x) - 1/2 = 0
  // so the root will be pi/6.
  System.out.println("So, pi is computed to be "
                    + 6*x);
  System.out.println(" And its real value is      "
                    + Math.PI);
}
else
  System.out.println("No convergence");
  }
}
```

9.3.4 The simplex method

The simplex method is a method of minimizing (or maximizing) a function over a region. It will work for regions in any number of dimensions, but we discuss it in the two-dimensional case for clarity.

Consider a function $f(x, y)$ of two variables defined over a plane. We consider a triangle in this plane. Our aim is to move the triangle towards a local minimum value of the function. To do so, we evaluate the function at all three corners. Next, we find the corner at which this value is largest. Assuming that the function varies smoothly in the area around the triangle, this implies that it is increasing in the direction of this corner from the centre. Therefore the function should be decreasing in the opposite direction. We reflect the corner in the opposite side of the triangle to obtain a new triangle, which has moved in the direction of decrease.

By repeating this procedure, we can 'walk' the triangle across the plane towards a local minimum. Finally, we come to a position where the triangle is sufficiently near a minimum that movement in any direction will cause the corner values to increase. At this point, we halve the size of the triangle, and repeat, homing in with greater accuracy at each decrease in triangle size.

The code for this example is available at `http://www.jscieng.co.uk/Code/NumComp/Simplex/`.

```java
public class Simplex
{
  // Constants for the method
  public static final double SHRINKAGES = 30;


  // The function to be minimized
  public static double f(double x, double y)
  {
    return (x-3)*(x-7) + Math.exp(y+2) + (y-1)*(y-3);
  }


  // The 'main' method actually implements
  // the simplex method.
  public static void main(String[] argv)
  {
    int i;

    // Set up array for the corners of the simplex
    // and insert initial values. First index is
    // which corner, second is which coordinate
    // of that corner (x, y, f).
    double[][] c = { { 0, 0, f(0, 0) },
                     { 0, 1, f(0, 1) },
                     { 1, 0, f(1, 0) } };

    // Count the number of times we shrink
    // the simplex.
    int shrink = 0;

    // Iterate until this has been
    // done enough times.
    while (shrink < SHRINKAGES)
    {
      // Find the highest corner
      int highest = 0;

      for (i=0; i<3; i++)
        if (c[i][2] > c[highest][2])
          highest = i;
```

```java
// Calculate the centre of the opposite face.
double cx = 0;
double cy = 0;

for (i=0; i<3; i++)
  if (i != highest)
  {
    cx += c[i][0];
    cy += c[i][1];
  }

cx /= 2;
cy /= 2;

// Try reflecting the highest corner in that
double rx = 2 * cx - c[highest][0];
double ry = 2 * cy - c[highest][1];
double rf = f(rx, ry);

if (rf < c[highest][2])
{
  // If this is lower than its current position
  // then move the simplex.
  c[highest][0] = rx;
  c[highest][1] = ry;
  c[highest][2] = rf;
}
else
{
  // Otherwise, we're near a minimum, so shrink
  // the simplex
  for (i=1; i<3; i++)
  {
    c[i][0] = (c[i][0] + c[0][0])/2;
    c[i][1] = (c[i][1] + c[0][1])/2;
    c[i][2] = f(c[i][0], c[i][1]);
  }

  shrink++;
}
}

// The method has terminated, so we're at a min.
System.out.println("The minimum is " + c[0][2]
                + " at x = " + c[0][0]
                + " and y = " + c[0][1]);
}
}
```

Note that it is easy to extend this method to handle functions of three or more variables: we move to using a tetrahedron for three variables or to similar extensions of the shape for large numbers. You should also be aware that this was a rather simplistic implementation of the simplex method. For more advanced work we can extend the method so that the simplex can also change shape. There are also faster but more complex algorithms available, such as Powell's method, which are beyond the scope of this book. See *Numerical Recipes in C* (Press, Flannery, Teukolsky and Vetterling, 1988).

9.3.5 Runge–Kutta methods

A standard numerical problem is the solution of an ordinary differential equation given initial value conditions. This is especially important since most differential equations do not have an exact algebraic solution so a numerical solution is the best available. The solution of differential equations given boundary value conditions is more difficult, and so is not discussed in this book.

An ordinary differential equation can frequently be rearranged so that the derivative at a point is written as some function of the x-value and the y-value:

$$y' = f(x, y)$$

Once it is in this form, we can imagine a stepwise method of solution in which we compute successive points by moving a short distance out from the previous point along the direction specified by the derivative.

The simplest example of this is the **Euler method**. If x_i are the x-values at each step, and these are equally spaced with a separation h, then we can compute the y-values y_i using the first two terms of the Taylor expansion:

$$y_{n+1} = y_n + hf(x_n, y_n) + O(h^2)$$

This method is somewhat primitive and is only first-order. However, a standard method used in numerical work follows a very similar algorithm. This is the **fourth-order Runge–Kutta method**. The algorithm is:

$$k_1 = hf(x_n, y_n)$$

$$k_2 = hf\left(x_n + \frac{h}{2}, y_n + \frac{k_1}{2}\right)$$

$$k_3 = hf\left(x_n + \frac{h}{2}, y_n + \frac{k_2}{2}\right)$$

$$k_4 = hf(x_n + h, y_n + k_3)$$

$$y_{n+1} = y_n + \frac{k_1}{6} + \frac{k_2}{3} + \frac{k_3}{3} + \frac{k_4}{6} + O(h^5)$$

This method produces an error term which is three orders of magnitude smaller than that from the Euler method at the expense of little additional computation. The function f needs to be evaluated four times as often for the same number of steps. However, it is found that the decreased error means that, even if we use a quarter as many steps, the result is still more accurate than that computed by the Euler method. You can think of the Runge–Kutta method as evaluating the derivative at the middle of each step and at both ends. An average is then taken, giving a much better idea of approximation to the behaviour of the derivative over the whole step.

We now write a simple program to solve the differential equation

$$\frac{\mathrm{d}y}{\mathrm{d}x} = x\sqrt{1 + y^2}$$

with the initial value condition $y = 0$ at $x = 0$. We compute the value at $x = 1$ using both the Euler and Runge–Kutta methods. We also compare these with the closed form solution

$$y = \sinh\left(\frac{x^2}{2}\right)$$

The code for this example is available at `http://www.jscieng.co.uk/Code/NumComp/RungeKutta/`.

```java
public class RungeKutta
{
  // The number of steps to use in the interval
  public static final int STEPS = 100;


  // The derivative dy/dx at a given value of x and y.
  public static double deriv(double x, double y)
  {
    return x * Math.sqrt(1 + y*y);
  }


  // The 'main' method does the actual computations
  public static void main(String[] argv)
  {
    // 'h' is the size of each step.
    double h = 1.0 / STEPS;
    double k1, k2, k3, k4;
    double x, y;
    int i;


    // Computation by Euclid's method
    // Initialize y
    y = 0;

    for (i=0; i<STEPS; i++)
    {
      // Step through, updating x and incrementing y
      x = i * h;

      y += h * deriv(x, y);
    }
```

```java
// Print out the result that we get.
System.out.println("Using the Euler method "
                    + "The value at x=1 is:");
System.out.println(y);


// Computation by 4th order Runge-Kutta
// Initialize y
y = 0;

for (i=0; i<STEPS; i++)
{
  // Step through, updating x
  x = i * h;

  // Computing all of the trial values
  k1 = h * deriv(x, y);
  k2 = h * deriv(x + h/2, y + k1/2);
  k3 = h * deriv(x + h/2, y + k2/2);
  k4 = h * deriv(x + h, y + k3);

  // Incrementing y
  y += k1/6 + k2/3+ k3/3 + k4/6;
}

// Print out the result that we get.
System.out.println();
System.out.println("Using 4th order Runge-Kutta "
                    + "The value at x=1 is:");
System.out.println(y);


// Computation by closed form solution.
// Print out the result that we get.
System.out.println();
System.out.println("The value really is:");
y = (Math.exp(0.5) - Math.exp(-0.5)) / 2;
System.out.println(y);
  }
 }
```

Note that it is easy to extend this method for vector differential equations. If y is vector-valued and x is still a scalar, then the derivative will also be vector-valued, so k_1, k_2, k_3 and k_4 all become vectors and the algorithm works exactly as before. Section 11.3 uses Runge–Kutta in this context.

It is also possible to construct **adaptive** versions of the Runge–Kutta method which automatically select an appropriate step size for the given integration. The **Runge–Kutta–Fehlberg method** is the most widely used adaptive method. Discussion of the actual algorithm, however, is beyond the scope of this book.

9.3.6 Least squares fits

The method of finding a least squares fit is commonly used in analysis of data. Consider a situation in which we have n pairs of readings (x_i, y_i) of two quantities and we suspect that the values of the two quantities are linked. We think that they are linearly related, so we wish to fit our data to a relationship of the form

$$y_i = ax_i + b$$

where a and b are to be determined. However, because we are using actual readings from experiments, we do not expect the fit to be exact. If we assume that measurements of the x_i are exact and that those of y_i are subject to normally distributed errors of variance σ^2, so $y_i \sim N(ax_i + b, \sigma^2)$, then we find that the maximum likelihood estimators for a and b are

$$\hat{a} = \frac{S_{xy}}{S_{xx}}$$
$$\hat{b} = \bar{y} - \hat{a}\bar{x}$$

where

$$\bar{x} = \frac{\sum_i x_i}{n}$$
$$\bar{y} = \frac{\sum_i y_i}{n}$$
$$S_{xx} = \sum_i (x_i - \bar{x})^2$$
$$S_{xy} = \sum_i (x_i - \bar{x})(y_i - \bar{y})$$

These maximum likelihood estimators minimize the sum over all points of the squares of the differences between the observed values of y_i and those predicted from the values of x_i.

The following program, which is available at http://www.jscieng.co.uk/ Code/NumComp/Squares/, implements this method to fit a line to some data.

```
public class Squares
{
  // The data to be fitted.
  public static final int N = 6;
  public static final double[] X =
    { 0.1, 3.7, 4.2, 6.3, 8.7, 9.8 };
  public static final double[] Y =
    { 6.0, 7.0, 7.2, 8.0, 9.3, 9.4 };


  // The 'main' method actually implements
  // the least squares fit.
  public static void main(String[] argv)
  {
```

```java
    int i;

    // Compute averages.
    double xbar = 0;
    for (i=0; i<N; i++)
      xbar += X[i];
    xbar /= N;

    double ybar = 0;
    for (i=0; i<N; i++)
      ybar += Y[i];
    ybar /= N;

    // Compute Sxx and Syy
    double Sxx = 0;
    for (i=0; i<N; i++)
      Sxx += (X[i] - xbar) * (X[i] - xbar);

    double Sxy = 0;
    for (i=0; i<N; i++)
      Sxy += (X[i] - xbar) * (Y[i] - ybar);

    // Hence find maximum likelihood
    // estimators.
    double a = Sxy / Sxx;
    double b = ybar - a * xbar;

    // Finally output some data about the fit.
    System.out.println("Line of best fit: y = "
                        + a + " * x + " + b);

    for (i=0; i<N; i++)
      System.out.println("At x = " + X[i]
                          + " would expect "
                          + (a * X[i] + b)
                          + " and measured "
                          + Y[i]);
  }
}
```

It is possible to extend this method to fit data to more complicated formulae, including those in which there are several variables per reading or in which we suspect a non-linear relationship between the variables.

WHERE TO GO FROM HERE

This chapter has been only an introduction to the issues of numerical computation and the standard algorithms used. If you are interested in this field, then the *Numerical Recipes* series of books are a popular source of numerical algorithms. At the time of writing (August 1998) versions are available for Fortran, C and Pascal. Unfortunately, a Java version is not yet available for this or any other popular text. Nevertheless, the *Numerical Recipes* books are accessible to the Java programmer since all algorithms are explained in detail before example programs are written. We would recommend *Numerical Recipes in C* (Press, Flannery, Teukolsky and Vetterling, 1988) since the two languages are similar enough that you will be able to understand most of the example code.

Programming practices

10.1   Introduction

This chapter is a brief introduction to some important ideas from computer science and software engineering. The first half draws on computer science to discuss what makes some algorithms better than others from that viewpoint and to give a few examples of standard algorithms. The second half moves on to software engineering to discuss how one should write large programs in a manner which makes them more likely to work and easier to maintain. The discussions will probably be at a suitable level only if you have not encountered these subjects before.

The sample code in this chapter assumes knowledge of Chapter 4 and of Section 5.2. All sample code is available from the website at `http://www.jscieng.co.uk/Code/ProgPrac/`.

10.2   Algorithmics

10.2.1   Order of execution

When we are comparing two algorithms which achieve the same task, we are inevitably forced to make a decision about which algorithm is better. There are several grounds on which we might make this decision. In the previous chapter, we discussed some of the issues determining the numerical accuracy of the results produced. Alternatively, we might find that our programming time is the constraining factor – we just want to produce something that works, and to do so as fast as possible. From a computer science viewpoint, the most important issue is that of the efficiency of the algorithms: we compare programs which satisfy our other criteria on the basis of their speed.

We could measure speed directly in terms of the time taken to run the program on given input data. A better alternative is to count the number of operations (for example, the number of additions, subtractions, multiplications and divisions) that are performed.

Table 10.1 Numbers of operations for two algorithms.

n	Operations for $100n$ version	Operations for $4n^2$ version
1	100	4
10	1 000	400
100	10 000	40 000
1 000	100 000	4 000 000
10 000	1 000 000	400 000 000

However, either of these approaches will only tell us about the behaviour of the algorithms in a specific case. A more useful piece of knowledge is how the number of operations is related to the size of the problem – one algorithm might be better than another for small problems but dramatically worse for larger ones.

The 'size of a problem' is rather hard to define in general. However, in many of the cases which matter, the correct measurement is clear. For example, if we are sorting a list then we want to know how the number of operations to sort it depends on the length of the list. If we are modelling heat flows in a metal object by considering a grid of points covering the object, each with an associated temperature, then we want to know what effect increasing the number of points in the grid will have. In both cases it is clear that we want to be able to solve the 'largest' problems that we can (sort the longest lists, simulate using the most points) and need an algorithm whose number of operations grows as slowly as possible as the size of the problem increases.

Consider the following program fragments, which use an array a:

```
// Iterate over all elements
for (int i=0; i<a.length; i++)
  <do something to the ith element>

// Iterate over all pairs of elements
for (int i=0; i<a.length; i++)
  for (int j=0; j<a.length; j++)
    <do something with the pair i,j>
```

In the first fragment, we iterate over the elements of the array. Hence, if there are n elements and each iteration takes 100 operations then the total number of operations is $100n$. In the second fragment, we iterate over every pair of elements. Because we perform two loops, one inside the other, if there are n elements and each iteration takes four operations then the total number of operations will be $4n^2$.

Next, imagine that the two fragments implemented different algorithms which carried out the same task. We have to decide which we will choose to use. Table 10.1 shows the total number of operations that each algorithm takes for varying values of n.

As we can see from the table, the first algorithm takes more operations for small values of n, whilst the second slows down more rapidly, and so takes more operations for larger values of n. The constants 100 and 4 were not significant for large values of n: the fact that the second algorithm took a number of operations proportional to n^2, whilst the first was linear in n, meant that the second was guaranteed to be slower for large arrays.

As we mentioned earlier, we are assuming that we wish to solve the largest problems that we can. This means that only the behaviour of the algorithms for large n is significant. Since the constant factors do not affect this, we omit them, and use the 'big-O' notation to say that the **order of execution** of the first algorithm was $O(n)$, whilst that of the second was $O(n^2)$.

We have now defined the fundamental measure against which algorithms are judged by computer scientists. An algorithm with a smaller order of execution is considered superior. Note that we can measure aspects other than an algorithm's usage of operations in this manner – we could also measure the use of data storage, for example, and would find that some algorithms require $O(n)$ storage during their computations, whereas some require $O(n^2)$ or more.

To emphasize how important orders of executions are, we consider the case of Fourier transforms. A Fourier transform expresses a function as a sum of sine waves representing the function's fundamental frequencies. Until the 1960s, the only well-known algorithm for computing Fourier transforms was $O(n^2)$ in the number of sample points on the function. A typical data set to be transformed could contain as many as a million points and this algorithm was so slow that transforms were little used. A better algorithm, the Fast Fourier Transform (FFT), was invented in the 1960s and achieved $O(n \log n)$ with a similar multiplicative constant. This algorithm is over 10 000 times faster for a data set of one million points, and suddenly made Fourier transforms practical to perform. They are now widely used in numerical work and are part of the fastest methods for a surprisingly wide range of problems.

There is an extensive theory of orders of execution. An algorithm may have different orders for best-case, worst-case and average-case input. We can also consider the actual problem and can sometimes produce a theoretical lower bound, below which no algorithm will be able to perform correctly. We can then discover whether the algorithm that we have is in fact optimal or if the potential for improvement still exists. In addition, as well as polynomial orders, such as $O(n^{3/2})$ and $O(n^7)$, there are algorithms with orders of execution such as $O(2^n)$ or $O(n^n)$. Just as higher polynomial powers are worse, so exponential expressions such as these are worse than any polynomial expression.

10.2.2 Examples

The discussion in the previous section was somewhat abstract, so we now turn to a number of small examples to demonstrate how orders of execution work. First of all, let us consider evaluating a polynomial,

$$P(x) = a_n x^n + a_{n-1} x^{n-1} + \ldots + a_1 x + a_0$$

If we assume that the a_i are stored in an array a then the naive way to evaluate the polynomial would be as follows:

```java
public static double power(double x, int n)
{
  double res = 1;

  for (int i=0; i<n; i++)
    res *= x;
```

```
      return res;
    }


public static double P(double x)
{
    double res = 0;

    for (int i=0; i<a.length; i++)
    {
        res += a[i] * power(x, i);
    }

    return res;
}
```

Note that this is an $O(n^2)$ algorithm. This fact is slightly obscured by the fact that power is a separate method, but nevertheless power is $O(n)$ and is itself called n times. This example demonstrates how easy it is to make mistakes during design – a much better algorithm for evaluating polynomials is Horner's method, which is implemented below:

```
public static double P(double x)
{
    double res=a[a.length-1];

    for (int i=a.length-2; i>=0; i--)
    {
        res *= x;
        res += a[i];
    }
}
```

This version is $O(n)$. You can even use it for evaluating fixed polynomials that are written out in full:

```
p = 15*x*x*x + 4*x*x + 2*x + 1;
```

becomes

```
p = ((15*x + 4)*x + 2)*x + 1;
```

which saves three multiplications.

As a second example, let us consider the factorial function. We can implement this directly with

```
public static double fact(int i)
{
    if (i>1)
        return i * fact(i-1);
    else
        return 1;
}
```

This method is said to be **recursive** – that is, it reduces the problem to an easier sub-problem and then calls itself to solve that subproblem. The method seems reasonable – it is $O(n)$ in terms of number of operations carried out, which is the minimum that we expect to achieve given the definition of factorial.

When we look more carefully, we see that this method is in fact $O(n)$ in memory usage as well. Each time we call a method, storage is allocated for its local variables. When a recursive method calls itself, this also happens – the different copies of the method may have different states at any given point, so they each need their own storage for local variables. The method `fact` does have a local variable, `i`. We have written the method in such a way that it calls itself repeatedly in a sequence n deep during calculation of $n!$. As a result, storage locations are needed for n copies of `i` and the memory usage is $O(n)$.

We can rewrite exactly the same program in **iterative** (non-recursive) form as follows:

```
public static double fact(int i)
{
    double ans = 1;

    while (i>1)
    {
        ans *= i;
        i--;
    }

    return ans;
}
```

This form is also $O(n)$ in operations but is $O(1)$ in storage – which means that it uses a constant amount of storage. This is preferable by far. In general, iteration and recursion have the relative behaviours that we have shown here: the same algorithm can be implemented in both ways, using the same number of operations, but the iterative form will be more efficient in terms of storage whilst the recursive form will often be easier to understand. The iterative form will often need extra variables, such as `ans` in the above.

10.2.3 Searching

Searching through an ordered data set to find a specific value is a classic problem in computer science. If we consider a set of n elements, then it is clear that we require at most $O(n)$ comparisons to find an element – this would enable us to check every element, one by one. We can also see that $O(\log n)$ is a lower bound on the number of comparisons needed: each comparison that we perform could show that the required element was either before or after the element that we have inspected. Therefore, at best it is possible to arrange m comparisons so that they are strictly independent and we obtain 2^m possible overall results. Hence, we cannot guarantee to find an element in a data set larger than 2^m using m comparisons. If $n = 2^m$ then $m = \log_2 n$, so the order of execution is logarithmic at best.

10.2.4 Example – binary search

Binary search is a simple algorithm which searches a sorted array using $O(\log n)$ comparisons. We proceed by dividing the area of the array that remains to be searched in half at each step. To do so, we compare the value to be found with the element in the middle of the area remaining. The result tells us on which side of that element our value would be found and so tells us which half of the area previously remaining to be searched we will find it in.

The following program implements binary search on an array. It is available at `http://www.jscieng.co.uk/Code/ProgPrac/Search/`. It uses some text input facilities from the standard libraries, which are explained in Section 5.8. These are not essential to the understanding of this program, and can be safely ignored.

```java
import java.io.*;

public class Search
{
  // The array to be searched.
  public static final int[] data
            = { 2, 7, 17, 32,
                  45, 76, 98, 101,
                  121, 143, 155, 187,
                  201, 257, 312, 345 };

  // A means of getting user input.
  // See Section 5.8 for details.
  // JDK 1.1 or later.
  public static final BufferedReader b
    = new BufferedReader(
        new InputStreamReader(System.in));


  // The 'main' method actually implements
  // binary search.
  public static void main(String[] argv)
            throws IOException
  {
    // The start and end of the area remaining
    // to be searched. The start point is
    // included, the end point is not.
    int startrem = 0;
    int endrem = 16;

    // Ask the user for a value to find
    System.out.println("Input a value to find");
    String s = b.readLine();

    int val = Integer.parseInt(s);

    // Perform binary search
```

```
while (endrem > startrem + 1)
{
  int mid = (startrem + endrem)/2;

  if (data[mid] > val)
    endrem = mid;
  else
    startrem = mid;
}

if (data[startrem] == val)
  System.out.println("Data was found");
else
  System.out.println("Data was not found");
  }
}
```

10.2.5 Sorting

Sorting a list of numbers is another classic problem. However, it is rather more difficult and there are many algorithms in standard use. We start by considering the order of execution that we might expect from an algorithm.

When we sort a list of n objects, we are effectively deciding what order they are currently in and then placing them in the correct order. Reordering the objects once we know where to put them is an $O(n)$ operation, since we can just copy each object into the correct place in a new array. We now only need to consider the issue of finding out which order they are originally in. There are $n!$ possible orderings for n objects, and the question of finding out which of these they are in is equivalent to searching the set of $n!$ permutations to find out which of these it is.

As we discussed in the previous subsection, searching a set of $n!$ objects takes $O(\log n!)$ operations. By Stirling's formula, this is approximated by $O(n \log n)$. Since this order of execution is higher than the $O(n)$ for the process of putting the elements into order once we know how they are permuted, the overall order of execution is also $O(n \log n)$ at best.

As we mentioned earlier, there are many algorithms for sorting. The simplest, **bubblesort**, is an $O(n^2)$ algorithm. This has led many people to suggest that it should not even be taught in order to protect programmers from the temptation of using it! We follow that policy in this book.

Of the remaining algorithms, **quicksort** is acknowledged to be one of the best and is implemented in many libraries. However, it is hard to explain and, although its average-case order of execution is $O(n \log n)$ with a very low constant, it has a worst-case order of execution of $O(n^2)$. As a result, we choose mergesort, which is usually considered to be inferior, as our worked example.

10.2.6 Example – mergesort

Mergesort is a sorting algorithm which is $O(n \log n)$ in all circumstances. It is probably the easiest of the $O(n \log n)$ algorithms to understand but has the drawback that it involves the allocation of more temporary storage than other algorithms.

To understand mergesort, consider merging two sorted lists to form a single sorted list of twice the length. This is an easy $O(n)$ process: at each stage we compare the elements at the heads of the two input lists, select that which is lower, remove it from its list and write it to the end of the output list.

Next, we consider performing such merging actions repeatedly. We start with n lists, each containing one element. Next, we merge these in pairs to give $n/2$ lists, each containing two elements. We repeatedly merge in pairs until we have a single list of length n. Since we double the size of our lists at each stage, it takes $O(\log n)$ merging cycles to obtain a single list. As discussed above, each merging cycle takes $O(n)$ operations, so mergesort takes $O(n \log n)$ operations in all.

The following program implements mergesort on an array. It is available at http://www.jscieng.co.uk/Code/ProgPrac/Mergesort/.

```java
public class Mergesort
{
    // The 'mergesort' method performs mergesort.
    // It calls itself recursively to sort the
    // subarrays.
    public static int[] mergesort(int[] data)
    {
        if (data.length == 1)
        {
            // If there's only one item then
            // it's already sorted.
            return data;
        }
        else
        {
            // Create two subarrays
            int halflen = data.length/2;

            int[] done = new int[halflen];
            int[] dtwo = new int[data.length - halflen];

            // Copy the data into them
            for (int i=0; i<halflen; i++)
                done[i] = data[i];

            for (int i=halflen; i<data.length; i++)
                dtwo[i-halflen] = data[i];

            // Mergesort the subarrays
            done = mergesort(done);
            dtwo = mergesort(dtwo);
```

```
// Create an array to return
int[] ans = new int[data.length];

// Merge the subarrays into it
int pone = 0;
int ptwo = 0;
int pans = 0;

// Repeat until we've transferred all data.
while (pans < data.length)
{
  if (pone < done.length)
  {
    if (ptwo < dtwo.length)
    {
      // If there's data in both arrays,
      // then transfer the lower head
      // to the output list
      if (done[pone] < dtwo[ptwo])
      {
        ans[pans] = done[pone];
        pone++;
      }
      else
      {
        ans[pans] = dtwo[ptwo];
        ptwo++;
      }
    }
    else
    {
      // If there's only data in the first
      // subarray then copy that.
      ans[pans] = done[pone];
      pone++;
    }
  }
  else
  {
    // If there's only data in the second
    // subarray then copy that.
    ans[pans] = dtwo[ptwo];
    ptwo++;
  }

  pans++;
}

// return the sorted array.
return ans;
```

```
      }
   }


   // The 'main' method actually
   // generates a random array and sorts it.
   public static void main(String[] argv)
   {
     // Pick a size for the array and create it.
     int size = (int) (100 * Math.random());
     int[] data = new int[size];

     // Fill it with elements.
     int i;
     for (i=0; i<size; i++)
       data[i] = (int) (1000 * Math.random());

     // Sort it.
     data = mergesort(data);

     // Print the sorted data.
     for (i=0; i<size; i++)
       System.out.println(data[i]);
   }
}
```

10.3 Software engineering

An engineering discipline concerns itself with the applications of an area of science. This means that engineers understand key scientific results but are concerned with successful application of these rather than extending the results themselves.

As an example, physicists can explain the principles behind a suspension bridge or a hydroelectric dam and can perform the computations needed during design. However, we turn to civil engineers rather than physicists to carry out such projects and to do so within a fixed schedule, providing given safety margins and using fixed resources. Similarly a chemist can choose suitable reagents and conditions for the production of polymers, but a chemical engineer designs the plant in which the reactions will take place.

Software engineering is the discipline that seeks to apply computer science to real-world projects and to produce useful results. A software engineer uses algorithms and techniques invented by computer scientists and puts these together to produce a specific computer system for a client subject to a completion date and a budget.

There may be stricter requirements as well as those of time and money. For example, when we consider **safety-critical** applications, such as aircraft fly-by-wire systems or nuclear reactor control systems, we need to develop methods for designing the system to ensure very high levels of reliability. We also need testing procedures which are capable of ensuring that these levels are met and may want to use formal methods to prove the correctness of parts of our program. Software engineering also tackles these problems.

Compared to the other engineering disciplines which we have mentioned, software engineering is immature. This is demonstrated every time a major software project runs over budget and over schedule. In fact, many large projects still fail completely. Nevertheless, over the 30 years in which software engineering has existed as a discipline many valuable lessons have been learnt.

The remainder of this chapter introduces some of the most basic of these lessons. It is useful both as an introduction to software engineering for those who hope to continue in it, and also for other programmers, who should find that these ideas help them to write programs that are more reliable and easier to maintain.

10.3.1 The design cycle

When a single programmer writes a short program which only they will use, there is no obvious need for any formal process. In general, the programmer knows what they want their program to achieve, can create a sensible structure as they write and will produce a program which they understand and can use to produce the desired results.

For larger projects, this kind of process does not work. Consider a software product that is being produced for a client in a different company. The software company has a team of programmers working on the project, over a time scale which may be measured in years. In such circumstances, all of the administration which was previously carried out inside a single programmer's head must now be made explicit.

For example, only the client actually knows what they need the system to do. This information must be recorded unambiguously in such a way that the programming team, who may not understand the client's business, will still be able to produce a system to satisfy these needs. Similarly, the members of the programming teams will not each be able to read all of the code that the others write. At any point, a specific programmer may be writing code that calls methods which a different programmer wrote (or even will write!). As a result, a formal design is needed, so that each programmer can refer to this and understand in overview how each portion of code that they write should behave and how the methods which they call will operate. Finally, once the product is complete, the client will need documentation to explain how it is to be used.

In fact, these techniques are applicable not only to large projects. Anyone who has done a sufficient amount of programming will remember looking back at old pieces of code and trying to work out what they do, how they do it and why that algorithm was chosen. Clearly documentation of some kind would be useful.

We now provide a brief overview of the **waterfall model** of the software development process. This was one of the first to be proposed, and is based on engineering practice in other disciplines. It is now thought to be inadequate in several respects, but it is nevertheless a sensible first approximation for a process and is the basis of the models used by most large companies. The waterfall model is illustrated in Figure 10.1. Note how each stage 'flows over' into the next, giving rise to the model's name.

The stages are as follows:

- **Definition:** The client is consulted and a formal specification agreed for the tasks

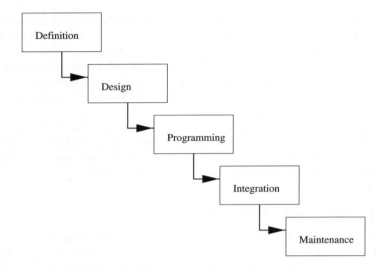

Figure 10.1   The waterfall model.

that should be accomplished by the product. This specification must be sufficiently detailed that the product design can be completed without further discussion and should cover issues such as the schedule, costs and hardware required to run the product. Internal deadlines are set for each of the subsequent stages.

- **Design:** The specification from the previous stage is turned into a design. This design gives an overview of the product's structure, and may go as far as specifying every method in the product, together with which arguments it takes and what it returns.

- **Programming:** Source code is produced, implementing the design. Following this, **unit testing** is performed – this is testing of individual methods and classes, possibly using additional code written specifically for testing purposes.

- **Integration:** The source code is finally all compiled into a single program. This is very different from the way that a typical amateur programmer works: the complete source code has been written before it is run for the first time as opposed to starting with a small program and gradually adding features. Following this, **system testing** is performed to verify that the units work together correctly.

- **Maintenance:** After the client has taken delivery of the product, any bugs that they find are corrected. This may require iterating through several of the previous phases. For instance, a bug may be caused by the design, in which case we will need to repeat the last three stages after fixing it. The development team should have a range of **regression tests** which check that any bug fix does not break other existing features and these should be run before every upgrade is delivered.

In practice, these stages overlap to a greater degree than is shown here. Nevertheless, these are worthy distinctions to aim for. We now discuss some of the important issues at each stage.

The major problem in the definition stage is discovering exactly what it is that the client wants. It is important to remember that the client will not be an expert on computer technology, and may not be able to formulate their needs in technical terms or even know what is possible. A very common problem is that the client adds requirements at a late stage, after the design is complete. Unfortunately, design decisions often make certain changes very hard to carry out at a late stage and many projects fail or are delayed due to this.

It pays to have a firm specification as early as possible. For some projects it is worth writing a demonstration system at the definition stage to show the client exactly how the product will behave. This demonstration should illustrate behaviour, but does not need to carry out any significant processing internally. Do not be tempted to modify the demonstration into the final product – design decisions in the demonstration system were taken to minimize effort, not to produce the best product.

Design can be carried out from several viewpoints. Two standard approaches are **top-down design** and **data-centric design**. In a top-down approach, we start by considering the task to be performed by a program. We produce a strategy for handling this which splits the large task into two or more smaller ones. Next, we repeat, splitting each smaller task into even smaller ones. After sufficiently many iterations, each of the tasks remaining is small enough to be implemented as a single method. By working our way back up the tree into which the tasks have been split we can see how to write control methods which call the basic methods to perform their tasks, then write methods calling the control methods to perform their larger tasks and so on.

Data-centric design starts by considering the data structures needed and the kinds of actions that we will want to perform on these. This fits in well with the concept of object orientation – we start by defining the classes that will be used to store data and deciding which methods they should have. Finally we carry out a top-down design for the actions that the program will need to perform, using our pre-existing knowledge of how the data is presented.

Regardless of which approach you use to design your product, it may be worth writing some sample code at the design stage to clarify technical issues before the approach that will be taken is fixed. In the most extreme case, it may be worth writing a complete first system to throw away before starting work on the real product.

The processes of programming, integration and maintenance are rather better understood by amateur programmers, so there is less to say about them at this point. However, there are still two important points to be made.

Firstly, there is the issue of documentation of code. A good design serves as a useful first level of documentation since it will outline the flow of data around the program and should allow a reader to move straight to the appropriate area of code for any specific task. However, it is equally important that the code itself should contain documentation in the form of comments. From a software engineering viewpoint, comments should be sufficient to allow a new programmer to take over maintenance of any section of the code without requiring additional explanations from its original author. For programmers working alone a similar level of documentation is useful – you will find it very hard to remember how your code worked when you look back on it after an absence of a year or more.

I suggest documenting code with comments before every method outlining its action and the meaning of the parameters and return value. You should also include additional comments at difficult points within each method. `javadoc` is a very useful tool in this respect. It allows you to write documentation alongside your code and then to generate documentation web pages from these files. This implements the concept of **literate programming** – that documentation embedded in code is much more likely to be kept up to date when the code changes than documentation stored in separate files. Refer to Section 4.4.4 for more information.

Secondly, it is important not to underestimate the time that will be taken during design and during the testing and debugging stages. Of course, testing and debugging come at the end of product development, so it is very tempting to absorb any scheduling slips earlier in the project by reducing the time available at this stage. Do not fall into this trap! Projects may well require a third of the total time or more for proper debugging (safety-critical systems will require more).

10.3.2 Modularization

An important issue that we have not discussed to date is how several people can work simultaneously on the same software product. Unlike other industries, it is fundamentally the case that allocating more people to work on a software product will not produce a proportional increase in speed of delivery. Adding each additional person causes communication overheads to increase, partially negating the work that the additional person can do. This situation is depicted in Figure 10.2.

Note how as the number of programmers increases the rate of code production starts to lag behind the expected value. The situation is even worse if additional programmers are added part way through a project – this situation is the subject of *The Mythical Man-Month* (Brooks, 1975).

In order to minimize the effects described above, we need to split projects into parts which are as cleanly separated from each other as possible. Each part can then be implemented independently of the others with little consultation between the programmers. This technique is called **modularization**. It is equally applicable to projects with a single programmer – clean divisions between different parts of your code allow you to understand a program much better than if the code is interlinked in a complicated manner.

We aim to achieve modularity during the design stage of a product. We carry out the design as stated earlier, but keep a lookout for areas (**modules**) of the program that can be largely separated from the remainder, leaving just a small number of methods in each part that the other uses. If we can find such modules, then, after we have defined the arguments, return values and actions of these few methods, the program has effectively been split into two.

Design, programming and unit testing of each module may continue, unaffected by progress in the other. For instance, one module could be fully coded and tested at a point when another was not even fully designed – as long as the second module contained the specified methods when it was complete, the first module would be guaranteed to work correctly with it. In fact, not only is this possible, but the design and programming of modules should be carried out as independently as possible to ensure that the modules do not use methods from each other apart from those specified in the design.

Modularity brings many other benefits. For example, consider a project in which it

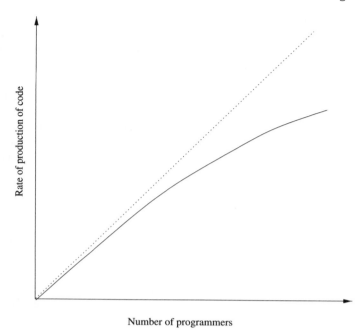

Figure 10.2 Rate of production of code versus number of programmers.

is discovered that one module's code is too slow. When we created this module, we defined which of its methods are provided to external modules. The result is that we can redesign the slow module from scratch, possibly with a totally different internal structure and using different algorithms. As long as we provide the same methods for external modules, the program as a whole is guaranteed to work.

10.3.3 Object orientation

As you will have realized, an object oriented programming style is ideal for implementing a modular design.

In a Java program, we can define separate packages for each of our modules. Next, we can define `public` classes which contain `public` methods as the interface visible to external modules. If we define other methods and classes at the default level of access control or below, then we actually prohibit code outside our module from using them – any attempt to do so will be stopped by the compiler. This is very useful since it eliminates the possibility that we will inadvertently write code violating the divisions between modules that we have defined.

Object orientation offers other useful features for modularizing programs. In earlier chapters, we have indicated that data stored in objects should be declared as `protected` or `private` and that access to it should be provided to external code through **accessor methods**. This practice allows us to modularize data structures more fully than would otherwise be the case: if external code cannot access data directly then even the format in which data is stored can be changed without causing problems if we provide the same set of accessor methods. This practice can be seen in action in the JNL: the matrix decomposition classes do not allow direct access to the parts of the factorization that they compute.

We can also use inheritance to our advantage: if we define an `abstract` base class or an `interface` then we are effectively defining a module – we list the methods that it will support. However, inheritance allows us to produce a variety of different implementations of the module, each of which `extends` the base class. Code external to the module will work unchanged with any of these implementations and we can even alternate between them at different points during the execution of a program.

WHERE TO GO FROM HERE

This chapter has been an introduction to ideas from computer science and software engineering. If you are interested in the issues of algorithmic order of execution that we raised, and would like to find out more about the theory behind this, then I would recommend *Algorithmics: The Spirit of Computing* (Harel, 1992) as an introductory text. For those interested in more examples of algorithms from computer science, I recommend *The Art of Computer Programming* (Knuth, 1981), a multi-volume work which devotes an entire volume to algorithms for searching and sorting!

Software engineering is also a large field, of which I have barely skimmed the surface. *Software Engineering* (Sommerville, 1995) is one of the many textbooks in this field, whilst *Object Solutions: Managing the Object-Oriented Project* (Booch, 1996) is a more specific work. I can also recommend *The Mythical Man-Month* (Brooks, 1975), which is a classic collection of essays on the author's experience at IBM, managing the System/360 project in the 1960s.

Physical modelling

11.1 Introduction

This chapter contains a number of example programs, each of which is somewhat larger than those covered in the remainder of the book. We use these examples to discuss a range of techniques for using numerical computations to model the physical world.

The examples in this chapter use graphics to display their output. Because of this, we assume knowledge of Chapter 7 and of all prerequisites for that chapter. All sample code is available from the website at `http://www.jscieng.co.uk/Code/PhyMod/`.

11.2 Discretization

When simulating the real world, we are faced with the problem that most of the quantities which we want to simulate vary continuously. For instance, if we wish to simulate the deformation of a beam when a load is applied to it, then we have a situation in which variables such as pressure, tension and position vary continuously throughout the body of the beam. In addition, if the system is not in equilibrium, then all of these quantities also vary over time.

One of the simplest methods of producing a computer model of such a system is to discretize the problem – we split some of the continuous variables into a number of discrete steps. For instance, in the case of the beam deforming under a load, we consider the beam as consisting of a large number of small pieces of metal. Each individual piece is given a position and each piece exerts forces on its neighbours.

Once this simplification has been made, we can apply Newton's laws of motion directly to the pieces. Each experiences forces from its neighbours and moves as a result. If we run such a simulation over a period of time then the results show the pieces hanging together as a coherent beam, being pulled away from each other where the beam is under tension and pushed together where it is under compression.

Note that we also discretize time in the construction of such models – we tend to operate in terms of small steps in time, computing the forces and velocities of each component before a step, moving it to take account of the step and then recomputing forces for the subsequent step.

When using models which simulate a parameter using discrete steps, you should bear in mind the issue of balancing rounding errors, discretization errors and a program's execution time which we discussed in Chapter 9.

 ## 11.3 Example – planetary motion

Our first example is a simulation of the three-body system of the Sun, Jupiter and a small asteroid moving in a plane. For such a system, the governing equations are Newton's laws of motion together with the formula

$$\mathbf{F} = \frac{Gm_1 m_2 \mathbf{d}}{d^3}$$

for the gravitational attraction felt by a body of mass m_1 from another body of mass m_2 at a relative displacement $\mathbf{d}$.

The current state of the system can be described by the positions and velocities of all three bodies. Given this information, we can compute the forces and therefore the accelerations of all of the bodies, so the problem reduces to integrating the differential equation for position over time.

At this point, the discretization that we will be required to perform becomes clear – we do not need to represent points in space by discrete variables, but will need to integrate numerically using a finite time step, and so are effectively discretizing time.

We now turn to the method that we will use to perform the integration. It turns out that the equations of planetary motion require integration by a method with a high degree of accuracy. If we use a low-order method then planets move in spirals, not closed orbits. We use the fourth-order Runge–Kutta method that we discussed in Section 9.3.5. Integration by Runge–Kutta requires a formulation in which there is a single (possibly vector-valued) variable to be integrated and its derivative can be computed at any point.

For our model, this means that we should not try to compute the behaviour of each body individually. Instead, we store the state of the entire system as a single vector, containing 12 entries. These 12 entries consist of six pairs of coordinates in the plane: the Sun's position, the Sun's velocity, Jupiter's position, Jupiter's velocity, the asteroid's position and the asteroid's velocity. We do not attempt to work in a centre of mass frame or keep any particular position constant. Given such a vector, we can compute all of the forces on all of the bodies and hence generate a derivative vector, again containing 12 elements in the form of pairs of coordinates in the plane: the Sun's velocity, the Sun's acceleration, Jupiter's velocity, Jupiter's acceleration, the asteroid's velocity and the asteroid's acceleration. This means that we have a single vector-valued variable to integrate, and so can use Runge–Kutta.

The discussion so far describes the system that we are modelling and the algorithm which we use to model it. The program performs one additional set of computations. The system which we are describing is a restricted form of the three-body problem (which has no exact analytical solution in general). We have restricted it to two heavy bodies with gravitational effects both on each other and on the asteroid. The asteroid itself is much smaller and has no significant gravitational effects on the other two bodies. This system can be solved exactly. Lagrange showed that, when the heavier bodies' masses are in the ratio 25:1 or more, there are stable positions for the asteroid. These **Lagrange points** are on the orbit of Jupiter, one sixth of the orbit either side of the planet. Observations have shown that these points are indeed marked by clusters called the **Trojan asteroids**.

Our model is sufficiently accurate to display this behaviour and, in the program that follows, we perform some extra computations to make it more obvious. Instead of displaying all three bodies as moving, before displaying their positions we perform a transformation so that the Sun is stationary at the origin and Jupiter is stationary on the positive x-axis. In this rotating coordinate frame we can see the asteroid oscillating about the stable Lagrange point.

The following program implements the simulation discussed above. It is available at http://www.jscieng.co.uk/Code/PhyMod/Trojan/. The statistics for the Sun and Jupiter are adapted from *The Greenwich Guide to the Planets* (Malin, 1987).

```java
import uk.co.jscieng.*;
import java.awt.*;

public class Trojan
{
    // Statistics concerning the Sun's orbit.
    public static final double SUNMASS = 1.99e30;

    // Statistics concerning Jupiter's orbit.
    public static final double JUPMASS = 1.90e27;
    public static final double JUPDIST = 7.78e11;
    public static final double JUPPERIOD = 3.74e8;
    public static final double JUPSPEED =
        2 * Math.PI * JUPDIST / JUPPERIOD;

    // The initial data for the asteroid.
    public static final double TRJMASS = 6.4e10;
    public static final double TRJANGLE = -1.0;
    public static final double TRJDIST = 8.2e11;
    public static final double TRJPERIOD = 4.2e8;
    public static final double TRJSPEED =
        2 * Math.PI * TRJDIST / TRJPERIOD;

    // The constant for gravitational attraction
    public static final double G = 6.67e-11;

    // The size of the steps in our integration
    public static final double STEP = 1e6;

    // The length of the trails that we leave
    // to indicate the asteroid's motion.
```

```java
public static final int HISTORY = 1000;


// Utility method to add two vectors. Do not
// use JNL, we cannot assume this knowledge.
public static double[] add(double[] a, double[] b)
{
  double[] c = new double[a.length];

  for (int i=0; i<a.length; i++)
    c[i] = a[i] + b[i];

  return c;
}


// Utility method to multiply a vector
// by a scalar. Do not use JNL, we cannot assume
// this knowledge.
public static double[] mult(double[] a, double b)
{
  double[] c = new double[a.length];

  for (int i=0; i<a.length; i++)
    c[i] = a[i] * b;

  return c;
}


// Computation of gravitational force on body a
// from body b. Body a is at (ax,ay) and has mass
// am. Body b is at (bx,by) and has mass bm.
public static double[] force(double ax, double ay,
                             double am,
                             double bx, double by,
                             double bm)
{
  // Calculate the displacement, its magnitude
  // squared and magnitude.
  double dispx = bx - ax;
  double dispy = by - ay;
  double dsqr = dispx*dispx + dispy*dispy;
  double d = Math.sqrt(dsqr);

  // Calculate the scalar size of the force.
  double fmag = G * am * bm / dsqr;

  // Create a vector of this size pointing
  // from body a to b.
```

```
        double[] f = { dispx * fmag / d,
                       dispy * fmag / d };

        return f;
}


// Compute the derivative of the current state of
// the system.
public static double[] deriv(double[] state)
{
    // The force on Jupiter from the Sun.
    double[] fjs = force(state[4], state[5], JUPMASS,
                         state[0], state[1], SUNMASS);

    // The force on the asteroid from the Sun.
    double[] fts = force(state[8], state[9], TRJMASS,
                         state[0], state[1], SUNMASS);

    // The force on the asteroid from Jupiter.
    double[] ftj = force(state[8], state[9], TRJMASS,
                         state[4], state[5], JUPMASS);

    // The derivative of the state. Positions of objects
    // have that object's velocity as their derivative.
    // Velocities have acceleration (calculated from force)
    // as their derivative.
    double[] ans = { // Velocity of the sun.
                     state[2], state[3],
                     // Acceleration of the sun.
                     (-fjs[0] - fts[0])/SUNMASS,
                     (-fjs[1] - fts[1])/SUNMASS,
                     // Velocity of Jupiter.
                     state[6], state[7],
                     // Acceleration of Jupiter.
                     (fjs[0] - ftj[0])/JUPMASS,
                     (fjs[1] - ftj[1])/JUPMASS,
                     // Velocity of the asteroid.
                     state[10], state[11],
                     // Acceleration of the asteroid.
                     (fts[0] + ftj[0])/TRJMASS,
                     (fts[1] + ftj[1])/TRJMASS};
    return ans;
}


// A method to change coordinate systems. Given
// the current state of the system, it returns a
// translated and rotated state in which the Sun
// has been moved to the origin and Jupiter
```

```
                  // rotated on to the x-axis.
                  public static double[] chngcoord(double[] state)
                  {
                    int i;

                    // Create storage to store translated state.
                    double[] tmp = new double[state.length];

                    // Copy all elements across unchanged.
                    // This is only correct for velocities.
                    for (i=0; i<state.length; i++)
                      tmp[i] = state[i];

                    // Then go back and copy positions across again
                    // translating them as we do so.
                    for (i=0; i<state.length; i+=4)
                      tmp[i] = state[i] - state[0];

                    for (i=1; i<state.length; i+=4)
                      tmp[i] = state[i] - state[1];

                    // Create storage for translated and rotated
                    // state.
                    double[] ans = new double[state.length];

                    // Take dot products with position of Jupiter to
                    // get new x-coordinates.
                    for (i=0; i<tmp.length; i+=2)
                      ans[i] = (tmp[i]*tmp[4] + tmp[i+1]*tmp[5])/JUPDIST;

                    // Take dot products with an orthogonal vector to
                    // get new y-coordinates.
                    for (i=1; i<state.length; i+=2)
                      ans[i] = (-tmp[i-1]*tmp[5] + tmp[i]*tmp[4])/JUPDIST;

                    return ans;
                  }


                  // The main method actually performs the integration.
                  public static void main(String[] argv)
                  {
                    // Set up the initial state of the system.
                    double[] state = { // Position of the Sun.
                                       0, 0,
                                       // Velocity of the Sun.
                                       0, 0,
                                       // Position of Jupiter.
                                       JUPDIST, 0,
                                       // Velocity of Jupiter.
```

```
                              0, JUPSPEED,
                              // Position of the asteroid.
                              TRJDIST * Math.cos(TRJANGLE),
                              TRJDIST * Math.sin(TRJANGLE),
                              // Velocity of the asteroid.
                              -TRJSPEED * Math.sin(TRJANGLE),
                              TRJSPEED * Math.cos(TRJANGLE) };

    // Rotate this to nice coordinates.
    double[] statechg = chngcoord(state);

    // Set up the array for storing trails showing
    // motion of asteroid.
    double[][] pastpos = new double[HISTORY][4];
    int i = 0;

    // Show a graphics window of the right size.
    SciGraph.showGraph(-3*JUPDIST, 3*JUPDIST,
                       -3*JUPDIST, 3*JUPDIST);

    // Keep looping until the user stops us.
    while (true)
    {
      // Perform Runge-Kutta integration.
      double[] d = deriv(state);

      double[] k1 = mult(deriv(state), STEP);
      double[] k2 = mult(deriv(add(state, mult(k1, 0.5))),
                         STEP);
      double[] k3 = mult(deriv(add(state, mult(k2, 0.5))),
                         STEP);
      double[] k4 = mult(deriv(add(state, k3)), STEP);

      double[] newstate = add(state,
                 add(mult(k1, 1.0/6),
                   add(mult(k2, 1.0/3),
                     add(mult(k3, 1.0/3), mult(k4, 1.0/6))
                     )
                   )
                 );

      // Rotate the result into nice coordinates.
      double[] newstatechg = chngcoord(newstate);

      // Draw the position of the Sun in yellow.
      SciGraph.line(statechg[0], statechg[1],
                    newstatechg[0], newstatechg[1],
                    Color.yellow);

      // Draw the position of Jupiter in blue.
```

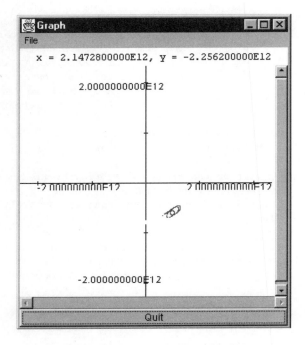

Figure 11.1 Trojan points of Jupiter.

```
SciGraph.line(statechg[4], statechg[5],
              newstatechg[4], newstatechg[5],
              Color.blue);

// Cover the part of the asteroid's trail that
// has expired in white.
SciGraph.line(pastpos[i][0], pastpos[i][1],
              pastpos[i][2], pastpos[i][3],
              Color.white);

// Record the new part of the asteroid's trail
// in its place.
pastpos[i][0] = statechg[8];
pastpos[i][1] = statechg[9];
pastpos[i][2] = newstatechg[8];
pastpos[i][3] = newstatechg[9];

// Draw this new part of the trail in red.
SciGraph.line(pastpos[i][0], pastpos[i][1],
              pastpos[i][2], pastpos[i][3],
              Color.red);

// Update the state of the system.
```

```
        state = newstate;
        statechg = newstatechg;
        i = (i+1) % HISTORY;
      }
    }
  }
```

Figure 11.1 shows the program running under Windows 95. Note how the asteroid moves in small loops about the stable point.

11.4   Example – AC circuit

Our second example of physical modelling is a simulation of an LCR circuit. This does not require any discretization – this topic will be picked up again in the next example – but does introduce an interesting technique. An LCR circuit contains an inductor, a capacitor and a resistor as shown in Figure 11.2.

We can use the theory of complex impedances on this circuit to show that if the input voltage is a sine wave of angular frequency ω (in radians per second) and peak voltage V, then the current that flows is a sine wave of angular frequency ω and peak current V/Z_ω where

$$Z_\omega = \sqrt{R^2 + \left(\omega L - \frac{1}{\omega C}\right)^2}$$

and a different phase from the input wave, lagging it by θ_ω (or leading for negative θ_ω, since $-\pi/2 < \theta_\omega < \pi/2$):

$$\theta_\omega = \tan^{-1}\left(\frac{\omega L - \frac{1}{\omega C}}{R}\right)$$

This behaviour effectively transmits frequencies in a range about $1/\sqrt{LC}$ and blocks all others.

The theory of Fourier series states that any periodic function may be expressed as a countable sum of sines and cosines at integer multiples of the function's period. We consider an input voltage which is a square wave of angular frequency Ω. For this waveform the appropriate result is:

$$V(t) = \frac{4}{\pi}\left(\sin \Omega t + \frac{\sin 3\Omega t}{3} + \frac{\sin 5\Omega t}{5} + \ldots\right) = \begin{cases} 1 & \text{if } 0 < \Omega t < \pi \\ -1 & \text{if } \pi < \Omega t < 2\pi \end{cases}$$

Because the theory of the LCR circuit is linear, we can treat each component of the series as acting independently of the others. As a result, we can apply appropriate scaling factors and phase lags to each of the terms and then add them together to obtain the waveform of the current (and also of the voltage across the resistor):

$$I(t) = \frac{4}{\pi}\left(\frac{\sin(\Omega t - \theta_\Omega)}{Z_\Omega} + \frac{\sin(3\Omega t - \theta_{3\Omega})}{3Z_{3\Omega}} + \frac{\sin(5\Omega t - \theta_{5\Omega})}{5Z_{5\Omega}} + \ldots\right)$$

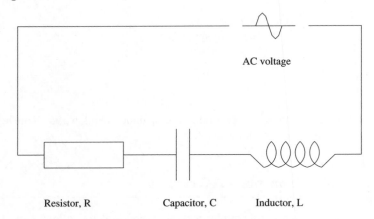

Figure 11.2   The LCR circuit.

This method of splitting a waveform into its component sine waves is of critical importance in further numerical work. As well as Fourier series, there is a more generalized concept of a Fourier transform, which may also be applied to non-periodic functions. The Fast Fourier Transform (FFT) algorithm, which enables Fourier transforms to be computed using available amounts of computer power, is one of the most important discoveries that numerical computation has seen. Unfortunately, it is also beyond the scope of this book, so I can only recommend further reading, such as *Numerical Recipes in C* (Press, Flannery, Teukolsky and Vetterling, 1988).

The following program uses the methods described above to plot graphs of the input and output waveforms for an LCR circuit with a square wave input voltage, given values of L, C, R and Ω. It is available at http://www.jscieng.co.uk/Code/PhyMod/LCR/. Note the use of separate classes implementing the Plottable interface to allow us to pass the functions to be drawn as arguments to functionPlot. This is explained in Section 7.4.4.

```java
import uk.co.jscieng.*;
import java.awt.*;


// The 'Wave' class is a wrapper for the method
// 'f' to allow it to be passed as an argument.
// It implements the initial input waveform.
class Wave implements Plottable
{
    // The frequency of the input waveform.
    public static final double OMEGA = 100.0/3;

    // The order of the term in its Fourier series
    // at which we stop evaluation.
    public static final double TERMMAX = 9;
```

```
  // The square wave itself
  public double f(double x)
  {
    double ans = 0;

    // Evaluate via Fourier series.
    for (int i=1; i<=TERMMAX; i+=2)
      ans += 4 * Math.sin(i*OMEGA*x) / (Math.PI * i);

    return ans;
  }
}


// The 'FilteredWave' class is a wrapper for the
// method 'f' to allow it to be passed as an
// argument. It implements the output waveform.
class FilteredWave implements Plottable
{
  // Internal storage for circuit parameters.
  private double l, c, r;


  // The constructor allows circuit parameters
  // to be passed in.
  FilteredWave(double lval, double cval, double rval)
  {
    l = lval;
    c = cval;
    r = rval;
  }


  // The filtered square wave itself.
  public double f(double x)
  {
    double ans = 0;

    // Evaluate via Fourier series
    for (int i=1; i<=Wave.TERMMAX; i+=2)
    {
      // A useful figure.
      double tmp = i*Wave.OMEGA*l - 1/(i*Wave.OMEGA*c);

      // The phase lag on this component of the series.
      double lag = Math.atan(tmp/r);

      // The factor dividing the magnitude of this
      // component of the series.
      double mag = Math.sqrt(r*r + tmp*tmp);
```

```
        // Evaluate the term and add it in.
        ans += 4 * Math.sin(i*Wave.OMEGA*x - lag)
              / (mag * Math.PI * i);
    }

    return ans;
  }
}


// The class containing the main method.
public class LCR
{
  public static void main(String[] argv)
  {
    // Show the graphics window, at a size that
    // will show two square waves.
    SciGraph.showGraph(0, 4*Math.PI/Wave.OMEGA,
                       -1.5, 1.5);

    // Plot the input waveform.
    SciGraph.functionPlot(new Wave(), Color.red, 1);

    // Plot the output waveform for a filter of
    // L=10, C=0.00001, R=1. This filter will let
    // components of angular frequency 100 through
    // unchanged, and will greatly reduce the magnitudes
    // of those much either side of this figure.
    SciGraph.functionPlot(new FilteredWave(10, 0.00001, 1),
                          Color.blue, 1);

  }
}
```

 ## 11.5 Example – heat flow in a solid

The final example of this chapter is a simulation of heat flow in a small square of thermally conducting material which is held in contact with a number of other objects at various fixed temperatures. The exact arrangement simulated is depicted in Figure 11.3 and we wish to compute the temperature distribution across the square in the steady state.

Although this particular situation is somewhat artificial, very similar techniques could be used to model heat transfer through a computer chip's cooling fins or other similar problems.

When we consider how to model this problem, we realize that we have too many continuously varying quantities – temperature and position – to model using simple techniques. As discussed at the start of this chapter, the solution is to discretize. In this example, we divide the square of material into a grid of smaller squares. We treat each

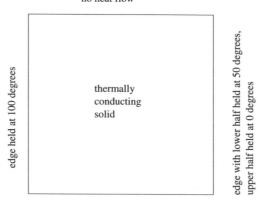

edge attached to insulator
no heat flow

edge held at 100 degrees

thermally
conducting
solid

edge with lower half held at 50 degrees,
upper half held at 0 degrees

edge held at 50 degrees

Figure 11.3 Heat flow in a solid.

of these as having a single temperature, not a gradient across it, and then consider heat flows between the grid squares to compute the steady state solution.

Experiments show that the amount of heat flowing between two objects is proportional to the temperature difference between them. This means that in the steady state each object is at the average temperature of its neighbours. As a result, if $t_{i,j}$ is the temperature of the grid square in the ith position on the x-axis and jth position on the y-axis, then

$$t_{i,j} = \frac{t_{i-1,j} + t_{i,j-1} + t_{i,j+1} + t_{i+1,j}}{4}$$

for all interior grid squares, and similar relations hold for those squares on the edges. This means that finding the steady state solution is equivalent to solving a very large number of simultaneous equations in the $t_{i,j}$. If we let the vector s contain data on all of the grid squares, then these could be written in matrix form (f represents the forcing term caused by heat flowing through the edges of the square):

$$As = f$$

Rather than solving this matrix equation directly, we do so using an iterative approach. If we split the matrix into diagonal and non-diagonal elements, $A = D + N$, then we can write

$$Ds + Ns = f$$
$$s = D^{-1}(f - Ns)$$

The second of these can be turned into an iteration (D is diagonal, so D^{-1} is easy to compute):

$$s_{n+1} = D^{-1}(f - Ns_n)$$

The **Jacobi method** states that this iteration will converge for 'diagonally dominant' matrices such as that in our problem.

If we now study the problem more closely, we see that the equation for $t_{i,j}$ above is in fact the Jacobi iteration if the values on the right-hand side are all from one iteration and are used to compute the next iteration's values on the left-hand side.

It is interesting to see that this method is exactly equivalent to simulating heat flow from an initial state until the steady state is reached. From this viewpoint, each iteration corresponds to a discrete time step. However, for the purposes of this problem there are better methods available.

The **Gauss–Seidel method** is justified by splitting the matrix into upper and lower triangular parts. When written in terms of the $t_{i,j}$, it corresponds to the Jacobi method, expect that the iteration is performed 'in place' – we update values of $t_{i,j}$ as we proceed as opposed to computing each iteration's values entirely using values from the previous iteration. This has the advantage of requiring half as much storage as the Jacobi method and also of converging more rapidly in most cases.

Finally, we can increase the rate of convergence again by **Simultaneous Over-Relaxation (SOR)**, which means that we over-exaggerate each change in a grid square's temperature by a factor of w where $1 < w < 2$. This can be thought of as working on the basis that as the method converges it does so consistently in the same direction, so we can save time by jumping further ahead at each iteration. For the best rate of convergence, the exact choice of w is important, and can be picked algorithmically by **Chebyshev acceleration**. In our example we set $w = 1.8$ which was determined by methods not in this book. For further information on the Jacobi and Gauss–Seidel methods, I recommend *Numerical Recipes in C* (Press, Flannery, Teukolsky and Vetterling, 1988).

The following program performs the Gauss–Seidel iteration to compute the steady state for our model. It displays the progress of the iteration using bands of colour to indicate the temperature gradients across the grid. It is available at http://www.jscieng.co.uk/Code/PhyMod/Heat/.

```
import uk.co.jscieng.*;
import java.awt.*;

public class Heat
{
  // The number of grid squares along each side of
  // the piece of material.
  public static final int SIZE = 100;

  // The number of Gauss-Seidel iterations to
  // perform between redraws.
  public static final int ITERPERSTEP = 100;

  // The number of redraws to perform.
  public static final int STEPS=10;


  // A method that applies the boundary
```

```
// conditions to the grid.
public static void setBCs(double[][] state)
{
  int i;

  // The left hand side is held at 100.
  for (i=0; i<SIZE; i++)
    state[0][i] = 100;

  // The bottom is held at 50.
  for (i=0; i<SIZE; i++)
    state[i][0] = 50;

  // Half of the right is held at 50.
  for (i=0; i<SIZE/2; i++)
    state[SIZE-1][i] = 50;

  // The rest of the right is held at 0.
  for (i=SIZE/2; i<SIZE; i++)
    state[SIZE-1][i] = 0;
}


// A method to perform Gauss-Seidel iteration.
// Note that we overcorrect by a factor of
// 1.8 because we are using SOR.
public static void iterate(double[][] state)
{
  double newstate;
  int i, j;

  // Iterate each of the squares in the middle
  // of the material. These are the average of
  // four neighbours.
  for (i=1; i<SIZE-1; i++)
    for (j=1; j<SIZE-1; j++)
    {
      newstate = (state[i-1][j] + state[i][j-1]
                  + state[i][j+1] + state[i+1][j])/4;
      state[i][j] += 1.8 * (newstate - state[i][j]);
    }

  // Iterate squares on the top edge. These are
  // the average of three neighbours.
  for (i=1; i<SIZE-1; i++)
  {
    newstate = (state[i-1][SIZE-1] + state[i][SIZE-2]
                + state[i+1][SIZE-1])/3;
    state[i][SIZE-1] += 1.8 * (newstate - state[i][SIZE-1]);
  }
```

```
  }


  // A method used by the graphical output.
  // We return a suitable colour for a temperature t.
  public static Color colorFor(double t)
  {
    if (t>86)
      return Color.magenta;
    else if (t>71)
      return Color.red;
    else if (t>57)
      return Color.orange;
    else if (t>43)
      return Color.yellow;
    else if (t>29)
      return Color.green;
    else if (t>14)
      return Color.cyan;
    else
      return Color.blue;
  }


  // The main method.
  public static void main(String[] argv)
  {
    int i, j, k;

    // Create grid and initialize all squares to 50
    // since most will end up near here.
    double[][] state = new double[SIZE][SIZE];

    for (i=0; i<SIZE; i++)
      for (j=0; j<SIZE; j++)
        state[i][j] = 50;

    // Apply the actual BCs to the edge squares.
    setBCs(state);

    // Show the graphics window.
    SciGraph.showGraph(0, SIZE, 0, SIZE, SIZE, SIZE);

    // For each redrawing step that we will do.
    for (i=0; i<STEPS; i++)
    {
      // Perform the correct number of iterations.
      for (j=0; j<ITERPERSTEP; j++)
        iterate(state);
```

```
            // Plot the temperature distribution,
            // displaying this as a colour gradient.
            for (j=0; j<SIZE; j++)
              for (k=0; k<SIZE; k++)
                SciGraph.point(j, k, colorFor(state[j][k]));
        }
      }
    }
```

WHERE TO GO FROM HERE

This chapter has introduced the idea of discretization and has discussed a few sample models of physical situations. These models have been longer than those in previous sections and the algorithms used have been more complicated and more comprehensively discussed. For a further discussion of these algorithms and many others, I recommend *Numerical Recipes in C* (Press, Flannery, Teukolsky and Vetterling, 1988).

APPENDIX A

Other resources

A.1   Introduction

This appendix directs you to further resources as you widen your understanding of Java and its scientific applications. It is divided into two sections corresponding to these two topics. In addition to the resources discussed here, you should consider reading any books listed in the 'Where to go from here' sections at the end of those chapters that interest you most. This book's companion website, at `http://www.jscieng.co.uk/`, contains links to other relevant sites. These are updated as more material appears, so you are advised to refer to them for the latest developments in each topic.

A.2   Learning Java

First of all, congratulations on reaching this appendix! If you have understood everything that we have covered then you understand virtually all of the language issues relevant to the use of Java for scientific work.

Nevertheless, we have omitted many important features of Java. The most glaring omission is that we have not discussed most of the standard library. As a rough indication of what we have left out, the JDK 1.2 comes with a fully functional cross-platform user interface and graphics library, the AWT, which includes reusable component support ('**beans**') and a user interface framework ('**Swing**'). The language also supports threaded code, complete with full thread synchronization primitives, a special abridged class declaration syntax ('**inner classes**'), calls to native code, networking, remote method calls, object serialization, Unicode text and much more.

There are literally hundreds of books describing these features. The most popular reference book for the entire language is *Java in a Nutshell* (Flanagan, 1997) and we can also recommend *Core Java 1.1* (Cornell and Horstmann, 1997). These books do not address scientific computing directly, but will help you start using the rest of Java. All of them, especially *Java in a Nutshell*, assume more knowledge than this book did. However, you should have reached a suitable standard to be able to read these by now.

Alternatively, the online documentation may be sufficient to answer your questions about the standard libraries. If you are using the JDK, then the documentation was installed in the subdirectory `docs` of the JDK directory. The file `index.html` in that directory would be a good place to start – you can open it in any web browser. For more advanced readers, source code for parts of the standard libraries is archived in the file `src.jar` in the JDK directory. You can expand the archive with the command '`jar xf src.jar`'.

Sun's website for Java is at `http://java.sun.com/` and will provide new versions of the JDK as they become available. Regardless of whether you use these, this website also provides a wealth of documentation, including the full text of several published books. The JDC forum on this website provides a knowledge base and access to Sun's technical proposals and documentation.

For example, at the time of writing (August 1998), there was a proposal under way to add keywords `strictfp` and `widefp` to distinguish between two versions of floating point arithmetic: the first would be rigidly defined, while the second would allow faster machine-precision arithmetic. This proposal had not been finalized, and so could not be discussed in this book, but will be of major importance to some areas of scientific programming. You can find out how this issue was resolved from the Sun website.

Finally, the `comp.java` newsgroups cover the latest language developments and `http://www.gamelan.com/` is a large repository of Java code that others have written.

A.3   Scientific applications

As we mentioned in the preface, this book's primary objective was to teach the Java language in a scientific context. The JSGL and JNL were included as useful libraries and we also provided basic introductions into numerical computation, software engineering and physical modelling.

Unfortunately, at the time of writing (August 1998), there are few books addressed to the scientific programmer using Java. Some suggestions for further reading were provided at the end of each chapter and there is little else currently available in print.

Online documentation is provided for both the JSGL and JNL: the JSGL documentation is available in the directory `docs` inside either the `JDK1.0` or `JDK1.1` subdirectories of the `JSGL` directory; the JNL documentation is available in the subdirectory `api` of the `JNL` directory. In both cases, the documentation is in the form of HTML and can be viewed in any web browser.

Visual Numerics, authors of the JNL, are another important source of information. Their website is at `http://www.vni.com/` and contains information about both the JNL and their other Java products as well as free downloads of new versions.

Finally, there are large number of other websites of interest to the scientific programmer. The majority of these are maintained by organizations which have been founded to represent our community and to push Sun for suitable additions to the language. The 'Java for Computational Science and Engineering' group maintains a site at `http://www.npac.syr.edu/projects/javaforcse/`. Its subgroup, the Java Grande Forum, are at `http://www.npac.syr.edu/javagrande/` and it maintains an excellent resource at `http://math.nist.gov/javanumerics/`. Further links, which are updated when more material becomes available, are listed on this book's website at `http://www.jscieng.co.uk/`.

APPENDIX B

Installation instructions

B.1   Introduction

This appendix contains installation instructions for the JDK, JSGL and JNL. More specifically, we cover the JDK version 1.2, the JSGL version 1.0 and the JNL version 1.0, revision F. We provide instructions to install these under Windows 98/NT and Solaris. We provide a section for each piece of software, consisting of a general overview of installation, followed by subsections with specific information for each operating system.

If you have no interest in the installation process and are using the exact versions and operating systems that we discuss then you should be able to turn straight to the relevant subsection and type commands exactly as listed. If you are a more experienced user or are installing different versions of the software, possibly under a different operating system, then the installation process may differ. You are advised to read the overview of installation, which may still be useful, but also to refer to the instructions provided with your software itself. You may find that the Solaris instructions are helpful for installation under other varieties of UNIX.

B.2   Installation of the JDK

Installation of the JDK version 1.2 on any system requires about 65 MB for the actual development tools and about another 80 MB if you choose to install the documentation. The JDK and documentation installation programs are available from Sun's website at `http://java.sun.com/`. I suggest that you download appropriate versions for your operating system before proceeding.

Installation will create a directory called something like `jdk1.2` (the exact name may include a sub-version number) and will install all files inside this. Under Windows, this directory should probably be created directly in `c:`, under UNIX it should probably be

/usr/local/jdk1.2. After this directory has been created and all contents copied into it, you will have to update your PATH environment variable to be able to access the tools that you have installed.

If you choose to install the documentation, this will be placed inside the JDK directory in a subdirectory called docs. All of the documentation is in the form of HTML, and so should be viewed with a web browser. Netscape Navigator and Microsoft Internet Explorer allow you to view local files using the 'Open File ...' option on the File menu. The file index.html inside docs is a good starting point; you might consider bookmarking it.

The source code for parts of the standard library is also available inside the JDK directory. This is archived in the file src.jar. In order to read it you will have to expand the archive using the command line by moving to the JDK directory and typing the command 'jar xf src.jar'. The jar command is part of the JDK, so you will only be able to perform this expansion once installation is complete.

Note that both the documentation and source code are intended as reference material for experienced programmers. You will probably not understand these before reading this book, but they should be helpful afterwards.

B.2.1 Windows 98/NT

Before installing the JDK version 1.2 you should remove any installation of a previous JDK from your system. This can be done by using the 'Add/Remove Software' control panel for versions of the JDK later than 1.1 or simply by deleting the installation directory for versions up to 1.0.2 (this will probably be the directory jdk1.0.x, directly inside C:). In addition, you should remove the old installation directory from your PATH, and unset the environment variable CLASSPATH. These are done by editing your autoexec.bat file under Windows 98 or using the Environment tab of the System control panel under Windows NT.

By now, you should have downloaded the automated installer from Sun's website. This is called something like jdk12-win32.exe (the exact name may include a sub-version number). You start the installation by running this program (by double-clicking on it or typing its name at a command prompt in its parent directory). The installation process will prompt you for a JDK base directory. This guide assumes that you choose the default option, placing the JDK in jdk1.2 at the top level of C:.

The installer only installs the development system. To install the documentation, you must unzip the archive jdk12-doc.zip, which is also available from Sun's website. This should be unzipped in the parent directory of the jdk1.2 directory which you just created. If you choose to place this where we specified, then you should unzip the documentation, restoring the saved directory structure, and starting in at the root of C:. This can be done using the Windows program WinZip or many command line utilities, such as PKUnzip. You must unzip restoring the saved directory structure. This is available as an option in the Extract dialog in WinZip or via the '-d' option in PKUnzip and will create a subdirectory docs of the directory jdk1.2 and place all of the documentation in there.

Finally, regardless of whether you chose to install documentation, you must set your PATH to include the subdirectory bin of the directory jdk1.2. The environment variable

PATH lists where the system will look for commands that you type. We need to add this directory so that commands such as `javac` will work. You can view your current PATH using the command 'path' from DOS. Under Windows 98, your `autoexec.bat` file (located at the top level of `C:`) should already contain a line of the form 'PATH = <current path>'. The <current path> will be a list of directories on your disk, separated by semicolons. Edit this file in a text editor to add

```
;C:\jdk1.2\bin
```

to the end of the list of directories, on the same line (use the exact JDK directory name for your system). Under Windows NT, you should edit your `path` using the Environment tab of the System control panel.

At this point, you should reboot your computer so that the change of PATH takes effect. After rebooting, to test this, move to a DOS window, and type `javac` or `java`. If the JDK has installed correctly then you will get some help information on these tools. Otherwise, the commands will not be found. If the commands succeed then you have finished installation. Otherwise, if installation failed, then use the 'path' command to check that the JDK directory is indeed in your PATH – this is the most common problem.

The complete installation process as performed from a command line might be something like this (assuming that you are running Windows 98, that the installation directory is `jdk1.2` directly inside `C:`, and that you have downloaded `jdk12-win32.exe` and `jdk12-doc.zip` directly inside `C:`):

```
C:\Windows> cd \
C:\> jdk12-win32
```

The installer now runs, and you specify the default installation point: the directory `jdk1.2` directly inside `C:`.

```
C:\> del jdk12-win32.exe
C:\> pkunzip -d jdk12-doc.zip
    <lots of output as unzipping takes place>

C:\> del jdk12-doc.zip
```

You should now use Notepad to open the file `autoexec.bat` inside `C:`. Change the PATH statement from

```
PATH <old path>
```

to

```
PATH <old path>;C:\jdk1.2\bin
```

If there is no existing PATH statement, then insert the line

```
PATH .;C:\jdk1.2\bin
```

Save `autoexec.bat`, exit Notepad and reboot the computer. After the reboot, typing `javac` at a command prompt should give some help information for this tool.

If you need further help with installation, then consult the documentation on Sun's website or talk to a local expert.

B.2.2 Solaris

This installation guide assumes that you will install the JDK into the directory /usr/local. This is a standard location for installing software that is not part of the operating system so that it will be accessible to all users of a system. This installation can only be done by a system administrator ('root'), since this directory is not world-writable. If you own your machine, you should perform the installation, as described below, as root. Otherwise, you should persuade your system administrator to do it for you. If this is not possible, you can perform the installation into your home directory by changing the references that we make to an installation directory from /usr/local to /home/<user name>.

Before installing the JDK version 1.2, you should remove any installation of a previous JDK from your system. This can be done by deleting the installation directory, which will probably be in /usr/local. In addition, you should remove the old installation directory from your path, and unset the environment variable CLASSPATH. These are probably both set in your ~/.cshrc file if you are using the C shell, or they may be set in a system-wide fashion by the system administrator.

By now, you should have downloaded the automated installer from Sun's website. This is called something like jdk12-solaris2.sh (the exact name may include a sub-version number and will include a processor type). You start the installation by moving this file into the directory in which you wish to install. Next, use the command 'chmod a+x <file>' to set the installer to be executable, and then use './<file>' to run the installer, which will create a subdirectory jdk1.2 of your current directory.

The installer only installs the development system. To install the documentation, you must decompress the archive jdk12-doc.tar.gz, which is also available from Sun's website. Move this to the parent directory of the jdk1.2 directory which you just created and execute the commands 'gunzip jdk12-doc.tar.gz' followed by 'tar xf jdk12-doc.tar'. This will create a subdirectory docs of the directory jdk1.2 and place all of the documentation in there.

Finally, regardless of whether you chose to install documentation, you must set your path to include the subdirectory bin of the directory jdk1.2. The environment variable path lists where the system will look for commands that you type. We need to add this directory so that commands such as javac will work. If you are using the C shell, then this can be done by editing your ~/.cshrc file to contain the line:

```
set path($path /usr/local/jdk1.2/bin)
```

Contact a local expert if you are not using the C shell. Alternatively, the system administrator will be able to set up the JDK so that all users can access it.

At this point, logging out and then in again will set your path to the new value, leaving the JDK ready to use. To test this, type javac or java at a command line. If the JDK has installed correctly then you will get some help information on these tools. Otherwise, the commands will not be found. If the commands succeed then you have finished installation. Otherwise, if installation failed, then check that the JDK directory is indeed in your path – this is the most common problem.

The complete installation process as performed from a command line might be something like this (assuming that you are using the C shell, that the installation directory is `/usr/local/jdk1.2`, and that you have downloaded `jdk12-solaris2.sh` and `jdk12-doc.tar.gz` directly inside `/usr/local`):

```
% cd /usr/local
% chmod a+x jdk1.2-solaris2.sh
% ./jdk1.2-solaris2.sh
```

The installer now runs and prompts you to agree with a licence agreement.

```
% rm jdk1.2-solaris2.sh
% gunzip jdk12-doc.tar.gz
% tar xf jdk12-doc.tar
% rm jdk12-doc.tar
```

You should now use a text editor such as pico, vi or emacs to add the line

```
set path($path /usr/local/jdk1.2/bin)
```

to your `~/.cshrc` file.

Log out, and log in again. After this, typing `javac` at a command prompt should give some help information for this tool.

If you need further help with installation, then consult the documentation on Sun's website or talk to a local expert.

B.3 Installation of the JSGL

These installation instructions cover the JSGL version 1.0. The JSGL is available from this book's accompanying website at `http://www.jscieng.co.uk/`. I suggest that you download an appropriate version for your operating system before proceeding.

The library is provided as a compressed archive. This expands to a single JSGL directory. This contains two subdirectories, `JDK1.0` and `JDK1.1`, containing the versions of the library for each of these versions of the language. The JDK 1.1 version also covers all later versions of the language. The JDK 1.0 version of the library is included for those platforms which do not yet have development tools for Java 1.1 or later. This version should also be used in applets (programs embedded in web pages), since, at the time of writing (August 1998), some major web browsers are not fully JDK 1.1 compliant.

Each of the `JDK1.X` directories contains two subdirectories. The first directory, `docs`, contains online documentation for the library. The other directory, `classes`, contains the actual library. The entire library is contained in a package `uk.co.jscieng` and the `classes` subdirectory is the base directory for the hierarchical structure in which this is stored: `uk` inside `classes` is the first level of this hierarchical structure.

To install the library, you should perform two actions. Firstly, you must uncompress the JSGL directory onto your hard disk. The exact location at which you do this is not important. I suggest a root-level directory JSGL inside `c:` under Windows, or `/usr/local/lib/JSGL` under UNIX. Secondly, you should set the environment variable `CLASSPATH`. This variable is used by the Java tools, such as `javac` and `java`, to find the `.class` files why it needs to run a program. The reason why you have not had to specify it so far is that the default behaviour is to search the location of the standard libraries followed by the current directory. Up until this point all of your programs have used only the standard library and their own files, so this behaviour has been sufficient.

B.3.1 Windows 98/NT

By now, you should have downloaded the compressed archive JSGL.zip from this book's website. To install this, you should unzip it in the parent directory of your preferred installation point. If you choose to place this where we specified, then you should unzip the file, restoring the saved directory structure, and starting in at the root of C:. This can be done using the Windows program WinZip or many command line utilities, such as PKUnzip. You must unzip restoring the saved directory structure. This is available as an option in the Extract dialog in WinZip or via the '-d' option in PKUnzip. The extraction can be done from the command line as follows (assuming that you wish to install directly inside C: and that you have downloaded JSGL.zip directly inside C:):

```
C:\Windows> cd \
C:\> pkunzip -d JSGL.zip
    <lots of output as unzipping takes place>

C:\> del JSGL.zip
```

Next, under Windows 98 you should use Notepad to open the file autoexec.bat inside C:. Add a line to set the CLASSPATH to search the appropriate version of the JSGL, then the current directory. This should look like:

```
SET CLASSPATH=C:\JSGL\JDK1.1\classes;.
```

or

```
SET CLASSPATH=C:\JNL\Classes;C:\JSGL\JDK1.1\classes;.
```

if you have already installed the JNL. Under Windows NT, you should set the CLASSPATH environment variable using the Environment tab of the System control panel.

At this point, you should reboot your computer so that the change of CLASSPATH takes effect. After rebooting, you should be able to use the JSGL from within your programs in exactly the same way that you have been using the standard libraries. import will locate the .class files using CLASSPATH.

If you have difficulty in using the JDK or the JSGL after installation, then check the exact value of CLASSPATH very carefully. If this seems to be correct then talk to a local expert.

B.3.2 Solaris

This installation guide assumes that you will install the JSGL into the directory /usr/local. This is a standard location for installing software that is not part of the operating system so that it will be accessible to all users of a system. This installation can be done only by a system administrator ('root'), since this directory is not world-writable. If you own your own machine, you should perform the installation, as described below, as `root`. Otherwise, you should persuade your system administrator to do it for you. If this is not possible, you can perform the installation into your home directory by changing the references that we make to an installation directory from `/usr/local` to `/home/

By now, you should have downloaded the compressed archive `JSGL.tar.gz` from this book's website. To install this, you should decompress it in the parent directory of your preferred installation point. The extraction can be done at the command line as follows (assuming that the installation directory is `/usr/local/lib` and that you have downloaded `JSGL.tar.gz` directly inside `/usr/local/lib`):

```
% cd /usr/local/lib
% gunzip JSGL.tar.gz
% tar xf JSGL.tar
% rm JSGL.tar
```

Next, you must set the `CLASSPATH` environment variable to search the appropriate version of the JSGL and then the current directory. If you are using the C shell then this can be done by editing your `~/.cshrc` file to contain the line:

```
setenv CLASSPATH /usr/local/lib/JSGL/JDK1.1/classes:.
```

or

```
setenv CLASSPATH /usr/local/lib/JNL/Classes:
               /usr/local/lib/JSGL/JDK1.1/classes:.
```

if you have already installed the JNL.

Note that in both cases the entire command should be on one line, with no gap after the colon.

Contact a local expert if you are not using the C shell. Alternatively, the system administrator will be able to set up `CLASSPATH` so that all users can access the JSGL.

At this point, logging out and then in again will set `CLASSPATH` to the new value. You should be able to use the JSGL from within your programs in exactly the same way that you have been using the standard libraries. `import` will locate the `.class` files using `CLASSPATH`.

If you have difficulty in using the JDK or the JSGL after installation, then check the exact value of `CLASSPATH` very carefully. If this seems to be correct then talk to a local expert.

B.4   Installation of the JNL

These installation instructions cover the JNL version 1.0, revision F. The JNL is available from Visual Numerics' website at `http://www.vni.com/`. I suggest that you download it before proceeding.

The JNL is installed in exactly the same way that we installed the JSGL in the previous section, so we will not repeat the entire installation instructions here.

The library is provided as a compressed archive. This expands to a single JNL directory with two subdirectories. The first directory, `api`, contains online documentation for the library. The other directory, `Classes`, contains the actual library. The entire library is contained in a package `VisualNumerics.math`, and the `Classes` subdirectory is the base directory for the hierarchical structure in which this is stored: `VisualNumerics` inside `Classes` is the first level of this hierarchical structure.

To install the library, you should perform two actions. Firstly, you must uncompress the `JNL` directory onto your hard disk. The exact location at which you do this is not important. I suggest a root-level directory `JNL` inside `C:` under Windows, or `/usr/local/lib/JNL` under UNIX. Secondly, you should set the environment variable `CLASSPATH`. This variable is used by the Java tools, such as `javac` and `java`, to find the `.class` files that it needs to run a program. The reason why you have not had to specify it so far is that the default behaviour is to search the location of the standard libraries followed by the current directory. Up until this point all of your programs have used only the standard library and their own files, so this behaviour has been sufficient.

If you require more detailed instructions than these, then you should read the instruction for installation of the JSGL in the previous section. The method used is identical apart from the names of the directories mentioned above.

Solutions to selected exercises

C.1   Introduction

This appendix contains solutions to all exercises set at the ends of previous chapters. They are listed in sections, each of which corresponds to a chapter containing exercises.

C.2   Chapter 2: Java from basics

2.1   The errors are:

- The class is not declared as `public`.
- The `main` method is not declared as `static`.
- The `main` method does not take the correct arguments.
- The variable `i` is not declared.
- The first `println` does not contain a '+' to join its last two sections together.
- The first `println` does not contain a '*' to multiply the last 9 and the `i`.
- The `if` statement uses the assignment operator '=', not the comparison operator '=='.
- The second `println` uses the wrong type of quotation marks.
- The second `println`'s line is not terminated by a semicolon.
- There is a missing '}' at the end of the program.

2.2   There is no output. a is greater than zero, so `isPositive(2)` is never executed. The '!' means that the first half of the `if` evaluates to `false`, so `isPositive(-5)` is executed, but generates no output because that section of the code is commented out.

2.3   a is `3.0` at the end because i and j are both integers, so `i/j` is evaluated by integer division.

2.4 Both 'a is seven.' and 'a is not seven.' are output because there are no `break` statements, so execution continues straight from the first case into the second.

2.5 Floating point numbers are necessarily an approximation to the mathematical ideal of real numbers, since they can store only finitely many digits. In this example, rounding errors in the 16th significant figure stop two logically identical calculations from generating identical results. Such rounding errors and methods for preventing their build-up are an important issue in scientific computing and are discussed further in Section 9.2.

C.3 Chapter 3: Java for C programmers

3.1 Unlike C/C++, there is a `boolean` data type, distinct from `int`, which is used in `if`, `while`, `?` and `for` statements. As such, 'if (!remainder)' must be replaced by 'if (remainder == 0)'.

3.2 Unlike C/C++, a function taking no arguments must be declared with `()`, and cannot be declared with `(void)`.

3.3 One of the most important functions of an object's destructor in C++ is to deallocate any memory that was allocated in the constructor. In Java this is no longer necessary because this memory will be garbage collected.

3.4 The class definition should not be terminated by a semicolon in Java. The `new` statement fails because calls to the default constructor must be explicit in Java: you must write 'new Complex();'.

C.4 Chapter 4: Advanced Java

4.1 The errors are:

- The classes `Five` and `Six` cannot both be `public` and be in the same `.java` file as each other.
- The class `Seven` is not `public`, so `Five.main` will be unable to call its `iterate` method.
- In `Seven.iterate`, the call to `Six.calculate` will not work – either the import statement must be changed or the class name must be fully qualified to allow the reference to be understood.

4.2 We choose a base directory and create subdirectories `d` and `e`. We place `Five.java` in `d` and `Seven.java` in `e`. We compile the program from the base directory with the command 'javac -depend -d . d/Five.java' and run it with the command 'java d.Five'.

4.3 The errors are:

- The array reference `table` never has an actual array created and associated with it. Use 'new int[5]'.
- `table` and `table2` are not the same. Arrays are indexed from zero, so `table` has all elements one place later.
- '==' compares the references, not the arrays. This means that even if the contents were identical, the `if` statement would fail.

4.4 The point made by this exercise is that neither pointers nor pointer arithmetic exist in Java. The closest that we can get is:

```
int[] i = new int[5];
int index = 0;

while (index < 5)
{
  i[index] = 0;
  i++;
}
```

4.5 `varone` exists once, and is accessed as `TwoParts.varone`. `vartwo` exists separately in every object of this class created. If `obj` is such an object, its instance of `vartwo` would be accessed as `obj.vartwo`. Similarly `methodone` is accessed as `TwoParts.methodone()` whereas `methodtwo` is accessed as `obj.methodtwo()`. `methodtwo` can use both the single instance of `varone` and the instance of `vartwo` associated with its own object. `methodone` can only use `varone`.

4.6 The errors are:

- `process` must have a `throws` clause since `preprocess`, which it calls, can throw exceptions and this method does not attempt to catch them.
- The `for` statement will cause an `ArrayIndexOutOfBoundsException` since array indices start from zero, so `l[l.length]` is one past the end of the array.
- `throw` must take an actual instance of an exception. As such we cannot 'throw BreakableObjects;', but must 'throw new BreakableObjects();'.

C.5   Chapter 6: Object orientation

6.1 The `divide` method is:

```
public void divide(Complex v)
{
  // Declare temporary storage for calculation
  Complex w = new Complex();

  // Calculate
  w.realpart = realpart * v.realpart
             + imagpart * v.imagpart;
  w.imagpart = imagpart * v.realpart
```

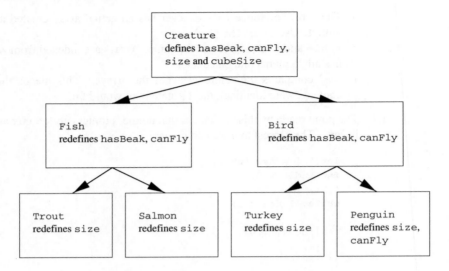

Figure C.1 A zoological database.

```
                         - realpart * v.imagpart;
       w.realpart /= v.realpart * v.realpart
                         + v.imagpart * v.imagpart;
       w.imagpart /= v.realpart * v.realpart
                         + v.imagpart * v.imagpart;

       // Copy value into this object.
       realpart = w.realpart;
       imagpart = w.imagpart;
   }
```

6.2 We define classes `Creature`, `Fish`, `Bird`, `Trout`, `Salmon`, `Turkey` and `Penguin` with the hierarchical structure shown in Figure C.1.

Note that the superclass defines all of the methods so that they can all be used on arrays of `Creature` objects. Below this, we redefine each method at the highest possible point in the hierarchy to obtain the maximum amount of code-sharing. For instance, `cubeSize` can be defined in `Creature` since it just calls `size` and cubes the answer. `hasBeak` is best redefined at `Fish` and `Bird`, while `size` is a feature of the individual objects. Note that we redefine `canFly` in `Bird` (presumably to return true!) even though `Penguin` will need to change this value. This is done with a view to expansion – for the vast majority of subclasses of `Bird` this will be a sensible default.

6.3 There are several possible solutions. One is:

```
class A
{
  int value1;
```

```
  A()
  {
    this(1);
  }

  A{int i}
  {
    value1 = i;
  }
}

class B extends A
{
  double value2;

  B()
  {
    this(3.0);
  }

  B(int i)
  {
    this(i, 3.0);
  }

  B(double d)
  {
    super();
    value2 = d;
  }

  B(int i, double d)
  {
    super(i);
    value2 = d;
  }
}
```

Note that 3.0 is used twice. This should probably be moved into a class constant to ensure consistency.

6.4   The divide method is:

```
public void divide(Complex v)
{
  // Calculate
  setModArg(modulus() / v.modulus(),
            argument() - v.argument());
}
```

6.5   We should make Creature, Fish and Bird abstract. The methods hasBeak, canFly and size should be declared as abstract in Creature. size should be defined as final in all four objects referring to specific animals. canFly should be final in Penguin. To scan through the array, we could write:

```
Creature[] creatures;

for (int i=0; i<creatures.length; i++)
  if (creatures[i] instanceof Edible)
    System.out.println(((Edible) creatures[i]).taste());
```

6.6 The code is:

```
interface Integrable
{
  double f(double x);
}

class Integrand implements Integrable
{
  double f(double x)
  {
    <function defined>
  }
}

public class Integration
{
  double integrate(Integrand i)
  {
    <perform the integration>
  }

  public static void main(String[] argv)
  {
    double d = integrate(new Integrand())
    ...
  }
}
```

Bibliography

Bishop J. (1998). *Java Gently*. 2nd edn. Addison Wesley

Booch G. (1996). *Object Solutions: Managing the Object-Oriented Project*. Addison Wesley

Brooks F. P., Jr. (1975). *The Mythical Man-Month*. Addison Wesley

Budd T. (1998). *Understanding Object-Oriented Programming with Java*. Addison Wesley

Cornell G. and Horstmann C. S. (1997). *Core Java 1.1: Fundamentals*. Prentice Hall

Cornell G. and Horstmann C. S. (1997). *Core Java 1.1: Advanced Features*. Prentice Hall

Dongarra J., Bunch J., Moler C. and Stewart G. (1979). *Linpack User's Guide*. Society for Industrial and Applied Mathematics

Etter D. M. (1997). *Structured Fortran 77 for Engineers and Scientists* 5th edn. Addison Wesley

Flanagan D. (1997). *Java in a Nutshell* 2nd edn. O'Reilly & Associates

Fox G. C., ed. (1997). *Concurrency: Practice and Experience* Vol. 9, No. 11. John Wiley & Sons

Harel D. (1992). *Algorithmics: The Spirit of Computing* 2nd edn. Addison Wesley

Jensen K. and Wirth N. (1974). *Pascal User Manual and Report*. Springer-Verlag

Kernighan B. W. and Ritchie D. M. (1988). *The C Programming Language* 2nd edn. Prentice Hall

Knuth D. E. (1981). *The Art of Computer Programming* Vol. 2, 2nd edn. Addison Wesley

Malin S. R. C. (1987). *The Greenwich Guide to the Planets*. George Philip

McCracken D. D. and Salmon W. I. (1988). *Computing for Engineers and Scientists with Fortran 77*. John Wiley & Sons

Niemeyer P. and Peck J. (1996). *Exploring Java*. O'Reilly & Associates

Plauger, P. J. (1994). *Programming on Purpose III*. Prentice Hall

Press W. H., Flannery B. P., Teukolsky S. A. and Vetterling W. T. (1988). *Numerical Recipes in C*. Cambridge University Press

Sommerville I. (1995). *Software Engineering* 5th edn. Addison Wesley

Watkins D. S. (1991). *Fundamentals of Matrix Computations*. John Wiley & Sons

Index